REDBOU1
HISTORY

By Alan Featherstone

Redbourn Books

Cover – front and back – Redbourn High Street from the north –
from a tinted postcard taken in about 1900

Published December 2001

by REDBOURN BOOKS
29 Crouch Hall Gardens
REDBOURN
Herts AL3 7EL

ISBN 0-9541948-0-2

Printed by
JENNER PRINT
1, Tower Business Park
Kelvedon Road
TIPTREE
Essex CO5 0LX

ACKNOWLEDGEMENTS

David & Celia Forbes	Checking, encouragement
Ralph Gould	Scanning assistance
Marjorie Hulance	Checking
Matthew Ling	Computer skills
Jim May	Computer help
Mel. Thompson	Publication/Computer help
David Cheetham	Checking [Church law]
Roy Craske	For various items of information
Peter Flitton	Checking [Mt Zion]
Gillian Harvey	Advice - Medieval period especially.
David Phear	Advice, [medical section]
Mervin Pritchard	For information relating to Vicars
Dr. Eileen Roberts	Advice - Priory/Alban & Amphibalus
Mary & Family	Reading, Indexing, Computer help and support
Diane Wiskin	Help with Parish Council records
Redbourn Village Museum	For the use archive material
Vicar & Churchwardens	For use of material in the Parish Chest
Staff of HRO other	Access and guidance in researching records
Record Offices, Libraries	Willing help in many ways
Geoff Webb	For photographs from his Redbourn Collection
Ron Such	For photographs from his collection
Richard Hogg	For photographs from the Markyate collection
Sue Flood	For help with Latin translations
The late Leslie Simpson	For many Latin translations over the years

Also many other people who have encouraged me with their interest in Redbourn's History for many years, and whose names I may have unintentionally overlooked

Other books published by the author:-
"St Mary's Church, Redbourn – Two Centuries of Pictures, 1786 –1986"
"The Mills of Redbourn" 1993

4

CONTENTS

PREFACE

The writing of this 'History of Redbourn' has been 'coming on' for a good many years and arises chiefly from my hobby of avidly collecting all and any information relating to Redbourn. This started almost from when we came to Redbourn in 1954 and certainly intensified after my retirement in 1988.

From time to time, when giving talks to various groups about aspects of village history, illustrating my talks with my ageing collection of slides, I have been asked if there was a book where further information could be found. My answer is generally to refer them to out of print books such as "The Story of Redbourn" written by a W.E.A. group under the leadership of Lionel Munby, and the late May Walker's delightful book "Redbourn", the only other detailed accounts being in County Histories, particularly "The Victoria County History of Hertfordshire" and John Cussan's "History of Hertfordshire".

I've tried to redress this shortcoming myself by writing articles about our history, mostly for the parish magazine, "Common Round"; such articles appearing under the title of "This and That about the Church" or "This and That about the Village". I have also written several booklets about the "Registers", "The Early History", "The Mills of Redbourn" and "Pictures of St Mary's Church".

My object here has been to produce a readable and comprehensive history, which I hope will appeal to villagers of all ages as well as to seriously interested readers of anything with a historical flavour. Though I have tried to touch on nearly every subject or occasion of interest, I realise that coverage of all of these may not always be as detailed as some might wish. This might indicate to readers that either there is more information available (in my files), or perhaps YOU know more than I do, and could thus add to my records – if so, I would welcome a call

Some items may have been omitted, either by intention or by accident. An example of the former, is the Recreational Training Centre planned by the Waifs and Strays Society at Nichols Farm in 1938/9 – nothing came of it because of the war, but I have details of what was planned.

The story, or history, of any village is not just one continuous chronological sequence of events, but a multitude of happenings, many occurring at the same time, and with overlapping backgrounds going back many years or even centuries. This is particularly so in more recent times when the activities of villagers cover a diversity of subjects.

Chapters 1 to 6 cover the period from pre-historical times to the end of the medieval period (at the Dissolution of the Monasteries). During the early period, primitive nomadic men probably stayed only long enough to hunt for food or perhaps to make sharp edged tools from the local flints. Iron-age farmers were the first permanent residents, building the "Aubreys" fortified site for their protection. No villa site is known in the parish to tell of Roman occupation and in fact nothing is known of habitation here until late in the Saxon period. But from then on, during the whole medieval period, the village developed under the Abbots of St Albans, who were its Lords of the Manor.

Subsequent chapters deal with the post-medieval period up to modern times. It is mainly in this period that a chronological sequence of chapters has been found impossible to follow. Thus the history of such subjects as the Church, the Chapels, the Schools and of course the People, their Homes and Occupations are all treated separately. However, to put each into a historical context, I usually adopt my favourite ploy of giving a quick glance back at the early origins of each subject. I have also tried to bring each subject up to date, ie. up to the new Millennium, or even slightly beyond.

Such a wide coverage presents many problems. Evidence from early times is mostly archaeological with relevant documents only appearing from the medieval times. These early documents, (often after translation) have to be scrutinised and bled for every slight hint that they might reveal - a job by no means yet complete. At the modern end of the scale, the reverse is the case. There is so much information that one really wants another lifetime to absorb it all. One valuable source does not comply with this observation - the National Census Returns. The full details in these are only released for public study when they become 100 years old, thus we eagerly await a detailed look at Redbourn in 1901.

It is hoped that the order of subjects I have settled upon will make for easy reading and understanding of our village history. Readers with particular interests may want to delve into those chapters or sections which most interest them, or even use this as a reference book.

I have used a mix of old and recent photographs as illustrations, mostly favouring the old as they give a better idea of Redbourn when it was smaller and retained its rural appearance.

Decimalization has not been adopted in this book – all linear and area measurements have been given in the same form as in the documents from which they were taken. Likewise monetary values are given as originally stated with no attempt to either decimalise or translate to modern values. If the reader is interested in pursuing this subject further I would recommend Lionel Munby's book "How Much is that Worth?" (Phillimore).

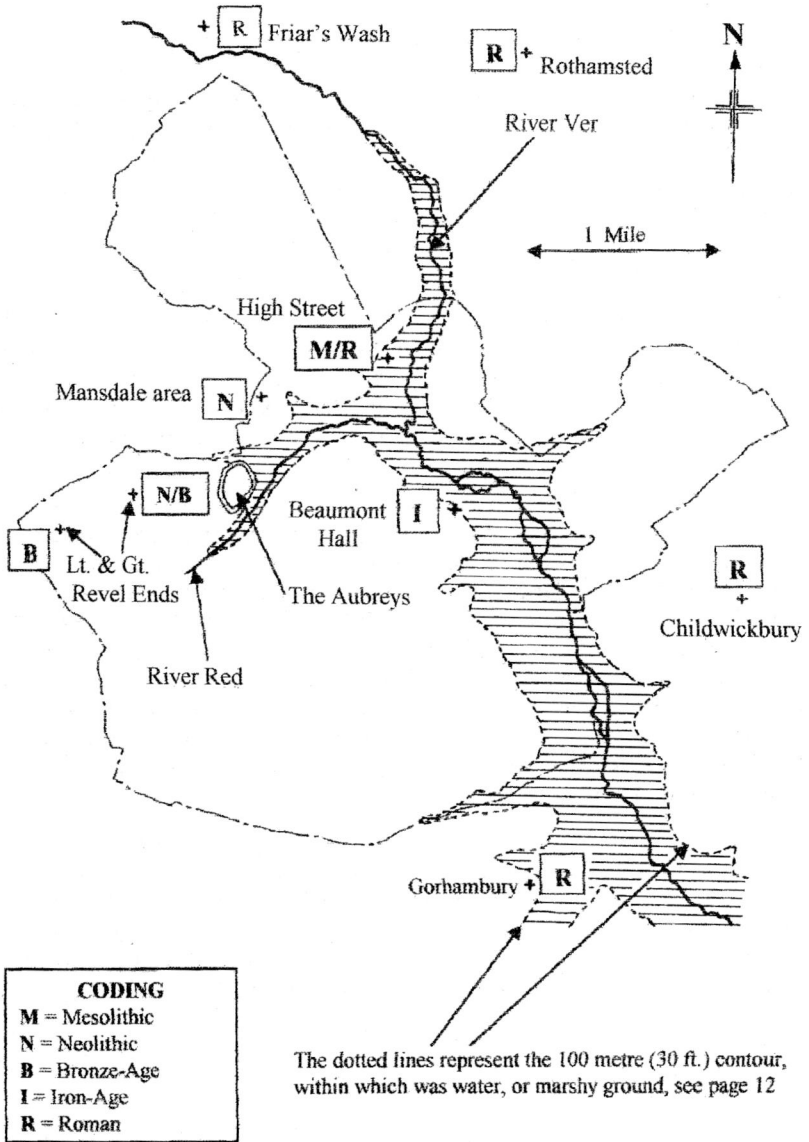

+ R Friar's Wash

R + Rothamsted

N

River Ver

1 Mile

High Street

M/R

Mansdale area **N** +

N/B +

Beaumont Hall

I +

B +
Lt. & Gt.
Revel Ends

The Aubreys

R +
Childwickbury

River Red

Gorhambury + **R**

CODING
M = Mesolithic
N = Neolithic
B = Bronze-Age
I = Iron-Age
R = Roman

The dotted lines represent the 100 metre (30 ft.) contour,
within which was water, or marshy ground, see page 12

Fig: 1.1 - Redbourn in Early Times
With known sites and archaeological finds marked

CHAPTER 1

FORMATION AND BIRTH OF THE VILLAGE

The landscape of this part of the country was formed jointly by the action of the sea and the glaciers that existed during the alternating warm and cold climatic eras[1]. The formation of the landscape and the natural resources which it provided, set the scene for the arrival of man. Over many millennia he learned to make use of some of these resources for his own benefit, but many more millennia passed before he established the permanent settlement which we know today as the village of Redbourn

During the last Ice-age, glaciers almost reached our doorstep - only the barrier of the Dunstable Downs keeping them at bay, forcing them to circle round to the east, from where they almost reached the area of St Albans. When the glaciers finally melted, a large lake was formed (near the present city), fed by water from the melting ice, which gouged out the main river valleys that we know today

CRETACEOUS CHALK

Before the last Ice age, much of southern England was covered by a shallow sea inhabited by millions of varied sea creatures. The shells of these, together with an ooze, formed from the remains of algae and other marine life over a period of about 30 million years, formed a layer of chalk some 200 to 300 feet thick. This layer lies beneath south-east England stretching from the south coast diagonally to the East Anglian coast. Evidence of this chalk can sometimes be seen locally when foundation trenches are dug, or in chalk pits, the best known of which is the old Lime works, now occupied by the Toxic Waste site about a mile south of the village. Fine examples of fossilised sponges, shells, sea urchins, ammonites and corals have been found in this pit

Chalk, and its contents, is one of the materials that man has learned to use since early times. Flints found in this chalk are silica-based stones, which are very hard and durable, but can be chipped and worked. Stone-Age man learned how to make them into useful sharp edged tools. Builders from Saxon times to the present day have also used them, either in their raw state, or after 'knapping' one side flat so as to make attractive, 'flush-work' walls (see examples in the church)

The chalk itself has been found useful for building, but must be quarried from lower layers where it is harder. The chief local source was at Totternhoe, hence its usual name, "Totternhoe Stone". It is also known as "Clunch"

A rarer local, silica based stone, formed from beach pebbles of the Eocene period, is a 'conglomerate' known as "Hertfordshire Puddingstone". (so named as it is found chiefly in this county and has the appearance of Plum Pudding[2]) This can often be spotted in the walls of churches, Redbourn included. Some, collected from village fields, have been used in the new Church Hall.[3]

A large block of Pudding stone was found during the building of Redbourn By-pass and can be seen near the Harpenden Lane Roundabout - *see Fig: 1.2.* Such large pieces may have formed early boundary markers. I have also seen it used as foundation stones for cottages in the village

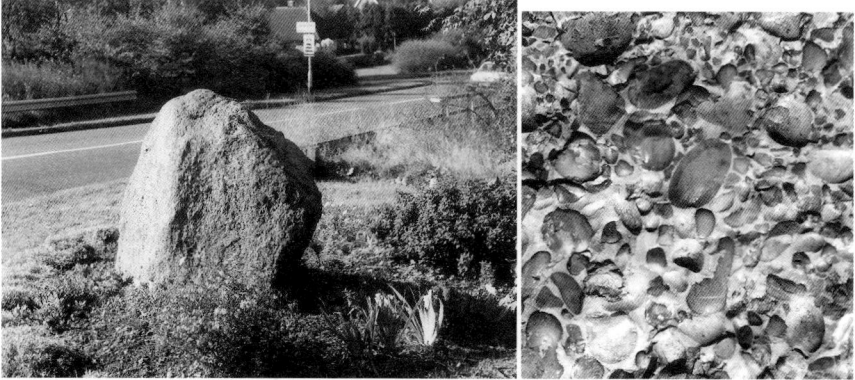

Fig: 1.2 - Puddingstone near Redbourn By-pass & close up of a similar stone

The softer, upper layers, of chalk could be used for 'marling' or 'chalking' the fields.[4] This was done by sinking a pit some 20 to 30 feet deep and 'spreading' the contents evenly around the field. When the job was finished the pit was back filled with unwanted materials, helped by subsequent ploughing around its edge. However, this was not always effective in plugging the hole and depressions often resulted, sometimes wrongly referred to as 'swallow holes'. At Revel End Farm one such hole collapsed and nearly engulfed a Tractor! [5]

STONE-AGE MEN

Our Stone-age ancestors were nomads, who wandered the land looking for food and water sufficient for their survival. We give these people the title of "Hunter-Gatherers" because of their style of living by **hunting** animals, birds or fish and by **gathering** fruit, plants or roots, which they found to be edible

It has been suggested that the landscape of Southern England in those very early times was a vast morass from Somerset in the west, to Kent and Essex in the east, with woodland and tangled scrub above the flood plain.[6] In this terrain there were no tracks until man, by repeated use, gradually formed well trodden paths

By sticking to higher ground, where vegetation was sparse, man could travel faster and further.   Such tracks have survived, usually referred to as 'Ridgeways'. Locally the 'Icknield Way' to the north of Redbourn is a good example, nearer is another, now called "Gaddesden Row"

The disadvantage of such high routes was that there was little water or food available. River valleys offered plentiful supplies of food in the form of vegeta-

tion, wildlife and water. The river Ver was one such valley that must have provided useful hunting for Stone-Age men

PALAEOLITHIC PERIOD

Men of the earliest Stone Age were not too skilled at making implements out of
the local flint; mostly trying to 'improve' suitable lumps by just breaking bits off
to give them sharp edges. Such tools are difficult to identify or date and I know
of no reliably identified finds for Redbourn

MESOLITHIC PERIOD

In this period the art of fashioning tools had developed considerably. Evidence of
flint-working has been found in Redbourn - *Fig; 1.3.*[7] These finds indicate that
early man camped near the river some 6000 years ago, (location in *Fig: 1.1*) and
chipped away at lumps of flint to produce a variety of tools. The evidence that he
left, showed not only examples of finished tools, but also the remains of larger
flint lumps from which tools had been chipped off (known as "cores") – the latter,
with the many chippings, proving that they were actually made 'on-site'

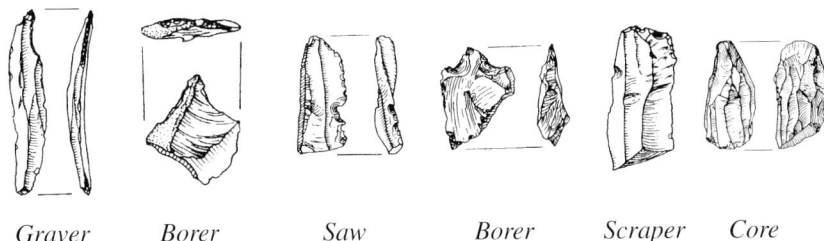

| Graver | Borer | Saw | Borer | Scraper | Core |

Fig: 1.3 - Mesolithic flints found in Redbourn

NEOLITHIC PERIOD

A fine axe head, dated between 2500 and
1600 BC, has been found on the opposite
side of the village (location in *Fig:1.1*) see
- *Fig. 1.4* [8] This is a much more refined
tool, it was carefully made to a slender sym-
metrical shape with a ground and polished
cutting edge. Such a tool, when fitted to a
haft of wood or Red Deer antler, is capable
of felling a 7-inch diameter tree in just 5
minutes. With this, and other developments
in hand tools, man was ready to change
from living off the land as a Hunter-
Gatherer, and starting to tame his environ-
ment by clearing the forests

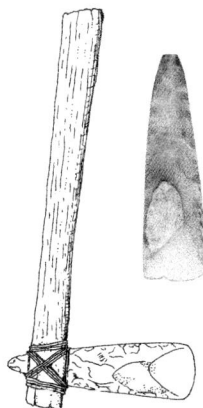

Fig: 1.4 – Neolithic Axe

Inset – Redbourn Axe head

THE BRONZE-AGE

With the discovery of how to make and
fashion metal into useful tools, man began to
take up a more static way of life, to plough and
plant the land and to keep animals for food.
However, it is typical of this age that little
evidence has survived. The find of greatest
interest locally is the cutting edge of a
Bronze Age axe head (see *Fig: 1.5*). The only
other find being a potsherd found near Watling
Street. [9]

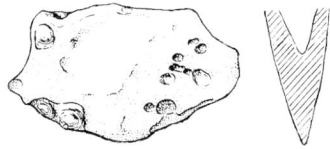

*Fig: 1.5 – Bronze Axe Head
found at Revel End*

THE IRON-AGE

Up to the coming of the Romans there were still tribes who roamed the land ready
to prey on the flocks and crops of the indigenous farming communities. Thus the
more peaceful farmers had a need to build defensible sites, inside which they and
their families could retreat for protection, if threatened. In Redbourn such a site
was built in the middle Iron Age, c.350BC, now known as "The Aubreys". The
name is derived from '**Auld Burh**' meaning '**Old Fort**'

The Aubreys has been referred to as a 'Hill Fort', but this is incorrect, as it
is not on a hill, but at the bottom of a ridge leading down from higher ground. It
is obviously intended to be defensive, having ditches and banks all the way round,
still about 14 feet deep in one position - *see Fig: 1.6*. Little archaeological investigation of the site has ever been made; Sir Mortimer Wheeler is supposed to have
viewed it and a Vicar, Rev. Lewis-Browne, said in 1899 that he was making some
excavations - but no reports were issued by either investigator [10]

More recently a well was investigated in the south-east bank by the
Redbourn Research Group (no longer in existence), who found evidence of an
ancient water level. By projecting around the relevant contour line the extent of
this water level can be clearly seen – shaded in *Fig: 1.1*. In this respect, a visit by
the Hertfordshire Natural History Society in 1907 is interesting as they reported
that parts of the site were then actually under water [11]

We must not think of this wide expanse of water as being clear and clean - it
would have been marshy, even boggy in places, and littered with all sorts of debris
such as dead trees, dead animals and even dead men. It is also probable that reeds
grew in the shallower parts and it is from these that the present village derives its
name - meaning **Reedy-Stream**, hence **Red Bourn**. I like to imagine that early
nomadic men also used this feature as a means of identifying the area, thus giving
our village a very early, pre-historic, name origin

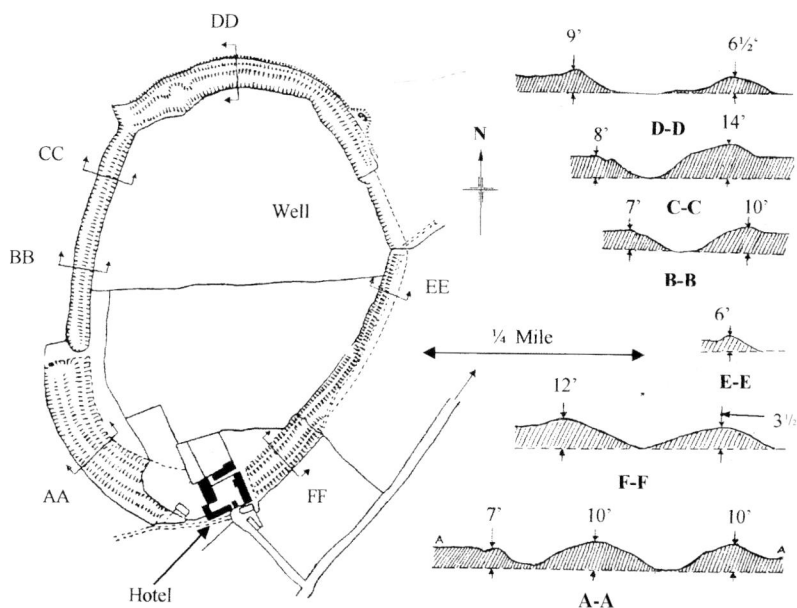

Fig: 1.6 – "The Aubreys" Iron-Age site

A piece of Folk-Law, or legend, has attached itself to the Aubreys recounting that when the Romans threatened a slaughter of Britons in the 3rd century AD, the local tribe hid their idol, a solid gold calf, somewhere in the Aubreys banks [13]

The Aubreys is not the only possible Iron-Age site in the village - aerial photo-graphy indicates marks near Beaumont Hall which could have been a farmstead in this period. [14] It is described as a *"rectangular...subdivided enclosure...with an imposing ditch and causeway on the east, facing the river"*

ROMAN

There are few indications of much Roman activity in Redbourn, apart from their great military road to northwest England and Wales, known to us today as "Watling Street". This was typically built in a straight line through what was to become our High Street some 1000 years later.

This road must have had quite an impact on the primitive landscape. All the trees were cleared to a total width of about 90 feet to reduce the risk of ambush (about the width of a 6-lane motorway with its hard shoulders). The road consisted of a base of large stones surfaced with those of smaller size, with drainage ditches each side, the cleared area was also ditched - see *Fig: 1.7* [15]

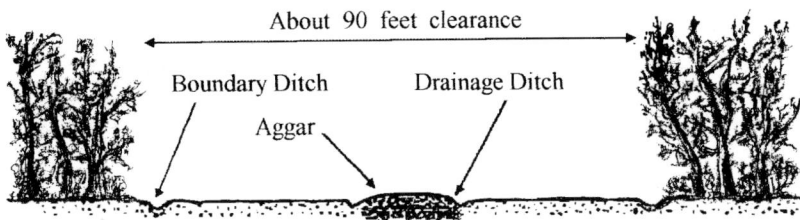

About 90 feet clearance

Boundary Ditch   Drainage Ditch

Aggar

Fig: 1.7 – Typical section through a Roman Road

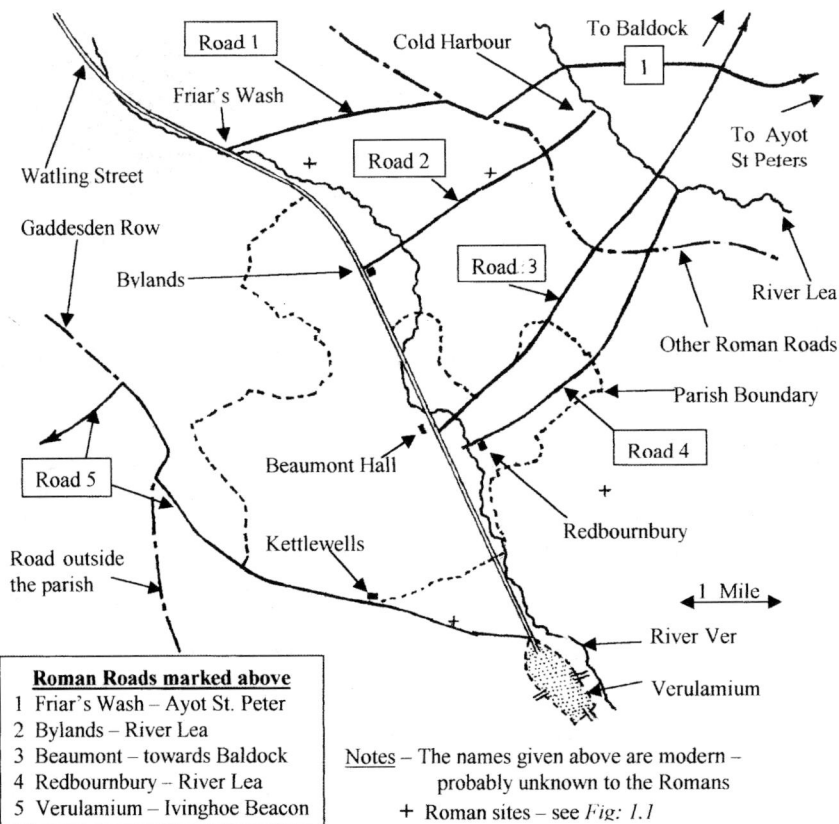

Road 1   Cold Harbour   To Baldock

1

Friar's Wash

To Ayot
St Peters

Watling Street   Road 2

Gaddesden Row

Road 3

Bylands   River Lea

Other Roman Roads

Parish Boundary

Road 4

Road 5   Beaumont Hall

Redbournbury

Kettlewells

Road outside
the parish   1 Mile

River Ver

Verulamium

Roman Roads marked above
1 Friar's Wash – Ayot St. Peter
2 Bylands – River Lea
3 Beaumont – towards Baldock
4 Redbournbury – River Lea
5 Verulamium – Ivinghoe Beacon

Notes – The names given above are modern –
          probably unknown to the Romans
+ Roman sites – see *Fig: 1.1*

Fig: 1.8 – Roman Roads in the Redbourn area

A group called "The Viatores" have studied and mapped Roman roads in the
South-east Midlands, their suggestions for local roads are shown above [16]

In spite of the known density of Roman Villas, it is rather surprising that one has not yet been found in the Redbourn Parish. The nearest are at Childwickbury, Gorhambury, Gadebridge and temple sites at Rothamsted and Friars Wash (*see Fig: 1.1*). Roman bricks used to build the corners (quoins) of Redbourn Church are another indication of a possible nearby villa (*see Fig: 4.5*). Other indications of suspected 'occupation sites' have been found near the High Street and during the building of Redbourn By-pass.[17]

The High Street investigation also provided a nice echo of marching Roman soldiers - a number of Hob Nails were found there - *see Fig: 1.9*

Fig: 1.9 - Roman Hob nail

A few Roman coins have also come to light in various parts of the village, including one of the Constantine period (307-333AD) shown in *Fig: 1.10* [18]

Fig: 1.10 Roman Coin

SAXON

The Saxon period is usually known as the 'Dark Ages' because of a dearth of contemporary written material. This is certainly true for Redbourn from Roman times to the reign of King Edward the Confessor

One debatable suggestion of Danish occupation cannot be entirely dismissed. Though the 'Danelaw' boundary is only about 5 miles away from a farm called "Dane End", it is thought that its name actually derives from being situated above a shallow valley (Old English 'Denu') leading down to the river Ver. Alternative spellings of 'Dean' or 'Dene' tend to support this conclusion [19]

There are several farms that bear the suffix 'End' (See also chapter 6). This is taken to denote that they were early clearings made into the basic forest. One of these, Church End, is considered to be the original site of the village; it is interesting to note its proximity to the earliest known habitation, "The Aubreys"

Church End is typical of a Saxon village siting - usually well clear of Roman roads or habitation, in this case about half a mile away from Watling Street

Perhaps some idea of what these small farm settlements looked like can be gained from reconstructions of Saxon villages such as that at West Stow, in Suffolk - here can be seen randomly spaced wooden, thatched huts, with a larger one for the Headman, all surrounded by an enclosing palisade

THE SAXON VILLAGE

Fig: 1.10 shows that these 'Ends' covered the whole area fairly evenly, but how they came together to form a parish, or Manor, is more difficult to understand. It is possible that protection offered by some Saxon thane, or nobleman, may be the key. Such Saxons were well armed and able to offer protection against marauders, but in exchange they expected payment from the villagers in the form of time spent labouring on the thane's own farm lands

By the end of the 11th century Redbourn had come under the control of a wealthy Saxon, Aegelwine Niger, or le Swarte (The Black) see *Fig: 1.11*. He was the first known Lord of the Manor, owning many other villages besides Redbourn. Some idea of his wealth is shown by the fact that he happily gave away four of his manors in the reign of Edward the Confessor (1042-7). The Charter confirming his gift of Redbourn to the Abbey (expecting the prayers of the monks for the good of his soul and those of his family) was given centuries later by Matthew Paris, that celebrated monk of St Albans Abbey. It was witnessed by the King, the Abbot, the Bishop of Dorchester and a long list of nobles. It reads thus [20]: -

"Let this be known to all the faithful, that I, Aegelwine the Black, with the agreement of my Lord King Edward do grant and dedicate to God and the blessed martyr, for the benefit of the monks serving him there, a piece of land consisting of 21 measures and one virgate in four places which we name: at Grenebeorge 5 hides, at **Reodbune 7 hides and 1 virgate***, at Langalege 5fi hides at Thwangtune 3fi hides, to the honour of God and St Mary and St Alban and all the saints at the church of the martyr Alban, for my soul and the soul of Wynflaedae my wife and the souls of my elders"*

Fig: 1.11 - Aegelwine and Wynflaeda
(By permission of The British Library)

The next Saxon evidence is also from a Charter, made about 20 years later, but this time by the Abbey of Westminster. This delineated the boundary of the joint parish of Wheathampstead and Harpenden, the portion that we shared with the latter being of course of great interest.[21] The common portion of this boundary is described between identifiable landmarks as follows: -

From *"langhecge thaet hit cymth to lippelane, from lippelane to secgham"*

This part of the common boundary is indicated on *Fig: 1.12*. "Long hedge" is long indeed, nearly 4 miles, of which 2½ miles borders Redbourn, from Beason

End to where there is now a roundabout on the By-pass. "Lippe lane" is now called Harpenden Lane and was the old boundary until it was changed to follow the Ver. The rest of the old boundary then followed Watling Street northward to "Secgham", meaning a meadow where sedge grows, which was near Friar's Wash

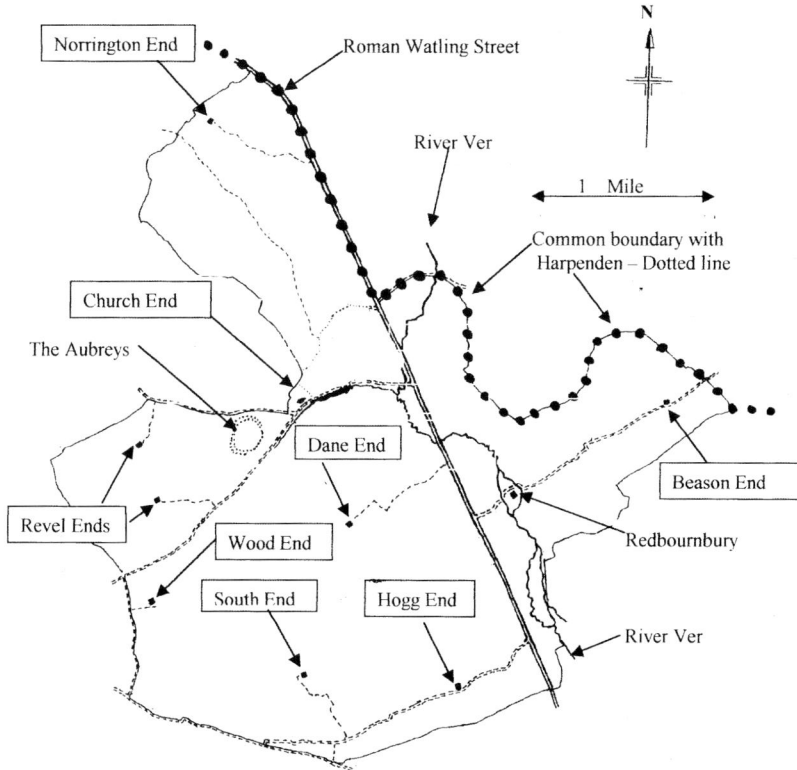

Fig: 1.12 – Redbourn in Saxon times

A Saxon spearhead found in Redbourn Churchyard (See chapter 5) could be linked to a warrior killed in a skirmish, such as that which might have led to the burial of the Golden Calf at "The Aubreys" (page 13)

As we have seen, the village was in existence in the middle 10th century, but it may have originated much earlier as suggested by the Rev. R. H. Fowler [22] :-
   "there was probably a parish here, and a church, long before the parishes of St Albans were established by Abbot Wulsin, in the middle of the 10th century"

<u>REFERENCES</u>

1   Most of the information for this section has been taken from - "The Geology of Redbourn", by D. A. Campbell, included in the Redbourn Programme for the Coronation (1953)

2   "Hertfordshire Puddingstone - St Albans City Museum, Information sheet No. 2

3   Collected by Mr John Harmer of St Agnells farm

4   J. R. Hunn - "Reconstruction & measurement of Landscape change" p184-5
    H. W. Gardener - "The Agriculture of Hertfordshire" p.127-8, Chalk Drawers p.108

5   H. W. Gardener - "The Agriculture of Hertfordshire" p.128

6   Sir William Addison - "The Old Roads of England" 1980, p.14

7   "Excavations in the City and District of St Albans 1974-76" - Excavations at Redbourn 1975 –pp.56-77. Also unpublished paper by Simon West - "A Mesolithic and later pre-historic site in Redbourn

8   Hertfordshire Archaeology V.I, p.119-20 - "A Neolithic Axe from Redbourn", F. D. Stageman

9   Evaluation Report GRE95, Simon West (in preparation) Also a pot-sherd found in the 'spoil' from a gas pipe trench near "Dolittle Mill" by Mr A. Dickinson

10 Transactions of the Hertfordshire Natural History Society - Vol. X

11 As 10, Vol. XIII

12 William Camden - "Britannia" many editions between 1586 & 1806, p.413

13 Mentioned in a leaflet issued by the Aubrey park Hotel in about 1993

14 David S. Neal - Excavation of the Iron-Age, Roman and Medieval Settlement at Gorhambury, St Albans, 1990, p.92

15 Richard W. Bagshawe - "Romans Roads", Shire Archaeology 1979, pp.12-17

16 "Roman Roads in the South-East Midlands" - The Viatores

17 "Excavations in the City and District of St Albans 1974-6" – C. Saunders & A. B. Havercroft, pp.56-77, Excavations at Redbourn 1975 - Harpenden & District Local History Society, Newsletter 33 January 1984, "Under Redbourn Roads" by W. S. Pierpoint

18 Roman coins found in a house at Church End & garden in Crouch hall Lane

19 "The Story of Redbourn" , 1962, p.3

20 Matthew Paris, "Chronica Majora", Rolls series of transcriptions Vol.6, p.28

21 "Wheathampstead and Harpenden" 1973, Part I, and p.3-4 and"Hertfordshire's Past", Vol. 4, pp.14-21

22 St Albans Archaeological and Architectural Society Transactions 1887, p.41

CHAPTER 2

DOMESDAY: INTRODUCTION TO MEDIEVAL REDBOURN

The Domesday Book made for King William the Conqueror in 1086 describes a parish little changed from Saxon times, yet now living under Norman rule. It thus gives a valuable picture of the early settlement at Redbourn, and a meaningful introduction to its medieval period. The book suggests a well established, thriving, agricultural community mainly held by the Abbot of St Albans, but with two other smaller holdings beyond his jurisdiction

Experts agree that the Domesday Commissioners did not visit every village and count every animal and measure each piece of land there. Rather, that they held courts in the major centres, locally such as St Albans, and took statements from the land holders, priests and perhaps selected groups of villagers

The original text of the main holding is shown in *Fig: 2.1.*[1] While *Figs: 2.2 & 2.3* give, respectively, translations and a comparison of all four entries

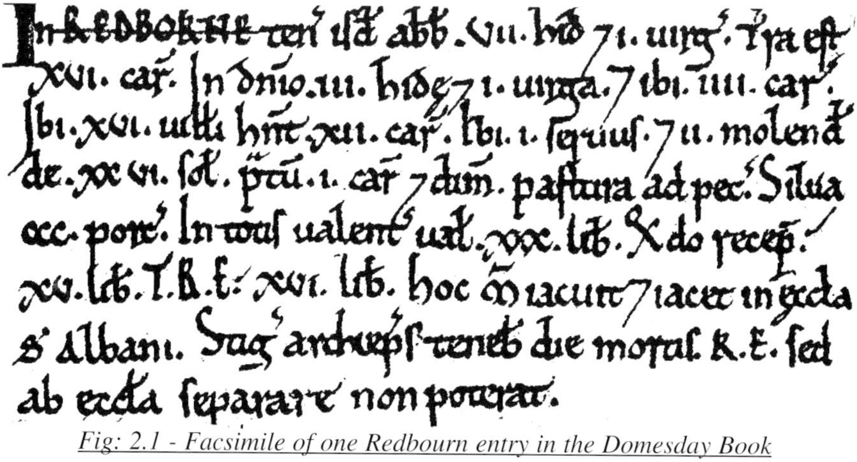
In REDBORNE ten' s'ca abb'. vii. hid' 7 i. uirg'. Tra est xvi. car'. In dnio. iii. hide 7 i. uirga. 7 ibi. iiii. car'. Ibi. xvi. uitti hnt. xii. car'. Ibi. i. seruus. 7 ii. molend' de. xxvi. sol'. ptu. i. car' 7 dim. pastura ad pec'. Silua ccc. porc'. In totis ualent' ual'. xxx. lib'. X do recep' xv. lib'. T.R.E. xvi. lib'. hoc m iacuit 7 iacet in eccla s' Albani. Stig' archieps tenebat die mortis R.E. sed ab eccla separare non poterat.

Fig: 2.1 - Facsimile of one Redbourn entry in the Domesday Book

The following comments result from my own studies, and is an attempt to present a reasonable assessment and explanation of the facts recorded by the Survey Commissioners

TENANTS AND SUB-TENANTS

The holders of the Domesday lands held them directly from the King, and were thus his 'tenants-in-chief'. Some of the lands were let out to sub-tenants, who were often Saxons whose families had worked the same land before the Battle of Hastings. The comments following concern each of the men appearing in the four entries for Redbourn given in *Fig: 2.2* overleaf

Abbot's Main Holding (10,10) – [Translation of *Fig: 2.1*]
> *In Redborne the Abbot also holds 7 hides and 1 virgate*
> *Land for 16 ploughs. In lordship 3 hides and 1 virgate; 4 ploughs there*
> *16 villagers have 12 plough. 1 slave.*
> *2 mills at 26s; meadow for 1½ ploughs; pasture for the livestock;*
>
> *woodland 300 pigs*
> *Total value £30; when acquired £15; before 1066 £16.*
> *This manor lay and lies in [the lands of] St Albans Church. Archbishop*
> *Stigand held it in 1066, but he could not separate it from the Church*

Abbot's Other Holding (10,14)
> *In Redborne Amalgar holds 3½ virgates from the Abbot.*
>
> *Land for 2 ploughs; they are there, with 2 villagers and 2 cottagers.*
> *Woodland, 200 pigs*
> *Value 30s; when acquired 20s; before 1066 40s.*
> *St Albans held and holds this land*

Count of Mortain's Holding (15,13)
> *In Redborne Ranulf holds fi hide from the Count. Land for 1 plough, but*
> *it is not there; only 2 smallholders*
> *Meadow for 1 plough; pasture for the livestock.*
> *Value 17s 4d; when acquired 20s; before 1066, 40s.*
> *Siward, a Freeman of King Edward's, held it; he could sell.*

Bishop of Lisieux's Holding   (6,1)
> *The Bishop of Lisieus has 1 virgate of land in Redbourne, Wigot*
> *holds from him. Land for ½ plough; it is there, with 1 smallholder*
>
> *Value 8s; when acquired 2s; before 1066, 10s.*

Fig: 2.2 - The four Redbourn Domesday Holdings

Note:- The above are translations as given by John Morris in:- "Domesday Book, 12 Hertfordshire"   (References in brackets are to this book)

THE ABBOT OF ST ALBANS, Paul de Caen, was the major landholder, not only of Redbourn, but also in the whole county, in which he had 20 manors. His Redbourn manor consisted of his 'demesne', or home farm, and the lands held from him by the villagers, subject to Labour Service etc. These villagers, or their forebears, had held their lands from previous Abbots and from Aegelwine the Black before he gave the land to the Abbey. Some of his holdings seem to have been self-contained farms, all of which were managed by Saxon sub-tenants, including:-
> *"In Redborne Amalgar holds 3½ virgates from the Abbot"*

AMALGAR. No hint is given of his status, but as he was obviously in charge of the farm, under the Abbot. This would have given him a higher status than the two villeins who also lived there

COUNT ROBERT OF MORTAIN. His half-brother, King William, granted him land in 19 English counties, principally in Cornwall, making him the largest land holder next to himself. Locally he had land in Hemel Hempstead, Berkhamsted and 10 other places in the county. One of his several castles was at Berkhamsted. A Saxon sub-tenant, Ranulf, looked after his Redbourn land:-

> *"Ranulf holds half a hide from the Count. Siward, a freeman of King Edward's, held it and he could sell"*

RANULF was a common name; there were four other Ranulfs in Hertfordshire. . One of them, described as *"a servant of the Count"*, held 30 acres of land at Berkhamsted - the normal amount for a villein to hold

SIWARD. The latter part of the above quotation shows that Siward was the previous sub-tenant, but as a "freeman" or freeholder he had the freedom to sell-up and move elsewhere if he so desired. However, the new Norman overlord had tightened up the old (feudal) system and taken away the freedom of his tenant (Ranulf) to do as he pleased with the land. Perhaps Siward was either killed at Hastings or had been deprived of his holding subsequently

BISHOP GILBERT OF LISIEUX, (in Normandy), was William's doctor. He held land in 6 English counties; this was his only Hertfordshire land. His Saxon tenant was:-

> *"Wigot holds from him (the Bishop). Alwin Hunter, Earl Leofwin's man, held it, he could sell"*

WIGOT was in a similar position to Ranulf, not being able to sell his land

ALWIN HUNTER, the previous Saxon sub-tenant was a freeman, able to sell his land and move if he so desired. This unusual name suggests that he was the same Alwin Hunter described at Watford as *"Queen Edith's man"*, ie. Tenant of Edward the Confessor's Queen

EARL LEOFWIN was brother to King Harold and died with him during the Battle of Hastings. He had 10 land holdings in Hertfordshire; these were re-distributed among 5 new Normans after the Conquest

INHABITANTS OF THE MANORS

Four classes of people make up the Domesday inhabitants of Redbourn:-

VILLEINS or villagers, were un-free men who held land in the 'Common', or 'Open' fields of the manor, while having to work the Abbot's demesne lands, as 'labour service', for much of their time, some of these may have been artisans such as blacksmiths, carpenters etc. [2.] Their average holding was about 30 acres [3]

OWNERS:-	ABBOT OF ST ALBANS		COUNT OF MORTAIN	BISHOP OF LISIEUX	TOTALS
TENANTS:-	ABBEY	Amalgar	Ranulf	Wigot	
INHABITANTS:-					
Villeins (Villagers)	16	2	-	-	
Cottars (Cottagers)	-	2	-	-	
Bordars (Smallholders)	-	-	2	1	
Serfs (Slaves)	1	-	-	-	
					24
ARABLE LAND:-					
Area (acres)	870	105	60	30	**1065**
(In Lordship)	(390)	-	-	-	
Ploughs (possible)	16	2	1	½	**19½**
OTHER LANDS:-					
Meadow - In terms of .. ploughs (oxen)	1½	-	1	-	**2½**
Pasture for	Livestock	-	Livestock	-	
Woodland for	300 pigs	200 pigs	-	-	
MILLS:-	2 Mills (26s)	-	-	-	**2 Mills**
VALUES:-					
In King Edward's time	£16	40s	40s	10s	**£20.10s.**
In 1066	£15	20s	20s	2s	**£17. 2s**
In 1086	£30	30s	17s.4d	8s	**£32.15s.4d**

Fig:2.3 - Assessment of Redbourn's Domesday Holdings

BORDARS, or smallholders, were of lesser standing than the villeins. They held about 5 acres or so of land and probably owed more labour service to the Abbot than did the villeins [4.] There were no Bordars in either of the Abbots holdings

COTTARS, as the name suggests were cottagers, and the lowest of the peasant cultivators having on average only about 4 acres of land, and obliged to do the more menial tasks for their Lord [5.] The name is indidicative that they lived in cottages away from the main village. At Redbourn there were only two, and these both lived on Amalgar's holding; suggestive of this being a small hamlet

SERFS, or slaves, were the property of the Lord, and the lowest order of inhabitants, having no land of their own. Some were employed as ploughmen, and per-

haps able to scrape enough money together to eventually purchase their freedom.
[6]. The only Redbourn slave was in the Abbot's holding - thus probably living at
Redbournbury, convenient for ploughing his master's demesne land

THE DOMESDAY POPULATION

It is obvious that the total population of Redbourn in 1086 must have been many
more than the 24 listed in the four survey entries - *see Fig: 2.3.* But these only represent the 'Heads of Households' and thus need to be multiplied by the number in
each family. The figure now generally accepted as an average for this is five. [7]
Thus to get a fair idea of the total population, the 24 families must be multiplied
by 5; however, this should not be applied until some corrections have been made
to allow for the following factors [8]:-

> Slaves should be counted as individuals, because they mostly had no
> families - for Redbourn there was just one
> No Priest or Miller is mentioned - they are thought to have been of
> villeins status, thus being included in the 16 for the main manor
> The three sub-tenants, Amalgar, Ranulf and Wigot need to be added
> (+3)
> An allowance for 'men missed', is normally taken as 5%, in this case +1

The figure of 23 (the slave omitted) can now be amended, (+3+1) making 27
heads of household, which when multiplied by 5 (plus the slave) gives.......

A REDBOURN POPULATION IN 1086 OF ABOUT 136 PEOPLE

ARABLE LAND

This is stated both as area and as the number of ploughs required to work it. That
given for the main holding includes both the demesne and the peasants' lands:-

> *"In Lordship (the demesne) 3 hides & 1 virgate (390 acres) and*
> *4 ploughs"...."the villagers have 12 ploughs" (for their 4 hides, ie. 480*
> *acres)*

A team of 8 oxen is thought to have been required to pull the heavy (Saxon)
ploughs; but obviously just 16 villagers would not have been able to rear and keep
nearly 100 beasts for all their 12 ploughs.[9] A suggested figure of about 3 oxen per
villein, makes a more likely total of 48 beasts thus giving ox teams of 4 per
plough. [10.] Medieval drawings often show such teams, *see Fig: 2.4.* These would
certainly have been more manoeuvrable and quite adequate for the small strips in
the Common fields, while full 8 ox ploughs would have been practical and necessary on the larger demesne lands

Fig: 2.4 - A Medieval 4-ox plough

The 480 acres of lands held by the 16 villagers, in the three or more Common fields, would have been divided into strips of about an acre. The direction of the strips being determined by the lay of the land and most practical to give the easiest access to the cumbersome ploughs. It was important that every strip in each field contained the same crop each year, with one year fallow - such plans had to be worked out and agreed by all the villagers. Also a tenth of their crops had to be given to the Lord as 'Tithe' and all grain had to be ground at the Lord's own mill

As payment for their land holdings, each villein had to work on the demesne lands for perhaps 2 days a week, and more at harvest times, fitting in work on their own strips in between.[11] They also may have had other dues or taxes to pay annually, or when a member of the household died, married or if land changed hands. Other duties may have involved the maintenance of roads, river courses etc.

OTHER TYPES OF LAND

MEADOWLAND is given in terms of the number of plough teams that its crops of hay could support. *"Meadow for 1½ ploughs"*. This only amounts to 12 acres, but taking a plough team as 8 oxen, was hardly enough to support the 16 villagers ploughs - even with their small 4 ox teams they would have required 64 acres [12]

This apparent dearth of meadow for plough teams is a common proportion in other Hertfordshire manors. Compared with 19th century figures, which could not have been too different from 1086, about 290 acres of meadow bordered the Redbourn rivers, *See Fig: 2.5* - enough to support their ox teams and their other livestock

PASTURE is stated vaguely as *"pasture for the livestock"*. In later centuries, pasture was normally situated around the farm dwellings, but most of the villagers' animals would quite happily have used what is now Redbourn Common, or strips in the Common fields when they were left fallow. Only two holdings had pasture - the same two that also had meadows

WOODLAND in Redbourn was only in the Abbot's two holdings, both given in terms of the number of pigs that they could support (all foraging for acorns and beech masts). The figures are rounded off to the nearest 100, and thus obviously must be estimates. A figure tentatively suggested for parishes in Bedfordshire is that 2fi acres was required per pig, giving the huge area of 1,250 acres.[13] It should be noted that this was not just one very large wood

A comparison of the figures given for adjacent parishes indicates the relative areas of woodland; showing that Redbourn was fairly well wooded in 1086. ie:-

Hemel Hempstead	1200 pigs
St Albans	1000 "
Flamstead	1000 "
Windridge (Gorhambury)	600 "
REDBOURN	**500** "
Wheathampstead (& Harpenden)	400 "
Sandridge	300 "

The first full map of the parish, made in 1841 (The Tithe Map), shows no great areas of woodland. However, evidence can be deduced from names, such as Nicholls Wood, Great How Wood, Pancake Wood; remaining tree groups, some-times called 'Springs' or 'Groves', which may be the remains of larger areas of trees. All these possibilities are indicated by lighter shading in *Fig: 2.6.* "Redding Wood" - from Redding or Ridding, is said to indicate earlier assarting, ie. wood clearance [14]

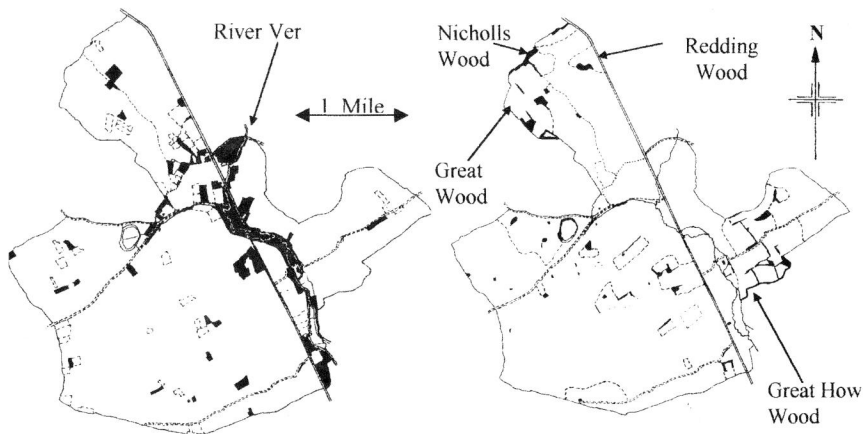

Fig: 2.5 - Suggested Meadowland   *Fig: 2.6 - Suggested Woodlands*
Note: Black areas are meadows and woods shown on 1841 Tythe map
The dotted areas are pastures or woods deduced from field names etc

AREA OF THE PARISH

The parish boundary with Harpenden was well defined by 1060 (see page 17), the rest of our boundaries with other parishes most probably being fixed by that time as well. This means that the parish area was also fixed and remained constant until the boundary changes of the last century

Thus it would seem logical that we should be able to relate the Domesday figures to the earliest reliable survey of the parish made for the Commutation of Tithes in 1841. In this survey the total parish area, excluding the Common, was 4515 acres

The figure given in Domesday was in terms of Hides and Virgates, equivalent to 1065 acres. However, this is now considered by experts to be an arbitrary figure on which taxation could be based.[15] A better figure to use relates to the number of plough teams employed to farm the arable land. It has been suggested that for fertile land 4 ox-ploughs were required for each square mile (640 acres).[16] On this basis the 19 fi Redbourn ploughs could farm 3120 acres of arable land.

This is remarkably near the figure of 3155 acres of arable land, given in the 1841 Tithe map.

MILLS

Only two mills are given for Redbourn in Domesday, both are in the Abbot's main holding; mills at this time were water driven, or occasionally handmills. It could be suggested that 'two mills' means two pairs of millstones in the same building, but at Redbourn there have been two quite separate mill buildings from ancient times [17]

The main mill was at Redbournbury adjacent to the manor house of the Abbey Chamberlain. The other, initially called "Bettespool", was on Watling Street less than a mile from the early village at Church End. Such mills, with their special mechanisms and planned watercourses, demanded particular skills and knowledge to create. The cost of such work would have been beyond the means of village people without the help of whoever was Lord of the Manor at the time There were only 5 other mills in the county which were valued more than Redbourn (Hitchin, Sacombe, (Bishops) Stortford, Watton and Wymondley), those at St. Albans being only of slightly higher value

VALUATIONS

The values given in Domesday are probably estimates of the amount of rent which could be obtained.[18] They are given for three significant dates:-

"T.R.E." = *Tempore Regis Edwardi* - In the time of King Edward the Confessor, ie. before 1066
"*When acquired*" - When re-allocated after the Conquest, ie. post 1066
"*Total value*" - At the time of the survey, ie. 1086

It will be noted that in the actual wording *(see Fig: 2.2)* these dates are given in reverse order; but I have chosen the chronological sequence as this makes more sense, *see Fig: 2.3*. The actual values mean little to us today because of the vast inflation over the intervening 900 and more years. However, they can be used to indicate value fluctuations since the Conquest, or as comparisons with other parishes

Most values, including Redbourn, show a drop after the coming of the Norman Conquerors. Some places show quite dramatic losses of value, perhaps due to pillaging by the invading army. This could have happened along the route taken by King William when he skirted around to the north of London - see Chapter 3. A further reason for loss of value at Berkhamsted may have been due to the Count fleecing the manor to pay for his castle there; the same picture can be seen on all his Hertfordshire holdings

In contrast, the Abbot's main holding in Redbourn shows only a slight drop in 1066, but then it nearly doubles its pre-conquest value. J. R. Hunn comments that *"something fairly dramatic had been going on in the Redbourn area between 1066 and 1086"*. He suggested that this might have been due to a reorganisation of the agrarian system, or to extensive woodland clearance, observing that the more regular appearance of the field systems might point to such work.[19'] Only two other Abbey holdings show such a dramatic increase, ie. Shenley and Sandridge. The other Redbourn holdings show losses after the conquest, but while two are showing signs of recovery, only that of the Count is continuing to drop

OTHER ITEMS TO NOTE

The area of the Abbot's manor was given as *"7 hides & 1 virgate"* - exactly the same area donated by Aegelwine the Black to the Abbey in the time of Edward the Confessor (see Chap 1); confirming that this really is one and the same manor

The entry for Redbourn, in common with many other Domesday parishes, does not mention either a Church or a Priest. This is not an indication that there was no church in the village, but rather that it had no monetary significance to the Commissioners. In the whole of Hertfordshire only 3 churches and 49 priests appear, out of 168 settlements

LOCATION OF THE HOLDINGS

The 'Manor of Redbourn' can be traced in many documents, mostly of post-Dissolution date. The earliest map of the manor is dated 1767, by which time it was in the hands of the Earls of Verulam.[20] This map shows the Manor lying south of the east-west roads to Harpenden and Hemel Hempstead; the manor of 1086 may not have been too different from this, with the villeins open fields mostly to the north

There is no hard evidence to locate where the other three Domesday holdings might have been. They were all later bought by the Abbot, and it would seem logical that he let them retain their separate entities, as small manors, rather than absorbing them into the mass of other Abbey lands

Therefore, we should be looking at farms which had attained manor status, such as - Butlers, St Aignels, Inges, (thought to be at Beeson End) and Lawrence (near Dane End)

The land held from the Abbot by Amalgar, has been suggested as probably lying east of the Ver on the higher ground above Redbournbury, ie. Beeson End.[21] Supporting this idea is the absence of any meadowland on this high ground and also surviving evidence of quite extensive former woods. Further it could be suggested that the 2 villeins and 2 cottagers here, as well as Amalgar himself, would have formed a small hamlet of about 5 cottages, fitting in well with Beeson End

The Count of Mortain's land contained both meadow and pasture, so it is likely to have been located beside a river. It could be suggested that it may also have been near his other lands at Hemel Hempstead. An obvious place would be somewhere along the river Red, towards the boundary with Hemel Hempstead, such as Wood End, Cross Lanes or perhaps Revel End

Finally the small holding of the Bishop of Lisieux. This is the most difficult to place; it has nothing like meadow or woodland to aid with its location, it could literally have been anywhere in the parish area. Perhaps consideration of a small manor such as Butlers, or Lawrence, might be considered

CONCLUSIONS

"Society portrayed in the Domesday Book had its roots in the British past; after 1086 it would change only slowly"

This interesting statement shows how important William's Survey really is to us today.[22] Applied to Redbourn it not only links our 'Saxon past' to the 'Norman present', but could largely hold true through much of the Medieval period or even longer. Confirming my earlier idea that Domesday gives us a useful introduction to the Norman and indeed the Medieval period of our history

The Survey is actually showing us a Saxon village of at least 16 dwellings, perhaps with a larger hut for the 'headman' among the villeins. This group of primitive wooden dwellings, somewhere in the Church End area, could have been protected by some sort of palisade. Besides this main nucleus of the parish, there were other smaller collections of buildings, or huts, in outlying parts where clearings had been cut into the wild woodland of primeval times. The location of many such clearings is thought to be indicated by the many 'Ends' that exist, an early example being 'Church End' *(For locations see Fig: 1.12)*

SPELLINGS OF THE NAME - 'R E D B O U R N'

Before looking further into our medieval history we should consider the name **REDBOURN**, its meaning and its many spellings through the ages

The 'English Place Name Society' state that it comes from the Old English **'Hreod-Burna',** translated as **'Reedy Stream'.** quoting Thomas Walsingham who, in the 15th century, stated - *"Redburn is derived from its reediness"* [23] A 'Bourn' is known to be a river having seasonal variations in level. This is true for both our rivers, but particularly for what we now call the **'River Red'**. William Camden, writing in the 16th century, called this river the **"Wemner"** or **"Womer"**, noting its reputation for foretelling disaster if it ran high or overflowed.[24] This is said to have happened just before both World Wars and also the General Strike .[25]

Latin Versions

REDBURNA	c.1042 TO 1098
REDBURNAM	11C. to 1423
REDBURNAE	15C.
REDBURNIA	1217
REDBURNIAM	13C.
RYDBURN	1562

English Versions

REDBORNE	1086 TO 1691
REDBORN	1577 to 1701
REDBURNE	1240 to 1728
REDBURN	1232 to 1842
RADBOURNE	1392
REODBUNE	c.1042
REDBOURNE	1402 to the Present day (incorrect use)
REDBOURN	1610 to the Present day (Modern version)

Strange spellings

REODBURNE	11C. to c.1060
RODBORNE	1346
REDBONE	1420
REDEBURN	1291 to the 16C.
REDEBOURN	1337
REDEBORNE	1428
REDDEBURNE	1428
RIDIBOWNE	1485

Fig: 2.7 - Different Spellings of 'Redbourn'

The alternative spellings of 'Bourn' and 'Bourne' appear in modern dictionaries; (meaning a stream, often seasonal). Personally I fancy the more picturesque spelling with a final 'e', but I must concede that **'REDBOURN'** is the correct modern spelling. Thus, in the case of 'REDBOURNE' I must, reluctantly, label its modern usage as 'incorrect' - See *fig: 2.7* for dated examples that I have found, in documents and in "The Place Names of Hertfordshire" [26]

REFERENCES

1   "Domesday Book - A Facsimile of the part relating to Hertfordshire"
2   "Domesday - A Search for the Roots of England" Michael Wood, p151
3   "Domesday Book - A guide" R. Welldon Finn, p38
4   As 2, p37.
5   As 2, p36.
6   As 2, p34
7   "Domesday England" H. C. Darby, 1977, p87
8   As 7, pp87-9 and as 2, p26
9   As 7, p125
10 As 2, p38
11 As 3, pp151-2 and "Fields" Richard & Nina Muir   REF ????
12 As 7, p138
13 As 7 p192
14 Story of Redbourn , p3 and Local History Encyclopaedia, John Richardson, A210
15 Thomas Hinde (Ed.) "The Domesday Book England's Heritage, then & now"
    1995, p.16
16 As 15, p.17
17 "The Mills of Redbourn" Alan Featherstone. p8
18 As 2, p78
19 "Reconstruction & Measurement of Landscape Change" Jonathan R. Hunn,
    1944, p77
20 CRO. Document ref - D/EV M39/P2
21 Victoria County History, Hertfordshire Vol. 1, p367
22 As 2, p167
23 Thomas Walsingham - "Gesta Abbatum" Vol. 1, p.54
24 William Camden - "Britannica", p.413
25 "The Common Round" (Parish Magazine), May 1965
26 "The Place Names of Hertfordshire", Cambridge University Press 1938, p78

CHAPTER 3

MEDIEVAL EVENTS

The chief source of information concerning significant Redbourn events in medieval times comes from the writings of monks of St. Albans Abbey, such as Matthew Paris, John Amundesham and Thomas Walsingham. They were mostly concerned with local and Abbey events, but often also give facts of wider importance, such as the Peasants Revolt, Wars of the Roses, visits of Royalty etc.

The national upheaval caused by the Dissolution of the Monasteries is recorded mostly in legal documents as this was more of a reorganisation of the lands, buildings and wealth of the English Monasteries - see chapter 6.

KING WILLIAM

After his triumph at Hastings, King William the Conqueror, did not make a direct approach to London to claim his Crown, instead he skirted around to the west and north. He was met en route by a party of nobles, which included Abbot Frederic the meeting taking place at Berkhamsted, where uneasy peace terms were agreed.

William soon found that Abbot Frederic was not to be trusted, being subsequently suspected of plots against his crown. The Abbot soon realised that he was in danger from the King, and fled to Ely.[1] As a consequence, William confiscated many of the Abbey lands and gave them to the Archbishop of Canterbury, including the Manor of Redbourn.[2]

For such a case Aegelwine the Black had embodied a curse into his charter.[3]:-

"If anyone should wish to transfer this our gift to some other purpose than that we have laid down, let him be deprived of the consolation of God's Holy Church, and let him be punished perpetually in the everlasting fires of the lower regions and share the dismal fate which befell Judas, Christ's betrayer"

The next Abbot, a Norman Paul de Caen, happened to be a friend of Lanfrac, the new Norman Archbishop, and had little difficulty in getting the confiscated lands restored. The Domesday Book briefly records these events:-

"This manor lay and lies in (the lands of) St Albans Church, Archbishop Stigand held it in 1066, but he could not separate it from the church".

NORMAN BUILDING ACTIVITIES

After their invasion, the Normans had rather obvious building priorities. It was vital for them to set up castles from where their nobles could control the land and its Saxon inhabitants; that at Berkhamsted for the Count of Mortain being a local example. Next they built, or re-built, monasteries and brought monks over from Normandy to manage them - St Albans Abbey came in for this treatment under Paul de Caen. Finally they replaced or rebuilt any 'unworthy' Saxon churches.

At Redbourn there is no tangible evidence of there having been a Saxon church but it can be argued that there was a small wooden structure here, and that it was replaced by the stone building which is the basis of the present church - (see chapter 4).

Note that Redbourn Priory came much later than this early building activity, it resulted from the thirst of the monks for relics of the saints - the relevant facts and fictions of this local creation will be discussed in chapter 5

CHRISTINA OF MARKYATE

Thomas Walsingham relates the strange story of the saintly virgin Christina, who, after being forced into marriage in c.1135, took refuge in a cell at Markyate, under the protection of the aged hermit Roger.[4]

Roger arranged for her to secretly meet Thurston, Archbishop of York, at Redbournbury, he annulled the marriage and enabled her to enter a nunnery. She eventually became Prioress of Markyate Nunnery, and in time, spiritual confident of the Abbot of St Albans and was famed as a prophetess and a worker of miracles.[5]

The better known part of her story concerns her visit to Redbournbury. Roger entrusted her to an aged couple, Godescal de Cadundene and his wife, but after receiving their commission they lost their horse in a dark forest and feared for their lives. However, by the prayers of Roger, a saddled horse miraculously appeared and took them safely home.

On the Rood Screen in Gateley church in Norfolk a figure is shown among other saints and kings; and entitled - *"St Puella Ridibowne"*- see *Fig: 3.1.* Puella is Latin for a maiden and is thought in fact to represent Christina of Markyate, and "Ridibowne" to mean Redbourn.[6]

Fig: 3.1- Christina of Markyate?
Screen in Gateley church, 1485

KING JOHN

Redbournbury was also the scene of another notable visit, but in this case an expensive one for the Abbey Chamberlain.

The troubles of King John are well known, principally his signing of the

Magna Carta and finally the loss of his valuables in the Wash just before his death in 1217. He was heading north to avoid confrontation with his angry nobles, but on his way personally commandeering equipment for the journey from the Abbey Chamberlain at Redbournbury, taking.[7] :-

"Three horses, two donkeys and a good new iron-clad cart".

The full cost was put at 50 shillings, the last item sounding particularly expensive. It is tempting to think that this cart would have been ideal for transporting his valuables, and maybe something that archaeologists are still hoping one day to recover and prove that the Wash really holds King John's secret.

The Chamberlain also had a duty to provide the Abbot with a horse whenever he travelled north to visit the Abbey cell at Tynemouth, but in this case he could expect its safe return.[8]

ROBBERY AT THE PRIORY

The mercenaries of King Louis of France, who joined the English Barons in their struggles against King John, came through Redbourn heading north to confront the King. They robbed and plundered whatever stood in their path. On the 1st of May 1217, Redbourn Priory came in their path and they looted it thoroughly, even taking the monks clothes - leaving them only in their underpants! [9]

One of their party, out for personal gain, secreted a silver-gilt cross which was said to contain a fragment of the true cross. He was immediately seized with a fit and had to be restrained, becoming completely mad by the time they reached Flamstead. The brave village priest barred their way into the church, dressed in white robes; in the ensuing confusion the cross fell from the man's cloak. Realising that this was the real cause of his madness, the soldiers entreated the priest to immediately return the cross to the Priory, and went on their way.

QUEEN ELEANOR

The passing of Queen Eleanor's body through the village on its way to London for burial in December 1290, is not recorded, but the village was on their route. St Albans was one of the stopping places, where hospitality earned the city its own 'Eleanor Cross' see Fig: 3.2.10 One can imagine the scene as the cortège passed by with all the villagers doffing their hats or kneeling to pay homage and respect to their King and his dead Queen.[11]

Fig: 3.2 - St Albans Eleanor Cross in
Cromwellian times

EARLY MIRACLES

The early medieval centuries were a time for miracles. I have told of that associated with Christina of Markyate; others relative to the founding of Redbourn Priory will be mentioned in chapter 5. Two others were associated with the Redbourn watermills:-

At Redbournbury, a disastrous fire was confined to just the mill [12]:-

"...a fire of unknown origin entirely destroyed the Chamberlain's mill at Redburne. This fire, fanned by an unbearable wind from the west, threatened the whole manor with ruin and devastation, but by the grace of God, and thanks also to the thickness and protection of the surrounding woods, it did no further damage".

This is some indication that there was much more woodland in this area than there is today.

About 50 years later, the other mill, "Bettespool", was the scene of a dramatic miracle with a happy ending [13]:-

"A certain 5 year old girl fell into the water at the mill of Bettespole and was quickly submerged. At the time the mill was grinding and the wheel was being rotated powerfully by an abundance of water. Thus the girl's body passed under the wheel, but although ground and tossed about, it remained whole and unscathed, at least by the mangling of the wheel. Many people rushed to the scene and when they saw the girl's mother clasping her daughter in anguish, they poured out a prayer to the proto-martyr, Alban, and lo and behold, while they were measuring and flexing her body, she began to revive and after a short time to show that she had fully returned to life".

Perhaps this is an early example of a way of resuscitating of drowned people, similar to that practised today.

THE ABBOT'S CUP

The writings of Thomas Walsingham tell of a minor but potentially embarrassing incident that occurred while the Abbot was celebrating the passion of St Alban. During the feast, John Aygnel of Redbourn approached the Abbot's table and claimed the privilege of being his Butler for the evening. He maintained that this was a right held by his predecessors as 'rent service' pertaining to "Dispensers Land" in Redbourn.14

The Abbot was quick to decline this offer, saying that he had never heard of it before. His friends tried to persuade John Aygnel not to press his claim to serve the Abbot, but he still insisted that this was his ancient right. After the feast a search of the Abbey archives revealed a charter which showed that there had been such a privilege, but it had been surrendered by a former tenant.

The 'Dispensers Land' was held partly by John Aygnel and partly by the Chamberlain. From its revenues it was customary to maintain a horse which the Abbot could use when he visited the far distant Abbey cell at Tynemouth. The 1841 Tithe Map shows "Spencers (Dispensers?) Field" as being part of South End Farm.

SONS OF REDBOURN
The practice of naming men after the place where they were born, or lived for a long time, sometimes gives us an insight to former inhabitants of Redbourn. Many such men appear in early writings, though care has to be exercised because there is also a Redbourn in Lincolnshire. Often such a derivation of a name is continued as a family name surviving to this day. A person with the name 'Redbourn' visited the Museum in 2001, he lived in Wokingham.

Many such natives of Redbourn appear in records from the 12th century; a useful source for these is in the Close or Patent Rolls kept in the Public Record Office. I offer the following names but there may be many more.[15]:-

Geoffrey de Redburne, son of William - held 2fi hides of land from the
    Abbot in 1259
Walter de Redburn - Appears in 1224, 1228 and 1229
William de Redburn - Charged with causing a death at Marlborough 1234
Adam de Redburn - His daughter, Matilda is mentioned in 1264
Brother Simon de Redburn - In an appeal case in Bedford in 1283
John de Redburne - Refectorer of St Albans Abbey, c.1308-26
Nicholas de Redbourn - Involved in a murder case in 1313
William de Redburn - Named in a document re liberties extorted from
    the Abbot in 1317
Brother John de Redburne - Also called "Pyk", involved in a dispute with
    the Vicar of St Peters re a Cross erected in that churchyard c.1335-49
William de Redburn - Pardoned for outlawery in Middlesex, 1346
Adam de Redburne - Mentioned in connection with the election of Abbot
    John de la Moote, 1396
Thomas Redburne - Killed by Robert Dycoun, 1350
Thomas Redburne - Proctor of Oxford, later Bishop of St David's

Of these early 'Sons of Redbourn', the last named was the most successful. He was educated at Oxford and was a good scholar and mathematician, becoming Proctor of the University in 1412. While Warden of Merton College he built a tower over the gateway. He also wrote "A Chronicle of England". Eventually becoming Bishop of St David's.[16]

A REDBOURN REVOLT

Seeds of discontent that later burst into life as the 'Peasants Revolt' had been fermenting in many places long before 1381. Redbourn was one such place, and held its own dress rehearsal some 50 years before the revolt staged by Wat Tyler. In about 1344 feelings in the village were very high against annual taxation, or tallage, which the Abbot had the right to impose 'at will' on their land holdings.

Leading villagers wanted a more lenient tax of 20 shillings overall, rather than 40 pence per head; they even collected the amount that they suggested and offered it to the Abbot. He refused the money, insisting that it was entirely his prerogative to choose what tax to demand from them.[17]

Villagers were able to find someone with sufficient knowledge of documents to be able to produce a convincing forgery of the charter of Aegelwine the Black and to embody into it the obligations that the villagers were prepared to offer. They even showed this charter to some important men in the neighbourhood, who were persuaded to support their cause before the Abbot.

The charter was duly produced for the Abbot to read, but he very soon spotted that it was a forgery. The forger had made the mistake of writing it in a mixture of English and French (Saxon and Norman), which had only been used since the Conquest and therefore could not possibly have been a Saxon document. The Abbot proved his point by producing the authentic charter and having it publicly read. At this point the intercessors acting for the villagers were acutely embarrassed and quickly denied any part in the plot.

The villagers were not to be subdued and continued to oppose being taxed at the will of the Abbot. They were immediately excommunicated, and the Abbot demanded that all the villagers should take an oath in court that they were now willing to pay taxes at the will of the Abbot and that - *"they were truly villeins in person and chattels"*

This was still not the end; some villagers would not be subdued in this way and declared their willingness to die for the cause. Consequently when the Chamberlain's servants came to distrain the culprits, the Bedel was seized and flogged. The Bailiff was then sent to arrest those involved, but all of them, except Adam de Rotherfeld, managed to escape, he was left to suffer for his companions in the stocks at St Albans.

The monastic account of the incident ends with a recital of all the village tenants, the land they held and how much they were to be taxed. This local 'Domesday list' is of great interest as it gives villagers' names for the first time and provides clear links to several farms later named after them. The list names 55 tenants, three of them paupers. Using this figure in the same way as for that of Domesday, **I can tentatively suggest a population in 1344 of about 275**

THE FLAMSTEAD TROUBLE

For some unaccountable reason to us now, the people of Flamstead in the 14th century claimed to have virtually the same rights to Redbourn Common as the local residents.[18]

The basic problem seems to have stemmed from the position of the Common, it was then called the Heath, which spanned their quickest route to market in St Albans, this can be seen from Fig: 3.4. Not only did they drive their herds across the Heath, and graze them en route, but they also asserted all 'common rights' (such as being able to dig up peat, clay or sand), saying that these belonged to Flamstead. They even tried to make Thomas Bedel (see *Fig: 3.3*) take down a house that he had built - *"near a footpath and the King's highway"* possibly where the house called - "The Heath" now stands.

Fig:3-3 Thomas Bedel
(By permission of the British Library. Add.MS.9063f.24b)

The Flamstead people extended their malice to the Priory, seizing a supply wagon carrying food and demonstrating outside the gates brandishing pitchforks, much to the alarm of the monks inside. The Prior's response to the hijacking was to purchase a "safe road" which ran *"from the mill at Betlespol to a lane called 'Heybriggelane'*, [Chequers Lane] *twenty feet wide"* - see *Fig: 3.4*

The Flamstead people were becoming arrogant and malicious, with the backing and support of their Lord, Thomas de Beauchamp, Earl of Warwick. The Abbot therefore, decided to call a public meeting to finally resolve the matter. Thus on the 15th of November 1383 the Earl of Warwick met the Abbot on Redbourn Heath, both with their councils and advisers in attendance.

The Abbot proceeded to demonstrate that all the land surrounding the heath belonged to him, also that the bones of Amphibalus had been found there and a Priory had been built to his honour. With such overwhelming evidence, the Earl had to admit that he had no rights to the Heath and that he had been misled by his officials into making false claims.

An agreement to this effect was drawn up and signed by both parties. However, the Abbot realised that, because of the geographical position of the Heath, the Flamstead people should be allowed some leeway. He agreed that they could still drive their herds across it to market, but that they were not allowed to stop and graze. They were also permitted to bring their sheep and dip them in the river, but only for two hours in any one day - a cottage on East Common, formerly an inn, commemorates this activity by its name - "The Sheep Wash".

LAW SUIT BY THE PRIOR OF ASHRIDGE

In 1380 the Prior of Ashridge started a lawsuit against the Abbot, claiming a half share in a road on the western edge of Redbourn - see Fig: 3.4 19:-

> "From Portdelle up to the Stone Cross which stand at the cross-roads, and from that place in the road up to the north up to Chalkdelle and thence to Holtsmere"

The Abbot reached a rather uncharacteristically hasty decision, perhaps because of a weightier problem looming at that time (see next section). It is difficult to imagine why this fairly minor road, about 6 miles from Ashridge should be of such interest to that Prior. The Abbot agreed, but subsequently it was discovered that the road had always belonged to the Abbot and that he should not have agreed to joint ownership.

THE PEASANTS' REVOLT

The problems the Abbot had experienced with Redbourn's forged charter, the Earl of Warwick and the Prior of Ashridge, all paled into insignificance when the fringe of the Peasants' Revolt struck St Albans in 1381.20 No doubt the people of the city and many villages in Hertfordshire had been avidly following the successes of Wat Tyler and his followers in Kent and East Anglia. On Friday June 14th they decided the time was right to join the revolt for their own ends.

Under the local leadership of William Grindecobbe, they sallied forth to petition the King and to seek the support of Tyler himself. They succeeded in both objectives, getting the promise of a letter from the King and also a promise of 'mob support' from the rebels.

They wasted no time on their return to St Albans early next day, and with growing support from the people of the city and surrounding villages, there was nothing the Abbot could do to resist them. A major cause of their anger towards the Abbot was his insistence on the exclusive use of his mills for grinding their corn, and his confiscation of all illegal hand mills used by the people. He had even paved the floor of his parlour with the stones thus obtained - this was their first target, so they entered the Abbey and ripped up this floor.

When the awaited letter from the King arrived the next day, it was publicly delivered to the Abbot. Though Abbot Thomas de la Mare tried to stand up to the rebels, he had to give way and produce charters. The rebels considered the Charters had restrictive conditions and. these were promptly and publicly burned - perhaps the charter of Aegelwine the Black was among them?

While all this was going on, some splinter groups seized the opportunity to go on the rampage in the city. In one of these groups men from Redbourn, combining with others from Berkhamsted, went looking for the Forest Warden -

Robert atte Chamber. He was obviously a very unpopular man, probably because he actively pursued any poachers on the Abbot's behalf. They could not find him, so they destroyed his house instead.

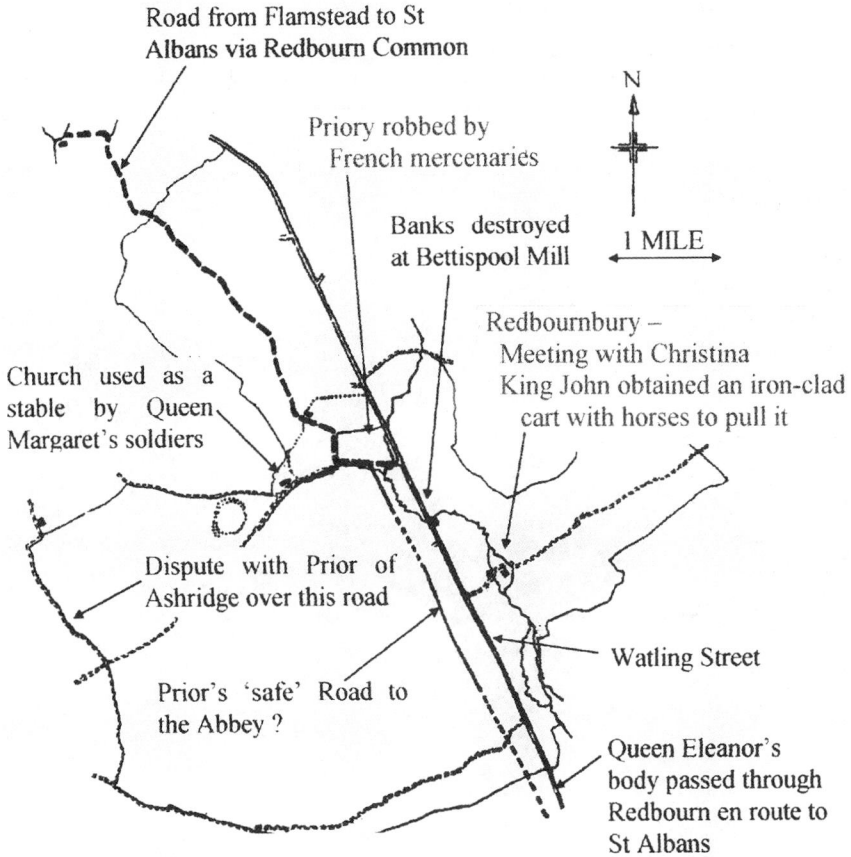

Fig: 3.4 - Problem areas for the Abbot at Redbourn

Other Redbourn people tried a more direct approach, and with the aid of some influential neighbours, they made their claims known to the Abbot. He agreed to consider these and to give his answer on the following Thursday. They were not too happy with such a delaying tactic and returned home intent on applying pressure by attacking Abbey property in the village.

It was nearly dark when they arrived in Redbourn, but without hesitation they roused all the men not previously involved with the events in St Albans. Their plan was to demolish the bank surrounding a meadow that they claimed had been illegally purchased to make the 'safe road' from the Priory to the Abbey. Walsingham described the event as follows.[21]:-

> *"Folly soon bred fools, and a large number of silly people were gathered together for the purpose of destruction of the embankment; and by their combined efforts the embankment was soon demolished in many places and razed to the ground; trees which had been growing on the bank were broken down and carried away".*

On Sunday came news of the death of Wat Tyler, but the rebels were now in full cry and not ready to give in. At this point the Abbot decided that it would be prudent to appear to give in, with the hope of regaining ground at a later time. Thus over the next few days he had charters drawn up to grant the demanded new rights of the villagers. Redbourn, Rickmansworth and Walden got their charters first, followed by 17 others within a week.

Each village had its own particular grievances, which were reflected by the individual charters. The main causes were with regard to their rights to graze, to fish, to hunt, to be able to use hand querns to grind their corn, and to have more freedom from the dominance of the Abbey.

As far as the mobs were concerned they had got what they wanted; the revolt was over, so they disarmed and returned peacefully to their homes.

This was not the end as far as the Abbot was concerned. When help arrived from the King, the rebels were arrested, tried and put to death, including the local leader, Grindecobbe. This action soon persuaded the people to give up their new charters and to swear oaths of fealty to the King. Thus were their new privileges annulled, and in addition they had to repair or pay compensation for all the damage that they had done to Abbey property. Finally the King's Treasurer, Sir Robert Tresilian, holding court in St Albans meted out prison sentences and fines without mercy. Thus was normality restored, much as it was before the revolt.

WARS OF THE ROSES

Some two and a half centuries after Redbourn Priory was plundered by the French, it was the turn of the church to suffer occupation and theft.

It is well known that St Albans was the scene of two fierce battles during the "Wars of the Roses".[22] The first, in 1455, apparently passed Redbourn by without any problems, the second, in 1461 was a different matter; the unruly army of Queen Margaret approached from the north, encamped and helped themselves to anything they needed

At Redbourn, the tradition has been passed down that they used the church to stable their horses. This is quite likely, but the story goes on to say that they stole the Font and the Altar table, which seems a little incredible.[23] Perhaps it is true - there is now no sign of a Norman font, the present one is of the Queen Anne period.

To conclude the story, Queen Margaret's army proceeded to attack and defeat the Yorkist army in the city, the decisive stage of the battle taking place on Bernard's Heath. Her victorious army proceeded to pillage and loot the city, the Abbey and the surrounding countryside - it is not surprising that there followed a severe food shortage in the district.

DISSOLUTION AND OTHER EVENTS
Other events in the Medieval period will be recounted in the next three chapters, ending with the Dissolution of the Monasteries.

REFERENCES

1   R L P Jowitt - "A Guide to St Albans and Verulamium, p55
2   Elsie Toms - "The Story of St Albans, p19
3   Matthew Paris - " Chronica Majors" Vol. 6, pp28-9
4   Thomas Walsingham "Gesta Abbatum" Vol. 1, pp100-1
5   "The Life of Christina of Markyate", Ed/Trans. C. H. Talbot, Clarendon Press 1959
6   I am indebted to Mr R. Craske and Mr & Mrs D. Kelsall for telling me about the screen painting in Gateley church
7   As 4, Vol. 1, p297
8   As 4, Vol. 2, p208; John Amundesham - Annales Monasterii S. Albani, Vol. 2, p319
9   As 3, Vol. 3, p16
10 "A History of St Albans" James Corbett, p32
11 Hertfordshire Countryside Vol. 14, No. 130, p.24
12 As 4, Vol. 2 p49
13 As 4, Vol. 2 p326
14 As 4, Vol. 2, p194
15 I retain the individual references for each name in my collection
16 Robert Clutterbuck - "The History and Antiquaries of Hertfordshire", Vol. 1, p.179
17 As 4, Vol. 2, pp 261-6
18 As 4, Vol. 3, pp 257-62
19 As 4, Vol. 3, p262
20 Most of this information is taken from "The Peasants Revolt in Hertfordshire 1381" - A symposium - Hertfordshire Publications, 1981; together with Thomas Walsingham's "Gesta Abbatum" Vol. 3, pp 328-30
21 As 4, Vol. 3, p.329
22 Gerald Sanctuary, "St Albans and the Wars of the Roses"
23 "A History of Redbourn Parish Church", guidebook 1958

CHAPTER 4

THE MEDIEVAL CHURCH

It is doubtful if discussion about the Domesday Commissioners was more than a seven-day wonder to the villagers of Redbourn. After all, they would still continue to have the same obligations and have to pay the same dues and taxes to the same Lord of the Manor, who was still the current Abbot of St Albans. Of far greater impact and lasting interest would have been when the Abbot sent his masons to build a new stone church for them at Church End.

From the very basic and simple three-cell building that he erected, it was to develop over the next four centuries into the more elaborate form that is still very much in use today. This chapter tells of how that church was built and developed through the medieval centuries.

THE SAXON CHURCH

It seems very likely that either Aegelwine the Black, or one of the Saxon Abbots, would have built a church at Redbourn for the hundred or so villagers. As most Saxon churches in counties, where building stone was scarce, were made of wood, archaeological evidence would be hard to find. However, the Tower may give us a clue to the existence of an earlier building.

A vital consideration when siting the tower would have been to choose firm ground on which to erect it. The obvious place would have been on the well compacted base of the old Saxon church, which may have been retained to house the congregation while the new nave was built nearby. The walls of the tower are some 3 degrees out of line with the Nave; usually evidence of a difference in building periods; in this case perhaps showing that the Saxon church had a different alignment, which had to be followed to take advantage of its firm base.

The tower contains a nice reminder of the Saxon builders who constructed the church under their new Norman masters. The String-course under the Belfry windows has 'billet and saw-tooth' decoration, which is said to represent timber and carpentry, echoing the favourite material and method of construction used by the Saxons –see *Fig: 4.1*

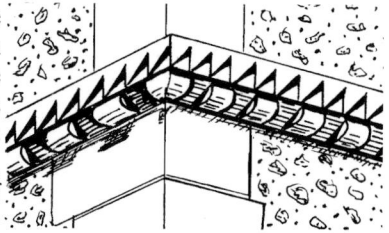

Fig: 4.1 – Tower String course

ORIENTATION

In most churches the Chancel faces the east, the rest of the building following the same alignment towards the west. However, measurement shows that the true alignment often varies by several degrees, both north and south. St Albans Abbey points about 20 degrees south, while Redbourn lies 8 degrees north of the true east.

It has been suggested that early masons used a lodestone as a crude compass, but did not allow for magnetic deviations - if St Marys had been made using such a device in the 12th century, it should point about 22 degrees to the south.[1]

A more likely idea has been developed by the Rev. Hugh Benson MA. based on an alignment with the point of sunrise on the day of dedication, (their Patronal Day).[2] There is no early historical evidence to support this theory, except from a note made by a captain in the Parliamentary Army, called Silas Taylor, who died in 1678.[3] -

> *"In the days of yore, when a church was built, they watched and prayed on the vigil of the dedication, and took that point of the horizon where the sun rose from the east; which makes the variation, so that few stand true, except those built between* (ie. at) *the equinoxes".*

The same procedure was described by William Wordsworth in 1823 in a poem about the erection of Rydal Chapel.[4]

Mr Benson gave many examples of churches that he had measured and which fitted his theory quite accurately. I too measured St Mary's church to find figures for its alignment. I then projected these to the horizon and found that the sun would have risen over Dudley Hill. This hill is 80 feet higher than the church and about a mile distant; which would have delayed the apparent time of sunrise seen from Church End. This geometry is shown diagramatically in *Fig: 4.2*

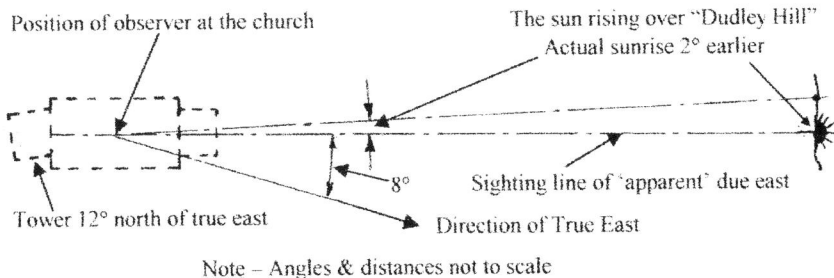

Note – Angles & distances not to scale

Fig: 4.2 – Geometry of the sunrise as viewed from the church on Patronal day c.1110

Two suitable dates fit a sunrise in the above direction in the 12th century, these occurred on 25/26th March and on 6/7th September. Interestingly these both fit with 'Mary Days' - March 25th the "Annunciation of Mary" and September 8th the "Nativity of Mary". These were found in tables supplied by Hugh Benson and allowed for the change from the Julian to the Gregorian calendar. Currently we celebrate our Patronal Festival on the 8th September, now known as the "Feast day of the Blessed Virgin Mary".

RICHARD BUILDS REDBOURN CHURCH

The builder of the 'new' church at Redbourn was the then Abbot of St Albans, Richard d'Albini. His predecessor, Paul de Caen, had rebuilt most of the Abbey in the Norman style, leaving Richard free to concentrate his building enthusiasm on country churches. The Abbot, not being able to consecrate or dedicate a new church himself, had to ask a Bishop to perform the ceremony. At that time St Albans Abbey had certain Papal privileges, and was exempt from the jurisdiction of its Diocesan Bishop, which was then Lincoln.

It was only through Thomas Walsingham noting such cases in order to prove, or justify this privilege, that we know who dedicated Redbourn church, and several others in the district; the relevant passage reads [5]:-

> *Herbert, Bishop of Norwich, dedicated the church of Redburne, Richard the priest being witness*

Walsingham does not give the actual date of the ceremony, but from a study of the lives of the Abbot and the Bishop, it is possible to make a reasonable suggestion of when it was. Firstly the two men were in their respective offices over almost exactly the same period:-

Richard d'Albini, Abbot of St Albans 1097-1119
Herbert Losinga, Bishop of Norwich 1091-1119

Quite a bit of correspondence between the two men has survived, showing that they met at public events on several occasions, making Herbert an obvious friend who Richard might invite to the Abbey. The date of his visit is not specified, but most likely it was in the middle years of his term, rather than later when Herbert suffered failing health. I have suggested a date of c.1110; Canon Davys also favoured this date in his lecture in Redbourn church in 1887.[6]

Fig:4.3 - Herbert Losinga
(Courtesy- Jarrolds of Norwich)

Some indication of the importance of Redbourn at that time was the statement that Flamstead was - *"a chapel belonging to the church of Redbourn"*. In c.1112 Abbot Richard - *"fraudulently sold it* (Flamstead church) *for his own benefit to Thurnot, to whom his predecessor, Leostan, had granted the manor"*.[7] This is further evidence that Redbourn church was already built by 1112.

THE NORMAN BUILDING

Fig: 4.4 shows my idea of what the church may have looked like when it was built in c.1110. Apart from an imaginary pyramid shaped roof, the surviving features of the Tower can be easily recognised, while the Norman Nave and Sanctuary have since been swallowed up by later building operations. The corner stones (quoins) were made with Roman Bricks, except for the Tower which had stone quoins. These can now best be seen on the north-west corner, *see Fig: 4.5*

Fig: 4.4 - Sketch of the church c.1110   *Fig: 4.5 - Roman bricks in the Nave*

There is absolutely no evidence of what the inside may have looked like; but usually churches at that time had no seating, the congregation standing or kneeling. The floors would have been bare earth, covered with straw, or reeds from the Ver. The Altar in the sanctuary would most likely have been of stone.

With the possible exception of the Chamberlain's Grange at Redbournbury, the church would have been the largest and most substantial building in the village. Thus it could have been used for all sorts of activities other than worship such as - public meetings, business, payments of debts or dues (such as one ordered to be paid in the Porch in 1662.[8])

It was not long before the stone masons were back to build the North Aisle. This is usually dated c.1140 because of the similar style and craftsmanship at St Mary's Hemel Hempstead, which was also built at that time.[9] *Fig: 4.6* shows the arcade in silhouette with the one remaining, blocked, Norman window visible beyond the centre arch. *Fig: 4.7* show the whole church in plan and section.

Fig: 4.6- North Aisle in silhouette
(Note- Norman Arcade and blocked window beyond)

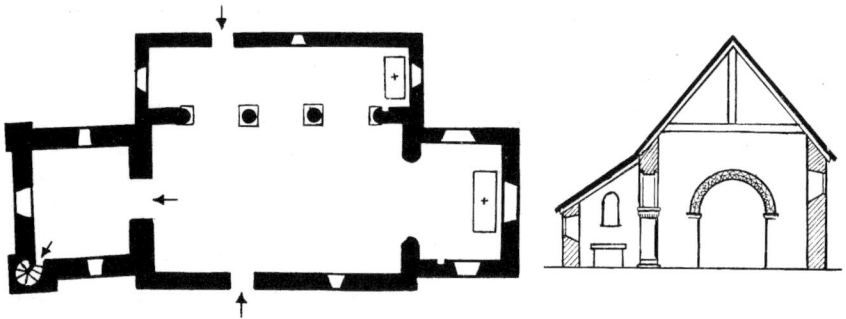

Fig: 4.7 - Plan & Section c.1140

MISSING EARLY ENGLISH

After this spate of early building activity, there is no definite evidence of building in the next style of architecture - "Early English". However, this is not entirely true as the columns and capitals of the Sedilia in the Chancel are certainly Early English (13th century). These are most likely features reused from elsewhere - possibly from one of the Priory Chapels which was of this period and had suffered a serious fire (see Chapter 5).[10]

THE DECORATED PERIOD

There were two extensions to St Mary's in this period - dated by the "Victoria County History" as c1340 and c.1350-60.[11] It will be noted that these dates put the work respectively before and after the Black Death of 1349. This dreadful plague killed nearly half the population, including most of the skilled stone masons. Thus it is not surprising to be able to detect quite a deterioration in the quality of craftsmanship in the later work, carried out by less skilled masons.

The earlier work consisted of an enlargement of the **Sanctuary** into a large Chancel with more room for clergy and clerks required by changes in the Liturgy at that time. In contrast, the new **South Aisle**, has poorly formed moulding especially of the arcade capitals; in fact the whole aisle has an outward lean - though in fairness this could be due to subsidence at a later date.

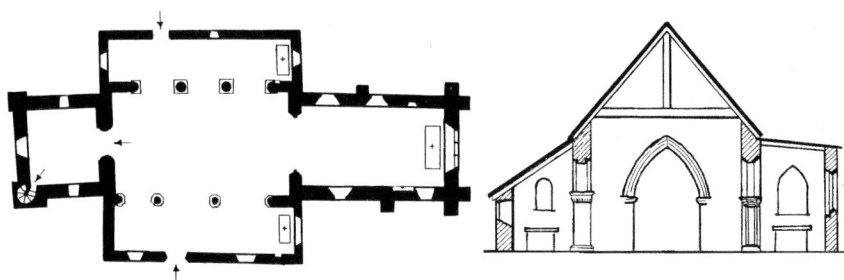

Fig: 4.8 - Plan and Section, Decorated work - 1340-60

Puzzling features of the Chancel are the uncharacteristically thick walls and massive buttresses; which are more like Early English work. This raises a question as to whether the Chancel had already been enlarged in the 13th century, which would also explain the Early English Sedilia. Further evidence of possible Early English origin has been found during recent repair work. A small length of window arch with a carved dragon on it, interestingly appears to be of this period.

THE PERPENDICULAR PERIOD

Early English and Decorated architecture, were replaced by the various Perpendicular styles, after the Black Death. The Perpendicular alterations and additions at St Marys all date from the latter part of the period, starting some 100 years and more after the South Aisle was built - see *Fig: 4.11*

The addition of a **Lady Chapel**, (*Fig: 4.9*) built on the south side of the Chancel, is dated by a will of 1448 which left money for - "*the principal window in the chapel of the Blessed Mary*".[12] Six years later a bequest towards "glazing", presumably stained glass, indicates that the chapel was finished. No medieval stained glass remains in the church; the existing window glass in the chapel is of 1936 and appropriately depicts St Mary, as would the 15th century window here. There was also tabernacle, probably richly carved and canopied, containing the figure of the Virgin Mary; as confirmed by a bequest for its painting in 1513.

Fig: 4.9 - The Lady Chapel with Priest's door

The use of the new chapel as a Chantry Chapel is shown by several bequests and from clergy referred to as *"Chaplains"*, (*"Capellanus Honoris" ie.* Honorary Chaplain), all occurring before 1448. The bequests asked for masses to be said for the dead, as 'Obits' (on the anniversaries of a person's death), or as 'Trentals' (30 Requiem Masses, said on successive days).

Wills between 1509 and 1525 show that the chapel was used as a meeting room for a Guild. The earliest benefactor was Thomas Peacock, who left 20 shillings to *"Our Lady of Yelde"* (Our Lady of Gild?) in 1509. The Peacock family were prosperous Yeoman farmers at that time. Richard Peacock, left money to the *"Broderhode* in 1512 and is commemorated by a brass in the chapel. This was probably a society formed for the protection and support of its members in sickness or hardship, rather than being a trade guild. The word "Brotherhood" was replaced in later wills by "Fraternity", and there appears to have been some difficulty in getting it established, as one will of 1513 says guardedly:-

"If the brederhode in Redburn be stablisshed and in condition to contynue..."

In 1547 King Edward VI ordered a list to be made of all Chantries, Gilds, and Brotherhoods etc. which had survived the Dissolution of the Monasteries.[13] The Redbourn entry does not mention the Brotherhood, so presumably it did not still exist, but three properties were listed which still provided money to pay for obits.

The **Porch** dates from about the same time as the Lady Chapel. Its roof is the same, probably the oldest in the church, see *Fig: 4.10*. Richard Bostoke's will of 1504 gives a glimpse of its former use by referring to - *"the leystow in the porch"*. A 'leystone' is more usually found in a Lych-Gate, where the bodies were rested just prior to burial.

Abbot John Wheathampstead did work in both the Church and the Priory, but the entries are sometimes puzzling - *"the construction of a certain wall made of stone which divides the Chapel from the Nave"*.[14] It has been suggested this refers to the wall that separated the Chapel from the Chancel, but which was later converted to the present archway.

Fig: 4.10 - !5th century Porch roof

The most important Perpendicular alterations to the church were described as *"a certain room built above the Nave"* (meaning the **Clerestory**) and - *"the work of the Holy Rood"*. For these the Vicar, William Bevyle, left 20 shillings in his will of 1478.[15] The two works were probably designed together so that the Clerestory windows would throw light on to the **Holy Rood** figures and lighten the Nave, which must have been very dark as it had no windows of its own.

The Medieval Rood would have been placed on top of the **Rood Screen** and must have been destroyed after the Reformation, see *Fig: 4.11*. The present Rood is purposely placed in a higher position; it was carved by a well know local sculptor - Sigfreid Peitzch, in 1990.

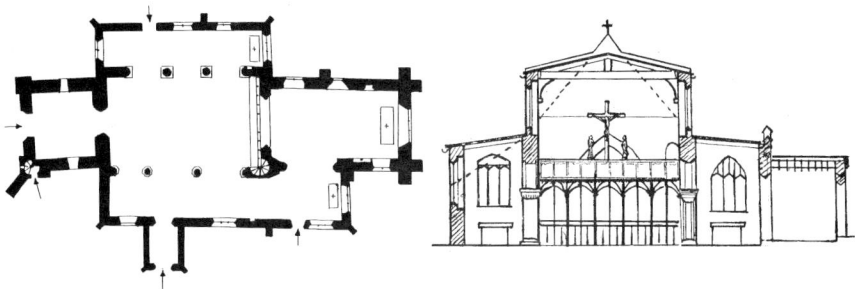
Fig: 4.11 – Plan and cross section in late 15th Century

There were many other Perpendicular alterations, such as buttresses, particularly that on the southwest corner of the tower, perhaps necessitated by the new external door to the Belfry, or to settlement cracks. Several windows were also enlarged in the same style in order to lighten the inside of the church.

"The south view of the church is distinguished against the north by brick battlements on a handsome arched and cusped brick corbel-table" This is how Professor Pevsner describes this beautiful feature running around the South Aisle and Lady Chapel. He dates it vaguely to the late 15th century".[16]

THE MEDIEVAL CHURCH COMPLETED

The final medieval alteration was financed partly by William Carpenter, who left 11 shillings in his will towards *"the new building and making of St John's ile"* (the **North Aisle**) in 1497. This new work replaced the old Norman 'cat-slide' sloping roof, shown in *Fig: 4.8*, giving more height so that larger windows, in the Perpendicular style, to replace the small Norman openings.

A problem arose because a small Norman window existed just where a new window was required. They solved this 'intrusion' by simply filling it in with rubble. This little window was rediscovered by the architect Oldrid Scott in 1913 who devised a way of propping up the arch so that the filling could be safely removed - see *Fig: 4.7*

Thus the medieval church was now structurally complete. It has since remained basically unaltered for nearly 500 years. Only with the addition of the new Transept Hall has this long period of building in-activity been broken.

INTERNAL ALTERATIONS

However, during the medieval period there were internal alterations, but of a less dramatic kind. Earlier in this chapter it was noted that the High Altar would have been of stone. This would always have been dedicated to St Mary; but bequests in wills show that other Altars existed. Those to 'John the Baptist' (North Aisle), and Our Lady of Pity (Lady Chapel) are easily located, but the locations of others are less certain. Those to Saints 'Stephen' and 'Lawrence' were possibly in the South Aisle, 'Katherine' and 'Nicholas' may possibly have been in front of the Rood Screen, but where was that to 'Saint Michael' ?

Seating, or rather the lack of it in the early church, has been mentioned. If there were pews in later medieval times, possibly with 'Poppy-head' finials, all traces were lost when box pews filled the church in later years - see Chapter 10. The insertion of stones, with brasses set in them, to cap vaults of the more wealthy parishioners, may have set a standard which eventually led to all the earth floors being paved by the end of the medieval period.

MEDIEVAL BEQUESTS

Medieval wills have already been mentioned as supplying information about parts of the church. Those making wills at this time seem to have been obsessed with securing a safe passage to Heaven. Besides prayers to be said for their souls, many gifts in money or kind went to the church for many things such as - building work, torches (for lighting), candles (at Images, Altars etc.), the maintenance of the bells or in one case for a new churchyard gate.

CHURCHWARDENS AND CONGREGATIONS

The most important part of a church is not its fabric or fittings, but the people who use the building for the worship of God. With the exception of the Vicar, the most important of these were the Churchwardens. This is an office whose origin is lost in antiquity, mention of medieval wardens is rare indeed. Their primary responsibility, as today, was to look after the church building and its goods, but in medieval times their duties extended beyond the church and churchyard into secular spheres, such as the care of the poor.

It would be nice to also look at the men and women who comprised the congregation in early days, but records of the church lives of these are also rare and usually only to be found in wills.

MEDIEVAL CLERGY

The account of the Consecration ceremony in c.1110 lists those present. Besides Bishop Losinga and Abbot d'Albini *"RICHARD THE PRIEST,* is given as *"being witness"* - could he have been the first Vicar of Redbourn?

Amongst the names given by Matthew Paris of monks who died during the early 13th century are - **"VALERIAN de REDBURNE"** (1218), **"ROBERT"** and **"MASTER SIMON"**, both of Redburne (1220).[17] All three appear to have been ordained priests; it is strange that they should all die within 2 years of each other.[18] However, I feel there is not sufficient evidence to conclude that any of them could have been Vicars here, thus I have not included them in *fig: 4.12*

A list of incumbents given in the Parish Magazine in 1948 starts dramatically with *"JOHN, murdered"*; however I think the author was confused with the next Vicar, another John. The first John <u>did</u> exist, he appears in a document of 1297, the supposed year of his murder, as *"JOHN, Vicar of the church of Redburn"*.[18] The later John was **JOHN TURNER,** or le Turnour, appeared in 1321 and 1327 as *"Chaplain of Redborn"*.[19] The account of his murder is given in the Parish Magazine (1933) and reads thus -

> *"In 1327, John Turner was Vicar of Redbourn, he, a poor man, came to a violent end, for he was robbed and murdered by one Geoffrey Foliet in about 1345. The said Geoffrey obtained the King's Pardon and was allowed to go free".*

Newcome, in his "History of St Albans Abbey", records the burial of a Vicar of Redbourn called - **"WILLIAM"** in St Albans Abbey during the reign of King Edward III (1327-77); he left 20 shillings for the privilege of burial there. [20] He probably came to Redbourn after John Turner's murder.

WALTER de BETTELOWE, or BERLOWE, appears in a grant of lands in 1358 at Hemel Hempstead. [21] He was described as *"late Vicar of Redbourn"*, and appeared jointly with *"John Ymaigne, Chaplain"* in the above grant. We can only guess if they both served over a similar period at Redbourn. They may both have seen the South Aisle built, perhaps worried by the masons lack of skill.

No names appear for the next 62 years, when **"SIMON the CLERK"** is seen as executor to a will he could have been Vicar of Redbourn.[22]

The next name **JOHN BARFOTE,** described himself as "Honorary Chaplain" in his will of 1430, but elsewhere he is given as Vicar. He had resigned the previous year, possibly due to ill health. In his will he mentions John and Richard as 'clerks', it is interesting to wonder if these were in fact 'singing clerks' who would have sat in the Sedilia in the Chancel.

There follows a quick succession of Vicars - **WILLIAM AYLEFE,** after Barfote in 1429, but resigned the next year. Then **JOHN COUPER** in 1430, who by 1433 had been replaced by **JOHN DAFTE**, In his will Dafte is described as - *"Vicarious Ecclesie parachialis de Redburn"*, (Vicar of the Parish Church of Redbourn) this stated also that he was buried at "Yseldon" (Islington?). Thus in just 4 years there were 4 Vicars of Redbourn.

WILLIAM BEVYLE, or Devile, after serving an unknown number of years at Redbourn, died in 1478. As has been stated, his will dates the addition of the Clerestory and the Rood Screen, referred to as the *"New work"*.[23]

ROBERT SMYTHE succeeded Bevyle and remained for 9 years. In monastic records he is referred to as 'Chaplain' and was *"subject to a pension of 50 shillings per annum"* some of which was due to a Priory in Wales.[24] -
> *"On the 3rd of March AD. 1486 (actually 1487) the right of Presentment to the Rectory of Angle in the County of Pembroke was given to Hugh, the Lord Bishop of St David's, on behalf of Sir Robert Smythe; subject to a pension of 23 shillings payable annually to the Priory of St Nicholas in that place; Sir Robert was Vicar of Redborn".*

It is difficult to understand the full significance of these pensions, or what Robert Smythe had to do with the Presentation of a Rector for Angle in Wales.

The title of 'Sir' accorded to him does not mean that he was a knight but rather it was an address of respect applied to clerics - in Latin it would appear as 'Dominus', meaning Sir or Master.

OWEN CHAPLAIN, was the next Vicar, and he too was subject to the 50 shillings pension deduction. The story of his appointment is an intriguing one.[25] In 1487 the Abbot had appointed **GERVASE BUCLOND** to be Vicar, but at the insistence of an Abbey official, Master Thomas Shenckwyne, he was persuaded to change his mind and appoint Owen Chaplain, instead - he was Thomas's cousin. What hidden facts behind this forced change of mind were not given, but it appears to have been a good choice as Chaplain stayed for ten years.

Date	Vicar	Other Clergy	Notes
c.1110	RICHARD, Priest		At the Church Dedication
d.1218-20		Valerian, Robert & Simon, Priests	Deaths recorded at Abbey
in 1297	JOHN ....?....		
1321-45	John TURNER		Chaplain - Murdered
1345+	WILLIAM ....?....		Buried in Abbey
d.1358	William BETTELOWE	John YMAIGNE	Chaplains
1420	"Simon the clerk"		See will on page 96
1429	John BARFOTE		Chaplain, d.1430
in 1429		JOHN & RICHARD	Clerks
1429-30	William AYLEFE		Resigned the living
in 1430	John COUPER		
d.1433	John DAFTE		
in 1433		WYSE & LANGRICHE	Clerks
in 1450		unknown	"Two clerks here"
d.1478	William BEVYLE		
1478-87	Robert SMYTHE		Resigned in 1487
1487	(Gervase BUCLOND)		Withdrawn
1487-97	Owen CHAPLAIN		Preferred nominee
1497-31	Robert WILSON		
1513-18		Alexander WALKER	Priest
1532-3	John SALTER		
in 1534		Thomas JORDAN	Curate
1538-9		Henry BURGHER	Curate
1538 D I S S O L U T I O N of ST ALBANS ABBEY			
in 1540	William BURY		
1544-7	Stephen BAILEY		Ex Abbey monk

Fig: 4.12 - Medieval Clergy

ROBERT WILSON is described as "Priest" or "Vicar" in wills from 1497 to 1531. In most of these he was a witness, possibly writing the will for the testators at their deathbed; occasionally he was also a beneficiary.

During five years of Wilson's incumbency **ALEXANDER WALKER,** priest, also appears. We do not known what his capacity actually was, but as the Brotherhood or Fraternity of Our Lady was active at that time, he may well have been Chaplain, or Chantry Priest.

Three wills between 1532 and 1533 give us the name of **JOHN SALTER**[26]. This is a new name not appearing in previously published lists of vicars - I am indebted to Mr Mervyn Pritchard for this name.

With the coming of the Dissolution I should finish this account, however, the next vicar is pertinent to the end of the medieval period and thus worthy of mention. He was **STEPHEN BAILEY** and had been a monk at St Albans Abbey, from where he was given a pension of £13.6.8d. [27] He appears in wills as Vicar between 1538 and 1546. However, this is rather puzzling as we also hear of **WILLIAM BURY**, "Parish Priest" in a will of 1540. [28] Bailey later appears at Bardfield, Essex, in 1548.[29]

The foregoing Medieval Clergy are listed in *Fig: 4.12*

There are a few men named as Curates in the Medieval period. They were THOMAS JORDAN (1534) and HENRY (or THOMAS) BURGHER, (1538-9). Other than their names, for which I am again obliged to Mr Pritchard, no further information is known.

THE VICARAGE

The Ecclesiastical Taxation ordered by Pope Nicholas IV in 1291, traditionally known as "Peter's Pence", included Redbourn Vicarage. This did not mean that a Vicarage house existed at that time (see Chapter 10 for Vicarage houses) - it was the value of the Benefice in terms of Tithes, Glebe lands etc. Redbourn was valued at £17.3.8d. The next valuation, nearly 250 years later, showed only a slight difference (£16.5.0d.), but by 1650 it had nearly doubled to £30.[30]

REFERENCES

1   "New Scientist" 3rd January 1974, pp.10 to 13; also letter in 24th January issue
2   "The Antiquaries Journal" Vol. XXXVI, July-October 1956, pp. 205-213
3   As 2, p.205
4   As 2, p.205 and Wordsworth's poem "Rydal Chapel"
5   Thomas Walsingham, "Gesta Abbatum", Vol. 1, p.148
6   Transactions of the St Albans Architectural and Archaeological Society", 1887, p.60
7   As 5, vol. 1, p.72 As 5, vol. 2 p.400
8   HRO. Miscellaneous ref. 76540
9   Susan Yaxley (Ed) "History of Hemel Hempstead", p.229
10 As 5, Vol. 2, p.400
11 "Victoria County History, Hertfordshire" D Warrand (Ed.), 1907, Vol. 1, p.368
12 As 9 Vol. 1, p369, note n
13 Rev J E Brown - "Chantry Certificates of Hertfordshire" p.37
14 John Amundesham - "Annales Monasterii S. Albani" Vol. 2, pp.264
15 As 14
16 Nikolaus Pevsner - "The Buildings of England - Hertfordshire", Second Edition, p.276
17 Matthew Paris - "Chronica Monasterii" Vol. 6, p.270

18   Calendar of Patent Rolls, 24/95 p.275
19   As 11, Vol. 2, p.399
20   Rev. Peter Newcome, Rector of Shenley - "The History of the Ancient Foundation called The Abbey of St Albans", 1795 - p.421
21   Catalogue of ancient deeds, Vol. 2 p.517, c.2411 - P.R.O.
22   "The Herts Genealogist and Antiquary", W Brigg (Ed.) Vol. 1
23   Archdeaconry of St Albans will 2AR28v
24   John Wheathampstead, "Chronica Monasterii S. Albani", Vol. 2 pp181 and 280
25   As 24 Vol. 2, p286
26   From a very useful list of wills compiled by Mr Mervyn Pritchard in about 1980
27   Herts. Advertiser 23rd April 1887, p3
28   As 26
29   As 27
30   J E Cussans - "History of Hertfordshire" Vol.3, p240

CHAPTER 5

REDBOURN PRIORY

Little more than half a century after the Norman church was built, a small priory was dramatically built only half a mile away, on Redbourn Common. To understand why, it is necessary to recount the story of St Alban and in particular of the Christian Priest who converted him. Both men suffered martyrdom for their faith; Alban's story is well known, but the largely fictional story of the priest, later known as Amphibalus, appeared some 900 years later. This chapter will start with a brief account of their stories and continue with the history of the Priory, founded in the honour of Amphibalus.

ALBAN AND AMPHIBALUS

Alban was a citizen of the Roman City of Verulamium. He gave shelter to a Christian priest who was being hunted by the authorities because of the success of his evangelising zeal in the area. While staying with Alban, this priest told him about the life, death and resurrection of Christ, and he was converted to the faith. When soldiers came looking for the priest, Alban helped him to escape, but was himself mistaken for the priest and arrested.

When brought before the judge, the mistake was soon realised; but before his release, he was required to prove that he was unaffected by the new teaching and would still worship the pagan Roman gods. Alban, already strong in the Christian faith, refused to worship at their altars. The judge then had no alternative but to sentence him to be beheaded outside the city walls; this was carried out on the hill where St Albans Abbey now stands (see *fig: 5.1*). John Morris puts forward a case for this having taken place in the year 209.[1]

Fig: 5.1 - The martyrdom of St Alban, (drawn by Matthew Paris)

Many accounts tell the story, including Bede's "History of the English Church and People". It was not until 1136 that the priest was actually named; this being arrived at by a complicated series of misunderstandings from earlier writings. A marginal note, which is now thought to have referred to the Caesar in charge at Verulamium by his nickname 'Caracalla', (meaning a long, German type, greatcoat) was somehow absorbed into the text, but altered to the word currently in use for such a coat - an 'Amphibalon'.[2] Geoffrey of Monmouth then adopted this in his own elaborated version and thereafter the error has stuck as "Amphibalus", and in the absence of his real name can only be accepted and used.

Thus the story stood until, at the request of Abbot Simon (1167-83), a monk called 'William' produced a largely fictional account of the lives of both Alban and Amphibalus. This was said to have been translated into Latin from an existing book, written in the vernacular tongue in c.590, this he called "Alia Acta" (Other doings).[3] After describing the well known story of Alban in dramatic form, William went on to tell the imaginary sequel of the escape of Amphibalus to Wales to there continue his mission.

The story continued with people from Verulamium pursuing him to Wales, binding him, and bringing him back to that city for trial. However, they stopped within sight of the walls of the city and were met by angry citizens intent on putting him to death there and then. This they achieved by the gruesome means of tying his entrails to a post, around which he was then forced to walk; this did not cause his death, so they whipped him, attacked him with spears and knives and finally stoned him to death (see *fig: 5.2*). William's final comment leaves the possibility for a disinterment at some future time:-

"....to be brought to light at some time or other - by divine action

Fig: 5.2 - The Martyrdom of Amphibalus (drawn by Matthew Paris)

The events that followed soon after William wrote his "Alia Acta" were recounted some time later by that famous 13th century monk, Matthew Paris, in his "Chronica Majora".[4] As if to fulfil William's prophesy that the bones would be discovered at some time in the future, Paris details happenings which led to this event. Being an artist of some standing, he also produced an illustrated account of the martyrdom of both saints, called "La Vie de Seint Auban".[5] Doctor Eileen Roberts describes this as *"the fullest and most sympathetic portrayal of all time"* [6] His version of the martyrdoms of both saints are shown in *Figs. 5.1 and 5.2.* The post around which Amphibalus had been forced to walk, is clearly shown. This became the 'attribute' by which he is mostly recognised, see the stained glass window in Redbourn Church - *Fig: 5.3*

Fig: 5.3 – Window in St. Marys Showing Alban, The Virgin Mary & Amphibalus

Paris starts the story of the discovery in his 'Chronica' by recounting how a citizen of St Albans, Robert Mercer, had a revelation in which he was visited by Alban himself, who showed him exactly where Amphibalus was buried:-

> *"This was a pleasant piece of open ground suitable both for pasture and also as a resting place for weary travellers. It was in a village called Redburn, almost three miles away from St Albans. On this open ground two hillocks stood out. They were called "The Hills of the Banners", because the public gather around there, when by long standing custom the faithful hold a solemn procession to pay their annual dues with respect to St Albans Abbey".*

When the Abbot was told the story, and heard that a crowd was assembling on Redbourn Heath, in anticipation of further developments, he sent some of his monks to guard the spot and to begin excavation of the "Mounds of the Banners" (can be translated as the "Hills of the Banners").

Much was made of the excitement at the scene and of the miracles and healings that took place. Some of these can be recognised as having been 'lifted' from other sources. He told how one called Algarus of Dunstable came with a large jar of ale to sell to the onlookers. When approached by a poor man begging for a drink - *"for the love of the martyr"*, Algarus flew into a rage, saying he had not come there for the sake of the martyr but to make a profit. At that moment, the jar fell to the ground spilling the ale; all the people were then able to drink freely, including the poor man. This miracle was assigned to the 'martyr's protection'.

The Rev. H. Fowler, in a lecture given at Redbourn in 1887 gave his opinion that the events taking place to discover the remains of Amphibalus were stage-managed from the Abbey, saying.[7]

> *"The invention was planned to take place 3 days after the feast of St Alban, preparations being made a week previously by sending monks with Robert to survey the spot and to appoint a watch. On Friday 17th June, preceding the feast, a fast and almsgiving were proclaimed in a special Litany. By these means a crowd was attracted to Redbourn and alleged miracles took place. On the day fixed for the Invention, Saturday 25th June (1178), Abbot Simon goes to Redbourn to celebrate Mass at the Chapel of St James. He gives orders to excavate…"*

On the day the Abbot celebrated Mass in this chapel, bones were found by the excavators and duly pronounced to be those of Amphibalus. They were taken in solemn procession to the Abbey, being met half way by monks carrying the shrine of St. Alban. At the place where they met, another miracle took place, the spot being later marked by building a small Nunnery dedicated to St Mary de Pré.

The contents of the interment were described by Matthew Paris in detail worthy of an archaeological report:-

> *"The blessed Amphibalus was found lying between and parallel with two companions, with a third companion in a place by himself at right angles to the others. There were also found near that place six of the companions of the aforesaid martyrs, so that with the blessed martyr Amphibalus, there were ten altogether. Among the remains of Amphibalus were found two large knives of the martyr's, one in the skull and the other in the breast".*

THE PRIORY IS FOUNDED

As well as making a shrine in the Abbey for the bones he believed to be those of St Amphibalus, the Abbot decided to hallow the spot where they were found by building a small priory there. We do not know when building started, only that it was inhabited during the reign of the next Abbot, Warin (1183-95).[8]

The existing Chapel of St James would have been used initially by the monks. Thus building could have concentrated on the domestic buildings, such as the dormitory, hall, toilet facilities, etc. However, it was obviously necessary to build a more worthy chapel eventually, and dedicate it to the memory of the martyr; such a chapel was not completed until 1215. As with St Mary's Church, it was not dedicated by the Diocesan Bishop (Lincoln) but by John Bishop of Ardfert (in Ireland). It seems that Bishop John had left his own diocese to reside in the Abbey there helping the Abbot with such work that only a Bishop could do. The Dedication was recorded by Thomas Walsingham as follows [9]-

> He…*"dedicated the church of the Blessed Amphibalus, Martyr, and his companions, for the honour and esteem of that place where the saint bore witness. The church was solemnly dedicated by Bishop John,…the Abbot himself was present. They were robed in full pontificals, and forty days Indulgence was granted by the then Prior there, Sir Gilbert de Sisseverne"*
>
> [An Indulgence is the exemption from temporal punishment. Note that the Prior was not a 'Knight', 'Sir' in this case was just a title of respect]

NOTABLE EVENTS AFFECTING THE PRIORY

In chapter 3, three events in the life of the Priory have already been told - the theft and recovery of a cross in 1217; high-jacking and threats to the Prior by the people of Flamstead just before the Peasants' Revolt; and during this revolt, the destruction of some of its enclosing banks. These events must have been very frightening for the monks living in the Priory and perhaps also for the villagers. Other happenings gave cause for celebration, or even for a public holiday, such as the excavation of "The Mounds" or the Dedication of the new Chapel.

Undoubtedly in the years after the finding of the bones of Amphibalus, there would have been much interest in the building activities that were taking place on what used to be part of Redbourn Heath. The Abbot himself would have visited on many occasions; indeed later Abbots were to treat the Priory as a rest home for themselves as well as for their monks.

One event that villagers may not have witnessed, but no doubt heard about later, took place at midnight on January 1st 1254, described by Paris as follows [10]:-

> *"About midnight…the moon being eight days old, and the firmament studded with stars, and the air completely calm, there appeared in the sky…the form of a large ship, well-shaped, and of remarkable design and colour. This apparition was seen by some monks staying at St Amphibalus* (the Priory)*…who were looking out to see by the stars if it was the hour for chanting matins. The vessel appeared for a long time, as if it were painted and built with planks; but at length it began by degrees to dissolve and disappear, wherefore it was believed to have been a cloud, but a wonderful and extraordinary one"*

Notice that they were looking at the stars <u>to see what time it was</u> - this would have required a good knowledge of Astronomy, in order to be able to tell the time from the position of different stars or constellations in the night sky. To do this accurately they would have also required a scientific instrument - such as an Astrolabe. In recent times the remains of such an instrument have been found near where it is thought the Priory was, see - *fig: 5.4*. This Astrolabe has been roughly dated to the 13th century, so it could well have been the very one used by the monks on that particular night. Science was a fairly common interest in monasteries - at a later time Abbot Richard Wallingford (1328-36) was well known in this field, in particular for the 'Great Clock' that he built in the Abbey

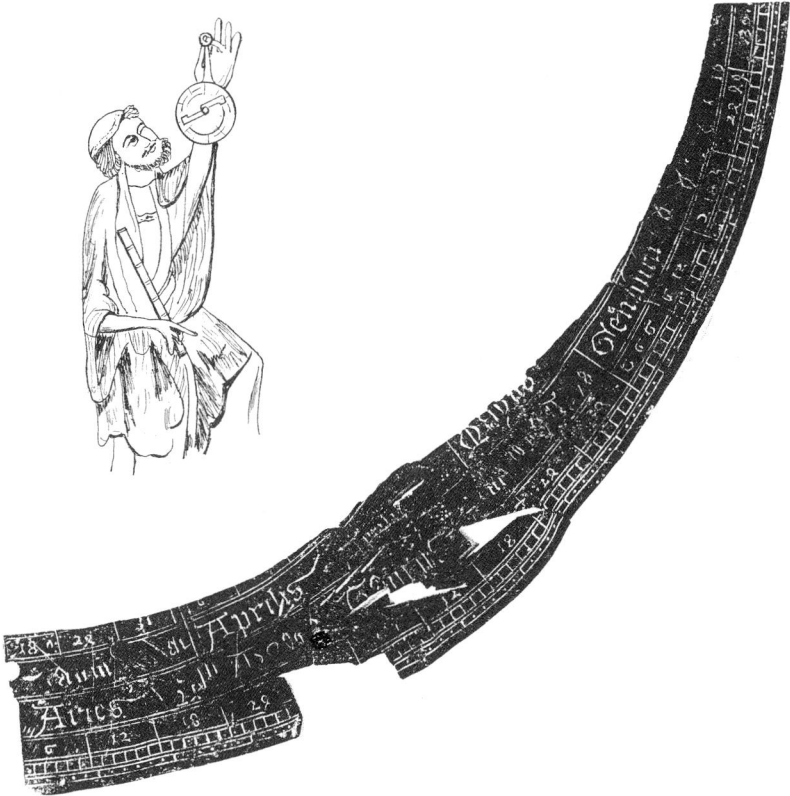

Fig: 5.4 – The remains of a 13th century Astrolabe

Found on the "Park Estate" in 1967 (Courtesy Verulamium Museum)
Inset - The method of using an Astrolabe to sight on the stars

A memorable day for both the people of Redbourn and of Flamstead was the 15th of November 1383, when a day-long meeting took place on the Common between the Earl of Warwick and the Abbot, with their respective advisers. The boundaries of the Common, then called the Heath, and of the Priory itself were toured by both parties and a final agreement to settle the 'Flamstead Trouble' was reached (see chapter 3, page 37).

EVERYDAY LIFE AT THE PRIORY

The Priory was initially intended as a convalescent home for sick monks, in order to avoid the spread of infection at the Abbey. Inevitably some died while at Redbourn, but as there was no cemetery there, instructions were issued in 1275 to ensure they were given the proper rites and taken back with dignity to the Abbey.[11] Transport was to be by a *"decent cart"*, and they were to enter the Abbey by St Germains Gate. As this gate was beside the Ver it would seem quite likely that some might have travelled by boat.

Somehow 16 monks were squeezed into the Priory at the time of the Black Death in order that they might escape infection; it is not known whether any actually died at Redbourn.[12]

At other times 3 or 4 fit monks were sent to the Priory to give them a month's rest from the discipline of Benedictine rule. It can be calculated that each monk in the Abbey would have got such a holiday at Redbourn every three years. This period of temporary relaxation was too much for some monks - they seemed to have gone a bit wild while at Redbourn, and as will be seen later, had to be disciplined and forbidden to indulge in all sorts of 'un-monk-like' activities.

It would not be surprising that some would reject a winter holiday on account of poor food and heating, the monks suffered great hardships and often had to shamelessly beg for sustenance.[13] Until sometime in the 14th century there was, incredibly, no kitchen at the Priory:-

> *"On a meat day...all they got was food hotted-up from what was left over by the convent; by the time this reached them it was cold and of little value because of the delay in transit"*

Abbot de la Mare ordered some improvements, probably including the building of a kitchen, but even with hot food, the cold conditions in the Priory must have been hard to bear. Abbot Michael Mentmore (1336-49) had granted two faggots a day between All Saints and the Purification of the Blessed Mary (November 1st to February 2nd). Abbot de la Mare changed this to 16 cart loads of fuel at Michaelmas (29th September) - it is difficult to see how these two schemes compared, but the latter presumably offered better heating for the Priory.

For Abbot de la Mare it was *"a special pleasure to him to stay in Redburne"*, he enjoyed the company of the brethren and lived with them on such an easy footing that his presence was not a burden to anyone.[14] However, he did expect standards to be maintained both of worship and in domestic habits:-

"They were expected to be punctual for Holy Communion and dinner; but if they had mistaken the time for a meal and came back late, he would rebuke them, not harshly or rudely, but with a kindly countenance and speech, encouraging them to keep good time - under penalty of paying for the wine"

The most welcome improvement seems to have been to provide separate toilets because:-

"Previously there was only one convenience for him (the Abbot) *and the monks, and the monks felt embarrassed to go there in his presence"*

It will be seen later how the provision of separate lavatories was part of more extensive provision made by Abbot de la Mare Redbourn.

His board and lodging at the Priory cost 5 shillings a week, but he decreed that while he was there 6 shillings could be spent on food; thus more than paying for his keep, perhaps also improving the standard of cuisine.

He also improved conditions in other ways - equipping the hall with couches and benches and providing tables, table cloths, a tapestry curtain etc., besides richly endowing the chapels with costly Frontals, one of gold-striped cloth, red silk curtains, Vestments, Chalices, Graduals and Lectionaries.

THE MONKS

None of the monks who stayed at Redbourn have their names recorded, however, we can assume that some of the well known monks, such as Matthew Paris, Thomas Walsingham, John Amundesham and others would have stayed there. Paris was a well-known artist, so we can imagine him spending much of `his time sketching and painting in the pleasant environment of the Priory grounds.

It has already been noted that some monks, when at the Priory, over-stepped the mark and *"could not contain themselves within the bounds of their freedom."* Abbot Wheathampstead complained that when…*"on vacation at Redbourn they should not indulge in immoderate holidays"* [15]

Three sets of Ordinances or Constitutions for monks staying at Redbourn were issued by Abbots Wallingford and Wheathampstead. On the principle that there is 'no smoke without fire', it can be accepted that these were not imagined transgressions but reflected incidents that had actually occurred, and were thus known to the Abbot. Thus they must give us a very good idea of the kind of things the monks 'got up to' at the Priory. The following is an edited list [16]:-

Travelling and general deportment

When travelling to or from St Albans they were to keep away from the King's Highway and use footpaths to avoid meeting strangers.

They were to walk 'in file', only in secluded places less than a mile away.

Monks were never to go about alone, or with a young boy.

Attendance at chapel -
> They were to attend regular daily services and when serving at the Altar were not to be neglectful, careless or slothful.
>
> The Prior was to 'stir up' the lazy monk from his bed and make him alert.

Meals -
> They were not to have meals elsewhere without permission.
>
> Meals were to be taken at regular times, and 'leftovers' given to the poor.

Behaviour -
> They were not to take the name of God in vain, or get used to swearing.
>
> They were not to speak rudely or deceive, but to speak politely.

Entertainment -
> They were not to entertain disreputable or suspicious characters.
>
> They were to avoid "excessive vigils", late drinking bouts, over-large meals, gadding about or too much recreation.
>
> No monk to have access to 'suspected places' or to introduce any person to the Priory who could give rise to gossip or slander.
>
> Conversations with women were prohibited, except in the course of duty, *"as this often dishonours a monk's good name"*

Hunting -
> The 'rule' (of St Benedict) forbade hunting, the Prior and Monks were not to keep hunting dogs or attend the hunt - not to career about through fields and woods or to jump across or tear down their neighbour's hedges.

The reaction to one set of rules issued by Abbot Wheathampstead, caused the monks to think their freedom was being threatened, complaining that:-

> *We have been free and we have remained free elsewhere, and we have passed our times at Redburn in freedom hitherto. It is, therefore, disgusting for our souls now to fall into bondage or to accept such a yoke...we, therefore, appeal to you* (Abbot Wheathampstead) *to leave us in that liberty since it is more to our liking than any innovation"*

It was recorded that the Abbot was much upset and *"railed against Monastic faults";* but nevertheless appears to have been later relaxed.

In the same year (1439) Wheathampstead went on to specify that *"the martyr Amphibalus be served with more devotion at Redbourn"*. On festival days *"especially every festival which is <u>kept by the people</u>...shall have both Vespers and Mass with note"* (ie. sung). This showed that villagers at times used the Priory Chapel as their own church. To help with the music he added two good singing clerks, who were also expected to serve the monks at table. The Prior was to be reimbursed for their board and wages with 9 shillings extra - from the Abbey Manors of Radwell and Burstone, from 3 houses in Slape and the *"Hilles of Sandrugge"*.[17]

THE PRIORS OF REDBOURN

The appointment of a Prior to a small Cell like Redbourn, did not seem to warrant a record in the Abbey annals. It is only from other events - like the election or the death of an Abbot, or other recorded happenings at which the Prior was present, that a name appears.

The Priory was occupied sometime between 1183 and 1195, but we do not know who was the first Prior. It has been suggested that Robert, one of the two priests of Redbourn who died in 1220 (see fig: 4.10), could have been the first Prior, but there is no evidence to support this idea.[18]

The first definite record is of Prior **GILBERT SISSERVINE** - he was among those present at the dedication of the chapel of St Amphibalus in 1215.[19] This is the same Gilbert who interviewed Robert Mercer, to whom the supposed burial place of Amphibalus had been revealed in a vision. Gilbert had been 'Master of Works' at the Abbey for some time before. Perhaps it was for this work, which probably included the building part of Redbourn Priory, that he was made Prior as a reward for past services rendered.

The next Prior that we know is **VINCENT**, his death is recorded in 1249, perhaps succeeding Gilbert Sisservine at some unknown date.

There may be a name or two missing in the 41 years after Vincent's death until Prior **GEOFFREY de ST ALBANS** appeared in 1290 when he had the honour of being one of the party chosen to carry the news of John de Berkhamsted's election to the King.

Twelve years later (1302), **RICHARD de HATFORD** was involved with the election of an Abbot, but in a rather shameful way. The Abbey Prior, John de Maryns, was proposed as the next Abbot, but Prior Richard, thought that <u>he</u> was a more suitable choice. The long case that he put up in Chapter to support his claim, was later described as - *"a frivolous file of documents which he foolishly composed"*. The election proceeded, so he wrote to the Archbishop protesting that the election was *"wrong"*, for this "folly" he was rebuked. When the new Abbot returned from his required visit to Rome in 1302, he deposed Prior Richard.

In c.1360 **JOHN WODEROVE'S** name appears. He had been Sub-Prior at the Abbey at the time of the Black Death, so it is tempting to think he may have been one of the 16 refugees evacuated to Redbourn Priory. It was he who purchased the 'safe road' to the Abbey after his supply wagon had been hi-jacked by the men of Flamstead.

At the conclusion of the 'Trouble with Flamstead' (see chapter 3), **WILLIAM de FLAMSTEAD** had been Prior for about 3 years. This seems a happy choice as he may have been able to placate the people of that village.[20]

At the election of Abbot John de la Moote in 1396, **WILLIAM WYLUM**, Prior of Redbourn, was present. His name appeared also on the letters of testimonial for the next Abbot - William Heyworth, in 1401.

THOMAS WENDOVER resigned from the Priory in 1427 and went to Beaulieu, in Bedfordshire where he died the following year.

There was then a quick succession of Priors. **HUGH LEGAT** succeeded Wendover, but in the same year he was discharged from the Priory and sent to Tynemouth where he died. **WILLIAM BRYTH** took over, but the next year he was succeeded by **RICHARD SMITH de MISSENDENE**, he came from Beaulieu, where he had been Prior for 20 years and Sub-Cellarer at the Abbey before that. One account of him says that he returned to Beauleau for a second term, until it was turned into a farm in 1435.

There is another long gap until in 1452, when **THOMAS WESTWODE** is named as being present at the election of Wheathampstead for his second term as Abbot; he was also at the election of Abbot Albone in 1465. He was named previously at the Abbey as *"Custos* (Custodian) *of the Lady Chapel"*.

A further Abbatical election in 1476 gives - **THOMAS ALBON**. Four years later, during a visit of the Abbot of Westminster, he was described as an 'inmate' of the Abbey. Whether this was a temporary residence, or whether Redbourn Priory was already closed we cannot tell, certainly it had become a farm some time prior to the Dissolution. Perhaps the arrangement was similar to Beauleau, which became a farm, but with occasional offices still said there.

There was mention of a Prior at the election of Abbot Ramrydge in 1492, but his name was not given. It has been suggested that there may have been 2 or 3 more Priors after Albon but there is no written evidence of their names.[21]

THE PRIORY BUILDINGS

Medieval monastic writings mention the Priory buildings, sometimes enabling dates to be ascribed to them. Physical evidence of medieval buildings appeared during building of the Park Estate, in the form of medieval stonework, mostly window tracery see *Fig; 5.7*. Three quite different stone heads were also found, one of which may have been meant to represent St. Amphibalus, see *Fig: 5.5*

THE CHAPEL OF ST JAMES. This existed near the "Hills of the Banners" before 1178, and was thus Norman in style. It was probably used initially for worship by the monks until a new chapel was built, to which it may have been attached. During the time of Abbot Thomas de la Mare (1349-96) it was described

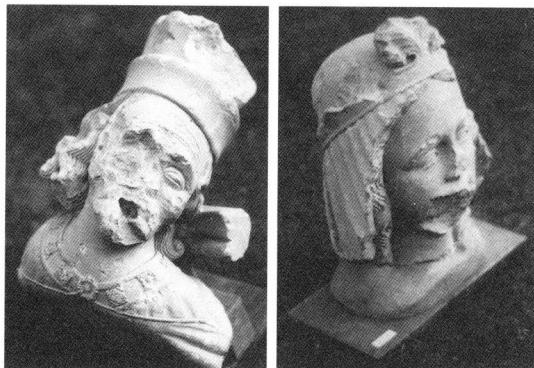

Fig: 5.5 - Stone Heads found on the Park Estate
thought to represent St Amphibalus (LHS) and a Lady
Benefactress or possibly Christina of Markyate (RHS)
(Both displayed in REDBOURN VILLAGE MUSEUM)

Fig: 5.6 Figure of Amphibalus
Formerly in the Abbey Cloister -
compare with head in Fig: 5.5
(Courtesy - Museum of St Albans)

as having been left in ruins for many years after a *"disastrous fire"*[22] Putting the rebuilding into the Decorated or early Perpendicular period - it was then re-dedicated by Archbishop Agathensis.

THE CHAPEL OF ST AMPHIBALUS. With the pre-existing chapel of St James available for services, the priority would have been to provide the domestic buildings to accommodate the monks. Later a chapel worthy of the Patron Saint would have become important. Such a chapel was dedicated in 1215, which puts it firmly into the Early English period.[23] It was equipped with a single bell.[24]

John Wheathampstead is well known for much building work during his two reigns as Abbot. At Redbourn he spent over £40 in 1438 on decorating the chapel (probably mural paintings), and improving the Altars [25] This chapel was still standing and with lead on its roof, as late as 1540 (See page 76).

THE CLOISTER. William Stubbard, who is buried *"near the Altar of St Osyth's......a former lay brother of the Monastery, a worthy craftsman in sculpture"* between 1421-40 built - *"the cloister at Redbourn"* and at the Abbey *"the Prior's chair, doors and sundry other laudable works"* all thus in the Perpendicular style.[26] The addition of a cloister shows that the little priory was developing like the larger monasteries; suggesting that it may now have become more than just a holiday home.

DOMESTIC BUILDINGS
Without the need for a Priory Chapel initially, (St James was already existing), work on its domestic buildings would be started soon after the discovery of Amphibalus in 1178. The priory is known to have been habitable between 1183 and 1195, thus dating them to the Norman Transitional period. The essentials

must have included a **HALL,** a **DORTER** (Dormitory) and a **REREDORTER** (Lavatory and Wash room), but as yet no Kitchen.

PRIOR'S QUARTERS. Much of the accommodation, including the Dormitory, seems to have been shared, even the Abbot had to share initially with the monks.

ABBOT'S ACCOMODATION. Until the time of Abbot de la Mare (1349-96) any visiting Abbot had to live and sleep with the resident monks. However, the monks expressed their embarrassment especially at having to share the lavatory with him. Perhaps this was the only excuse that de la Mare needed to improve his personal accommodation there. He spent 100 marks (£66.13.4d.) and built a *"a beautiful room with windows in three sides"* siting it above the Common Lavatory with 'en suite' facilities.[27] Being built during his abbacy, puts it in the Decorated or Perpendicular style of architecture.

KITCHEN. Repairs were made in the time of Abbot Wheathampstead, prior to 1438. [28] This shows that it was already existing and old enough to require attention, probably by then 50 years or more old, thus dating it to about the mid 14th century, and in either the Decorated or Perpendicular style.

INNER PORCH. Suggests an anteroom of some kind, perhaps part of the hall.[29]

THE GROUNDS. It was only during the time of Abbot Wheathampstead that the Priory grounds were mentioned. As part of improvements at Redbourn the enclosure of the **OUTSIDE COURTYARD** is given in 1438.[30] At a later, unspecified date, - *"repairs to the stone walls surrounding the outside courtyard"* costing £7.18s.4d, are mentioned.[31] Men from Flamstead threatened the Priory outside the **GATE** near the Heath (See page 37). This locates one gateway, but there was another on the south giving access to the Prior's safe road to the Abbey.

THE DISSOLUTION AND AFTER

When Henry VIII was declared supreme head of the Church in England in 1534, the first year's income, or 'first fruits', from monastic property were ordered to be paid to the Crown. Therefore, a detailed list was prepared of all ecclesiastical property, called the "Valor Ecclesiasticus".[32] The entry for Redbourn Priory gave its value as £9.2s.0d, with the tithes 1/10th of that amount.

After the Dissolution, the Court of Augmentations was set up to manage and dispose of the monastic properties seized by Henry, they produced figures on which the sale prices of properties were calculated. The Priory was much more highly valued here than in the 'Valor' - a feature common with other places. The Court figures are much more detailed and include the Manor farm, the Priory farm and rents from its properties; some of which were not included in the earlier valuation.

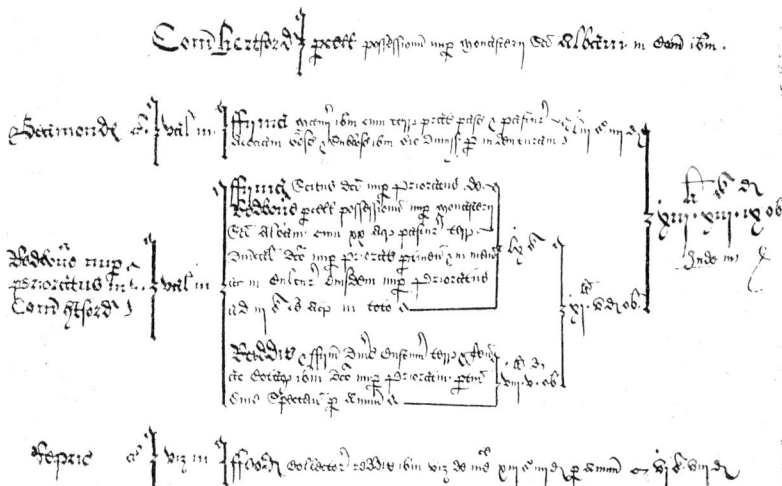

Fig: 5.7 - Part of the Court of Augmentations 'Particular' for the sale of the Priory in 1540 [33]

[Courtesy of the Public Record Office]

A transcript of the above document is as follows:-

"County of Hertford | parcel of the possessions of the late monastery of Redburn

Beamonds | value in	*| the farm of the Manor with lands, meadows*		*53s. 4d*
	| pastures, rights of pasture, woodlands and coppices		

The late Priory | value | the farm situated at the former Priory, with

20 acres of pasture, the demesne lands belonging and cultivated by the Priory - at 2 shillings the acre   *60s.*

Rents and dues of customary tenants of lands and Tenements and cottages belonging, per annum   *£8.0.5½..*

     (Sub Total)   *£11.0.5½*   (Total)   *£13.13.9½.."*

The 'Particular' continues thus:-

     "Fee for rent collector, half of 13s.4d.(1 Mark)   *6s.8d.*
Net Balance p.a.   *£13.7s.1½.*

     For a tithe of the revenues, payable to the King   *£1.6s.9d.*

     There remains over and above £12.7s.6d which is rated after 20 years purchase amounting to the sum of £240.7s.6d.

     Notice that the sale price was based on rents over a 20-year period, totalling £240.7.6d. This was the price paid by John Cocks and his wife, Eleanor, in 1540 - becoming Tenants-in-chief, to the King, and having to pay him tithe. The document was signed by the man responsible for engineering the Suppression and disposal of the monasteries for Henry VIII – THOMAS CROMWELL.

The Court of Augmentation document ended with two "memos" about the property, one a note about the trees in the grounds, the other showing that the Priory chapel was still standing and with lead on its roof:-

" *there ben no woods, butt onely certeyn oks, elmes and aisshes aboute"*
"...there remaynethe certyn leade upon the chapell of the priory"

Eighteen years later John Cocks sold it to Sir Richard Rede (see chapter 8), who passed it to his son, Innocent, the family holding it for three generations.[34] It was eventually sold to Sir Harbottle Grimston of Gorhambury in 1655.[35]

When Sir Richard took over the Priory he is said to have used its stones to build a new home for himself, called "Place House".[36] References to this house are few - one is in his own will, but the most interesting is in a biography of Francis and Anthony Bacon, by Daphne du Maurier - called "The Golden Lads".[37] du Maurier, who researched authentic documents, located "Place House" as being - "*bounded by the village street on one side and the large expanse of village green on the other*" This fits in very well with **The Priory" house,** whose garden used to extend to the Common.

The site of this house is more of a mystery than the Priory itself; perhaps the favoured position is where the Georgian house called "The Priory" now stands in the High Street. The name itself suggests a possible connection with the former Priory, but a medieval stone 'feature' in the garden wall of a house behind it, (formerly within its grounds) and a report of foundations being seen in its garden add even more interest. see *fig: 5.8.*[38]

Perhaps when "Place House" itself became ruinous, it gave rise to the name of the adjacent passageway called "**The Ruins**" (in later times "Tottens Alley").

A very unlikely underground connection has been suggested running from "The Priory" house to the Church, beneath the avenue of trees across the *Fig:5.8 - Garden feature* Common. The supposed opening into this from the cellar in "The Priory" actually looks more like a storage alcove, to me. Quite why a secret underground passage should be required between the Priory and the Church is a mystery.

Both Alban and Amphibalus had Heraldic Arms attributed to them in the mid 15th century. These appear, together with those of St Oswin, in St Albans Abbey Presbytery dating from the time of Abbot John of Wheathampstead's second abbacy, - see *Fig: 5.9*

Fig: 5.9 - Heraldic Arms attributed to Alban and Amphibalus
(**Photograph by D. Kelsall**)

On east facing wall of the Presbytery: King Oswin (left), Alban (centre), Amphibalus (right)

DOCUMENTARY EVIDENCE OF THE PRIORY'S LOCATION

Having concluded this account of the Priory's history, the question of where it was, must now be tackled; the actual site having been lost since the destruction of monastic property after the Dissolution. For this, documentary evidence is most important, while physical clues are scant; but together they can be used to make what I hope will be some convincing suggestions.

The major clue was totally destroyed when the monks dug out the two burial mounds on the Common to find the remains of Amphibalus in 1178, and then proceeded to erect the priory buildings on the land where they had been. However, Matthew Paris provides some useful descriptions of the pre-existing site and also records that the earlier chapel of St James stood nearby, giving a rather strange and unearthly reason for its existence [39]:-

> *"This chapel had been built long ago in honour of the martyr on account of the frequent displays of heavenly light which had appeared to shepherds keeping watch there over their flocks by night"*

Two, more earthly, reasons can be suggested. Firstly it was quite a common practice to build a church to sanctify a pagan site; the fact that the Hills of the Banners were used as a public meeting place could hint at such an early take over. Linked with this, its dedication to St James, (associated with pilgrims) strongly suggests that the chapel may have been provided for pilgrims on their way to the shrine of St Alban in the Abbey.

Matthew Paris provides us with four useful facts about the site [40]:-

· *"It was in a village called Redburn, almost three miles from St Albans.*
· *"...a certain heath, uncultivated of old"*
· *"This place possessed a pleasant piece of open ground suitable both for pasture and also as a resting place for weary travellers"*
· *"On this open ground...two mounds stood out, they were called the Mounds of the Banners"*

From these facts given us by Paris it is apparent that the site of the discovery, and later of the Priory itself, was:-

· On the main road, over 3 miles from the gates of St Albans - thus roughly in the area of Fish Street farm.
· The fields of Fish Street farm near the road were shown as grassland on the earliest map of the area, thus 'uncultivated' land.
· For the mounds to have 'stood out', they must have been slightly higher than the main road - there is a slight slope up to the farmhouse.
· Such a pleasant piece of grassland near the road would have been attractive to travellers to rest before the final stage of their journey.

There is no chance of confirming this hypothesis because the whole area is now occupied by new housing and the old farmhouse itself.

Further medieval documentary evidence comes from Walsingham describing the enclosure of part of the Common for the priory site [41]:-

"The Abbot...had enclosed a certain part of the Heath, about a third, with hedges and ditches on all sides"

The interesting part of this is the proportion that he gives for the area of the enclosure. It must be remembered that the common was much larger in the 12th century than it is now, thus we are looking for a third of this larger area. The early area has in later centuries been further reduced because of the encroachment of houses around the edge. An unwritten law allowed a house to remain if it had been built and a fire lit in its hearth within 24 hours.

One obvious case is "The Heath" on the corner of Lybury Lane, earlier suggested as the place where Thomas Bedel tried to build a house (see Chapter 3). Other cases of encroachment are apparent from a study of large-scale maps, *Fig: 5.12* is my assessment based on the 1841 Tithe Map. The most prominent area is, of course, that containing Fish Street farm and its various Park Fields, all indicating former uncultivated, or park land.

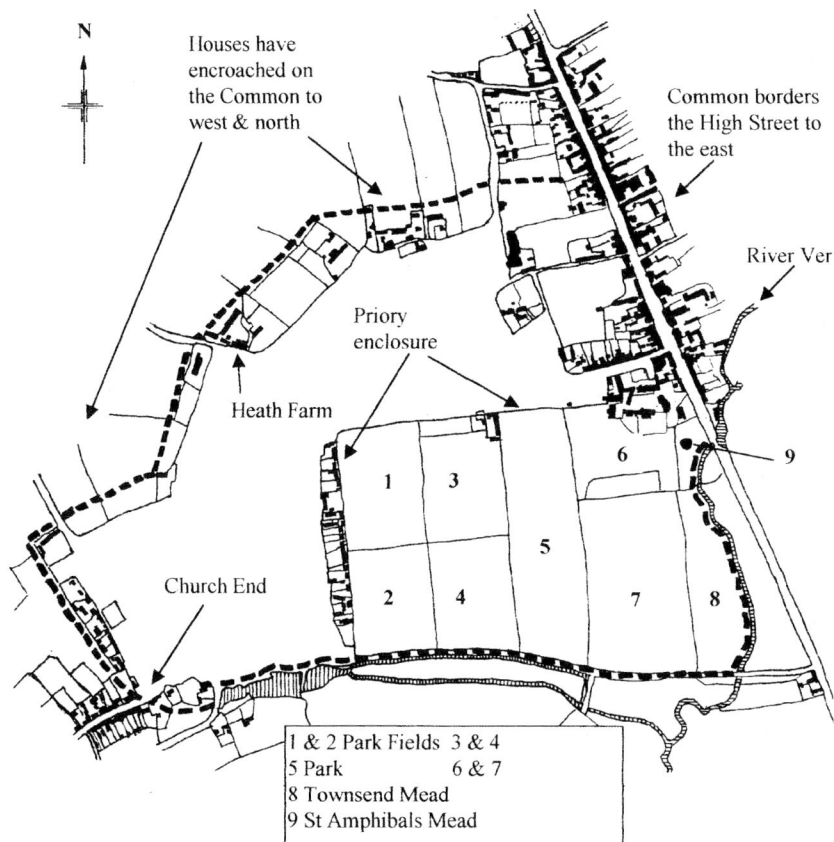

N

Houses have
encroached on
the Common to
west & north

Common borders
the High Street to
the east

River Ver

Priory
enclosure

Heath Farm

Church End

1

3

2

4

5

6

7

8

9

1 & 2 Park Fields 3 & 4
5 Park   6 & 7
8 Townsend Mead
9 St Amphibals Mead

Fig: 5.10 - Suggested features of the Common in Medieval times

Measuring the area of this suggested medieval Common we get a
conservative 89 acres, with the area of Fish Street Farm and its land 33 acres; this
includes "Amphibals Mead", but not "Townsend Mead". This is surely near
enough to the medieval claim that *"about a third of the Heath"* was enclosed.

In his lecture at Redbourn in 1887, the Rev. Fowler suggested that the avenue
of Elms from Church End to the Ruins passage, actually led to the Priory gate.[42]
He further suggested that former priory properties extended along the High Street,
Lamb Lane, and north to Crouch Hall. He drew a line along the back of the North
Common houses, but included the "Bees Nest" which he thought would have been
the Prior's apiary (this is incorrect - the house was only known as the "Beesnest"
from about 1839, having previously been called the "Blacknest").

One hundred years later, Dr. Eileen Roberts, in her lecture in Redbourn Church gave a much more likely and accurate suggestion, pointing to the fields formerly part of Fish Street Farm.[43] She noted that most of these fields had 'Park' in their names, this denoting an enclosure of land. The field names were - Upper Park, Lower Park, The Park, Plough Park and (two) Park Fields, see *fig: 5.10*

Another statement of the area is given a 'Particular' for the grant of the Priory to John Cocks, by the Augmentation Office in 1540 - see *Fig: 5.7* [44]:-

> *"The farm situated at the former Priory of Redborne....with 20 acres of pasture, the demesne lands belonging, at 2 shillings the acre*
>
> *...   ...£3.0.0d"*

These figures can be compared with those given for the Fish Street farm area on the Tithe Map:-

Court of Augmentation	1841 Tithe Map
20 acres of pasture	25 acres grassland & meadow
£3 at 2s. per acre, i.e. 30 acres	31½ acres = 6½ arable + the above

These areas are so close, even allowing for inaccuracies of measurement in early times compared with the accurate 1841 map, I think it shows that this area is indeed the most likely site of Redbourn Priory and its grounds.

PHYSICAL EVIDENCE OF THE SITE

So much for documentary evidence; but there is also much physical evidence of medieval remains in the same area. The main evidence is the finding of much medieval ecclesiastical stonework of the 12th to 15th century, though unfortunately no actual building plans have been recognised.

These were found during the building of the "Park Estate", in 1966-7. Archaeological work was carried out by the, then newly formed, Redbourn Research Group, with some outside help. Their resources were sadly inadequate to cover the whole of this potentially important site, the existence of which was completely unexpected until initial ground clearance began.

Because of my role as surveyor for the Redbourn Research Group, I am able to show a plan of the site, never previously published (*Fig: 5.12)*, but unfortunately no authoritative report has yet been prepared. However, my understanding of the findings is that they indicated a farm of about the 16th century with some early ditches and filled wall foundations. A well of about the 16th century was completely dug out and in the bottom the base of a tree pump was found - see *Fig: 5.11*. its decayed remains are now in the care of the Redbourn Village Museum. It is interesting to note that the Rev. Fowler shows a well, sited near Fish Street farm, called "St Amphibals Well".[45]

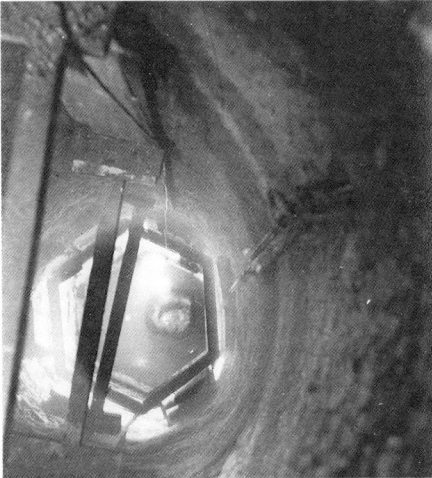

Tree Pump in the bottom of the well

Tree Pump removed from well

Base of small column

Beaded decoration

Floor tile fragment of St. Peter with the 'Keys of the Kingdom

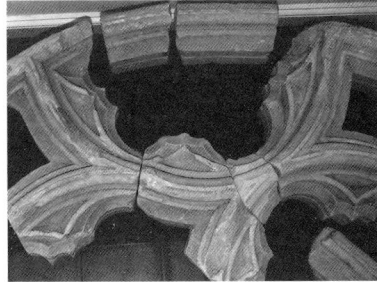

Some tracery fragments assembled in the Museum

Fig: 5.11 - MEDIEVAL AND OTHER FINDS FROM THE "PARK ESTATE"

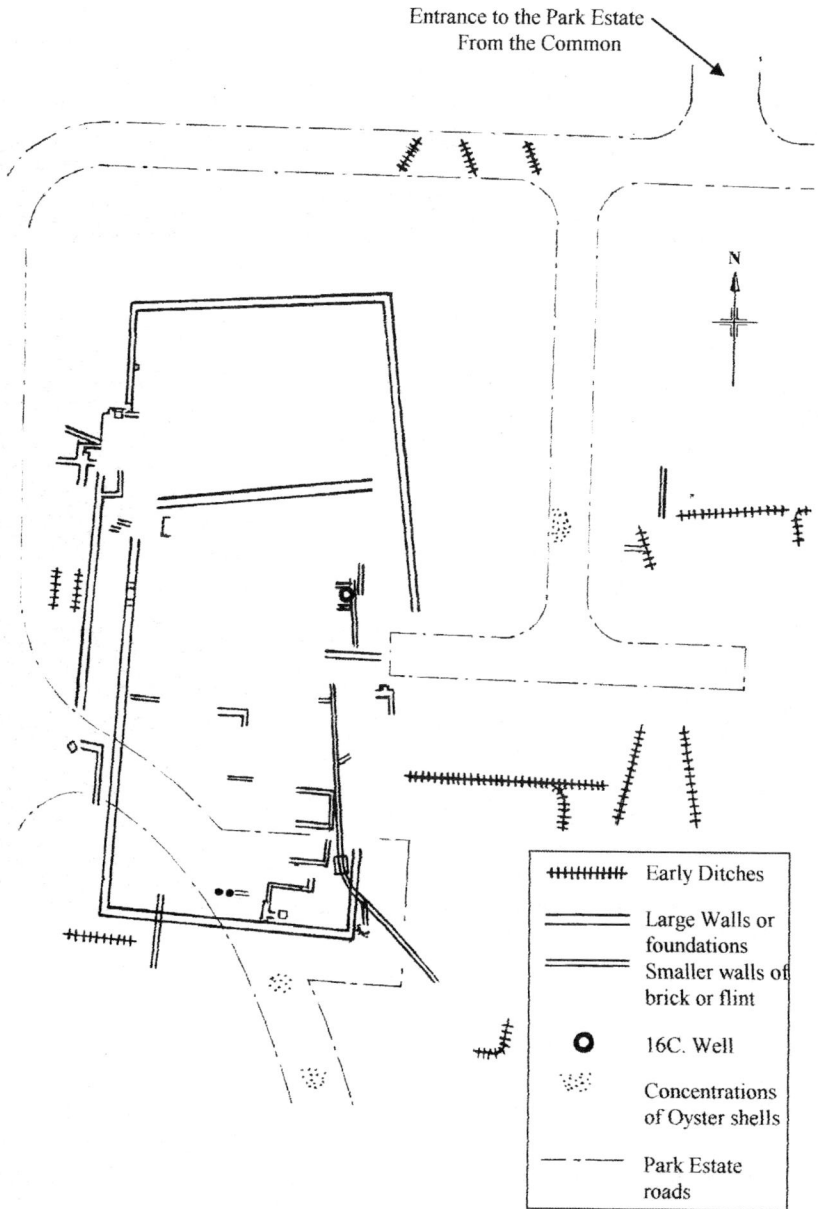

Entrance to the Park Estate
From the Common

N

Legend:
- ++++++++ Early Ditches
- ═══ Large Walls or foundations
- ═══ Smaller walls of brick or flint
- **O** 16C. Well
- Concentrations of Oyster shells
- - - - Park Estate roads

Fig: 5.12 – Archaeological features found on the PARK ESTATE, 1966-7

Redbourn Research Group at work

Top of the well

Corner foundations - Tudor

Base of large Medieval column

Long brick gully, diverted to left

Bed of Oyster shells

5.13 VIEWS OF THE EXCAVATIONS ON THE PARK ESTATE

THE "MOUNDS OF THE BANNERS"

The validity of the monks claim that the human remains they had found in the "Hills" were actually those of Amphibalus has been refuted by Thomas Wright F.S.A.[46] In a paper he read to the Society of Antiquaries in 1849, his opinion was that many of the so-called relics of saints kept in monasteries were in fact taken from barrows or graves of early times. As an example of such a discovery he cited the happenings at Redbourn and pointed out that burials in the Roman period, in which Amphibalus lived, did not normally contain weapons. Whereas in Saxon burials it was common for a large knife, or spearhead to be found by, or under, the skull, with another knife near or below the breast :-

> *"Among the remains of Amphibalus were found two large knives of the martyr's, one in the skull and the other in the breast"*

The above is from the description of the grave goods given by Matthew Paris (see page 59) showing that the bodies found are more likely to have been a Saxon chieftain and his followers, killed in some local skirmish, rather than a Christian missionary of Roman Verulamium.

Two wooden Shrines, or Coffers, were kept in the Priory to contain holy relics of Amphibalus; among which were two large knives. [47] One of these could easily be the Saxon spearhead that was found in the churchyard in 1907 see *Fig: 5.14*. [48] Perhaps it was buried for safety after the Dissolution, maybe by an ardent Vicar.

Fig: 5.14 - Saxon Spearhead found in Redbourn Churchyard

CONCLUSIONS

I have spent a lot of space detailing the most likely location of the Priory because I think it is important to correct earlier misconceptions, but also because I feel that this will round off an otherwise enigmatic account of a 'lost' site.

The case centres on an area of the medieval Heath, or Common, shown in *Fig: 5.10*, but points to the Fish Street farmhouse as being the most likely location of the main Priory chapel. In this respect it is interesting to note that the orientation is very roughly east west as were most churches. A less likely idea is that the farm buildings formed a roughly 'cloister-like' square to the south See *Fig: 5.15*, however, this is quite a common layout of local farms which have no ecclesiastical connections.

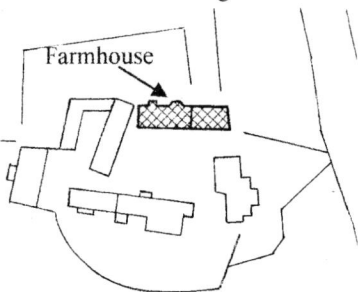

Fig 5.15 - Fish Street Farm 1841

However, the most convincing evidence to my mind comes from a survey of 1696, referring to [49] :-

> *"that Capital messuage called ST. AFFABLES CHAPPEL, alias ST. JAMES CHAPELL, most commonly (called) FISHSTREETT FARME"*

Fig; 5.16 - Fish Street Farm, 1964

REFERENCES

1   Hertfordshire Archaeology 1968, Vol. 1, pp. 1-8 John Morris - "The date of Saint Alban"

2   Arthur Swinson, "The Quest for Alban", Fraternity of the Friends of St Albans Abbey, 1970, p40

3   As 1, "Other Doings (Alia Acta)" translated by Leslie Simpson with an introduction by Dr. Eileen Roberts

4   Matthew Paris - "Chronica Majora", Rolls Series Vol. 2, pp.301-308

5   Matthew Paris - "Illustrations to the life of Saint Alban"

6   Eileen Roberts - "Images of ALBAN" p.109

7   HRO. D/ESa.130 - Lecture notes of Rev. Henry Fowler for his lecture in Redbourn Church

8   Thomas Walsingham - "Gesta Abbatum", Rolls Series Vol. 1, p.211

9   As 8, Vol. 1, p289

10 Matthew Paris - "Historia Angulatum", Rolls Series, Vol. 3, p.61

11 As 8, Vol. 1, p.452-3

12 Sir William Dugdale - "Monasticon Angulatum", p.526

13 As 8, Vol. 2, p.397

14 As 8, Vol. 2, p.399-400

15 John Amundesham -"Annales Monasterii", Vol. 1, p113

16 Abridged from -"Gesta Abbatum" (ref. 8) Vol. 2, pp.202-5 (1326-35); "Annales Monasterii" (ref. 16)Vol.1, pp.102-15 (1423) and Vol. 2, pp.203-12 (1439)

17 As 15, Vol. 2, p. 207

18 Herts Advertiser April 23rd 1887 - "Cells of St Albans, author unknown

19   Unless otherwise referenced mentions of the Priors of Redbourn taken from:-
      Walsingham's "Gesta Abbatum" vols. 1,2 & 3
      Amundesham's "Annals Monasterii" vol. 1
      Wheathampstead's "Registrum Abbatae" vols. 1 & 2
      Most references also occur in the Victoria County History, Hertfordshire" vol. IV,
      p418
20   As 12, p.209
21   Herts Advertiser 1887, article about "Redbourn Cell" by unknown author
22   As 8, Vol. 2, p..400
23   As 8, Vol. 1, p.289
24   As 8, Vol. 2, p.400
25   As 15, Vol. 2, p. 200
26   As 15, Vol. 1, p.440
27   As 8, Vol. 2, p.399
28   As 15, Vol. 2, p.200
29   As 8, Vol.2, p.203
30   As 15, Vol. 2, p.200
31   As 15, Vol. 2, p.264
32   "Valor Ecclesiasticus", Temp. Hen. VIII, 1810-34 Vol. 1 PRO. - Ref. Press 6/107,
      p.451
33   PRO. Ref. E.318/Box 8/294
34   PRO - Patent Rolls C66/928m20, C66/1055m12
35   HRO. Ref. II.M.14
36   Mentioned in his will - PRO. Ref.PROB.11/58
37   As 56 and "Golden Lads" by Daphne du Maurier, p92
38   Reported to me personally by Miss Ann Skillman
39   As 4, Vol. 2, p.307
40   As 4, Vol. 2, pp.302-3
41   As 8, Vol. 3, p. 260
42   As 7, Lecture notes and sketch by Rev. H. Fowler
43   Lecture reprinted in "The Abbey Link" Autumn 1997, p.10
44   PRO. Patent Roll, Ref. C.66/690m21
45   As 42
46   "Archaeologia" of Society of Antiquaries of London, 1849, Vol. 33,pp.262-
      8, Notices relating to the Antiquaries of St Albans, by T. Wright F.S.A.
47   As 8, Vol.1, p.282
48   Gerish Collection in HRO; box 62; Levelling of the churchyard took place
      in 1907
49   Gorhambury Manorial Records, HRO. Ref. I.68

CHAPTER 6

MEDIEVAL REDBOURN

This chapter sets out to update the picture given of the village by the Domesday Survey (chapter 2). As in earlier chapters, monastic records have to be chiefly relied on, in particular the taxation list made after the failed Redbourn Revolt of c.1344 (Chapter 3) and a Rental of 1455 [1], (See *Fig: 6.1*) The latter is of special interest and value as it updates the Norman Survey of nearly four centuries earlier and gives an almost complete account of the village, its tenants and their holdings. This must be one of the most important Redbourn documents surviving.

Court Rolls survive, but only from 1514. These mostly concern exchanges of land, but occasionally give other glimpses of the period - like that of an illegal Horse Mill in 1522 (see page 89). Wills are another source. From 1420 these were under the control of the Church, through the Archdeaconry of St Albans. Though basically personal, they sometimes give information about other people, properties, customs and gifts to the church.

Finally, the redistribution of Monastic property in the village after the Dissolution, will be considered and its new 'lay' owners seen. In a similar way to the Domesday enquiries, the Dissolution may have made little difference to villagers' lives. The Priory had already been closed several years, and the management of the Manor was probably still organised by the same local men, but now under a different, non-resident, Tenant in Chief.

THE MANORS OF REDBOURN

> *"...a little commonwealth, whereof the Tenants are the members, the Land the bulk, and the Lord the head"*

This is one definition of a manor, written in 1607 by John Nordon, in "The Surveyors Dialogue". A more traditional picture is of open fields, centred on a manor house, a church and the villagers' cottages. This does not entirely hold true for Redbourn. For a start, the Lord of the Manor, except for a brief period, always lived elsewhere. It is true that the village houses clustered near to the church, but management was centred over a mile away at Redbournbury.

For the whole medieval period, the various Abbots of St Albans were the Lords of the **MANOR of REDBOURN,** with their Chamberlains managing it from the grange at Redbournbury. In 1538, just before the Dissolution, the Abbot leased the manor for 60 years to Henry Beech; then in 1550 King Henry gave actual ownership to Princess Elizabeth. She later leased it to Sir Richard Rede, for three generations of his family - they were the only <u>resident</u> Lords of the Manor, see also chapter 8. Court books and rolls exist from 1514 to 1940.[2]

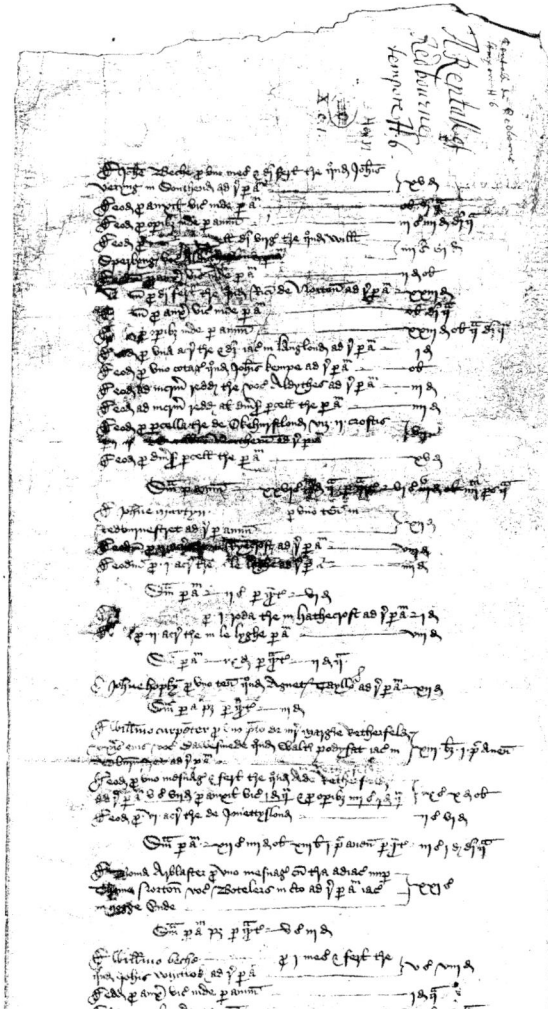

HEADING:-
"A Rentall of Redbourne Tempore H.6 [Henry VI] *33.H.6* [1455]

FIRST ITEM:-
John Beche
For 1 mess(uage) & ½
ferl(ingate) of land, late
John Veryng's in Southend
at rent pa 15d
For Sheriff's Aid ³/₄d
For Labour Service 3s.4³/₄d

SUB TOTAL (Line 18) -
Sum pa. 26s. ⁴/₄d
Per. quarter 6s. 5½d
4ᵗʰ quarter pay 5d

[Does not add up to Sub Total]

Fig: 6.1 - Part of the Rental of the Manor of Redbourn, 1455

Written in the time of King Henry VI, it consists of 4 membranes of parchment, sewn together to make a roll 8 feet long, the Latin text is written on both sides and consists of 534 lines showing the holdings and rents payable by each tenant of the Manor of Redbourn.

The 1455 Rental does not always give figures for the extents of tenants' holdings, but the likely areas can be deduced by comparing similar rents. The following figures total about 1514 acres but do not include the Demesne land.

Arable land	285	acres
Meadow and pasture	27½	"
Woodland	4	"
Land in Common fields	366	"
Crofts (small closes near a dwelling)	155½	"
Tofts (Site where a house may have been)	120½	"
Wicks (A specialised farm, ie. a Dairy)	6	"
Cotlands (about 5 acres or less)	17½	"
Land associated with dwellings	531	"

It is obvious from this list that the manor consisted of roughly the same sort of holdings that we saw in the Domesday Survey; ie. arable or plough lands of the villagers in the Common Fields, also meadow and pasture. The Crofts, Tofts and Wicks were smallholdings; the Cotlands, which would have included a humble cottage, were held by cottars in return for labour services to the Lord. The "land associated with dwellings" (my description) provides clues to the types of properties existing at that time - see section on village buildings, page 88.

After the Dissolution the manor passed to King Henry's children, starting with Princess Elizabeth. Charles, Prince of Wales, found it a useful financial resource in 1628 when he used it to clear some debts to citizens of London by transferring it to trustees of the Mayor.[3] In the following year they leased it to Henry Meautys of Gorhambury, who purchased the Reversion in 1652.[4] Since that time, subsequent owners of that house retained the manor until it was bought back into Royal hands by the Crown Commissioners in 1931.[5]

A survey map of the estate of James Grimston, of Gorhambury made in 1767 shows the manor of that time lying mainly south of the east-west roads between Harpenden and Hemel Hempstead. The area totalled 5115 acres, but by that time several large farms were in different hands, as can be seen from Fig: 6.2

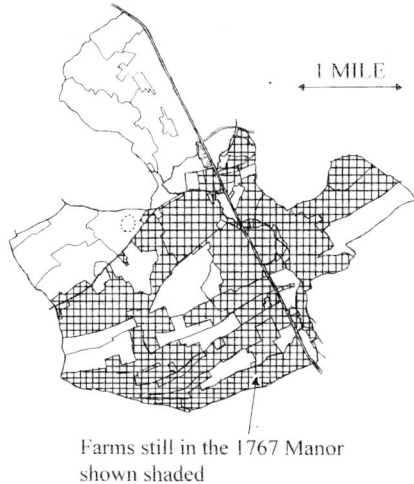

1 MILE

Farms still in the 1767 Manor shown shaded

Fig: 6.2 – The Manor of Redbourn 1767
Based on a Survey by E. L. Davis

The second main manor was created for the Priory after its foundation. This was known as the **MANOR of the PRIORY, or ST AMPHIBALS MANOR**. The earliest information is from the Court of Augmentation 1540, (page 69) [6]:-
>   *"The farm situated at the late Priory"* valued at £3 plus £8 in rents.
>   *"The Farm of the Manor"* called "Beamonds", valued at £2.13.4d

These two entries show that the Priory had two different entities, ie. The PRIORY MANOR which comprised the old Priory buildings and the adjacent land, whereas St. AMPHIBALS MANOR was purely Beamonds Farm (now Beaumont Hall). Court records survive from 1587 to 1920.[7]

Besides these two main manors, there were also three smaller ones -

ST AGNELLS MANOR: Its records exist between 1629 and 1874, being contained within the court books of Flamstead manor, in which parish it partly lay.[8] However, it existed before 1454 when it was bought by the Abbot from Joan Spendlove for £18, including an annual pension to her of 40 shillings [9]. At the Dissolution it was granted to John Cokkes who also purchased Redbourn Priory and its manor [10]. It subsequently passed through several hands, including the Ferrers family, but it is in the papers of Sir John Sebright of Beechwood, near Flamstead, that the above court record books are found.

MANOR OF INGES: This probably originated from land owned by William Inge in 1303 [11]. Its court rolls exist between 1639 and 1858. A Rental of 1785 included "The Bole" (later the Punch Bowl), also certain fields and meadows, now difficult to locate [12]. The last surviving document is notice of a court to be held in the Punch Bowl in 1858.

LAWRENCE MANOR: Court rolls exist from 1527.[13] Its lands were small and very scattered, but centred on Bottom House farm, and included the Red Lyon, Rose & Crown and Lamb inns, several cottages and *"certain alms houses called the Church House"* at Church End, also six closes of land.[14] The final document, dated 1786, stated that as there had been no courts for 60 years, all its copyhold lands should be considered as freehold, thus winding up the manor.[15]

A farm, also referred to as a manor, was **BUTLERS**, but only between c.1545 and c.1600.[16] There is no documentary evidence of manor courts, so the title could have been assumed by owners of the Farm, possibly for status reasons.

REDBOURN ENDS

The earliest farm in Redbourn was established by Iron Age men at the Aubreys - see chapter 1. There is no evidence to link these early settlers with the farmers of later ages, in fact about 1400 years separates the Aubreys from the emergence of Redbourn as a farming community under Aegelwine the Black. His early manor probably consisted of a number of scattered and isolated settlements. Such settlements are thought to be evidenced today by farms whose names bear the suffix of 'End', suggestive of a clearing cut into the wild forested landscape.

The fact that none of the Redbourn 'Ends' are described as such in documents until the mid 15th century is no denial of their very early origins. The families after whom six appear to be named, can be traced back to the late 13th or early 14th centuries, but this is not to say that they were not differently named by the original farmers in Saxon times. In "The Place Names of Hertfordshire" (English Place Name Society, Vol. XV) the medieval origin of many farms are suggested, mostly deriving from the name of an early owner. Where no source reference is given it can be found in the above book. For the location see *Fig: 6.3*

BEESON END - Adam Bestney appeared in the taxation list (c.1344), the present spelling has evolved from his name.

CHURCH END - A title suggesting the existence of a church here, perhaps from Saxon times - see chapter 4. It has always been considered to be the early 'centre' of the original village. The nearness to the Aubreys may also be significant, but no physical link has been established between the two.

DANE END - Its possible Danish connection, or its situation above a Dene, has been discussed in chapter 1. It first appears as a name in 1294 and also in the taxation list, but in these cases the farmer is named after his farm, ie. Roger ate Dene.

HOGG END - John Hog appears in 1307, also Nicholas Hog in the taxation list. It is also tempting to link it with the Domesday woods for 500 pigs.

NORRINGTON END - Alice de Northington is seen in 1296, when it was known as Northington before becoming Northampton and finally Norrington End.

REVEL END - Its earlier name was Rutherfield End, from Adam de Rutherfeld of 1307 and also in the taxation list. The name is said to suggest an 'open space' for cattle. Revel End is a 16th century version, alternating with Rotherfield for about 100 years. The suggestion that it may derive from an alternative spelling, Retherveld, and indicate the holding of revels here, is not supported by documentary evidence. There are two Ends of this name, Great and Little Revel Ends.

SOUTH END - Though nearly in the south of the parish, it probably owes its name initially to Adam Bisouthe, 1314. In the 17th century it briefly appears as Southes (ie. Mr. South's farm).

WOOD END - No 'Wood' family can be found, so this may indeed originate from a Domesday Wood, though the name only appears from 1523.[17]

HOLTSMERE END should not be included in this list as the farmhouse and most of its land, lies in Flamstead parish.

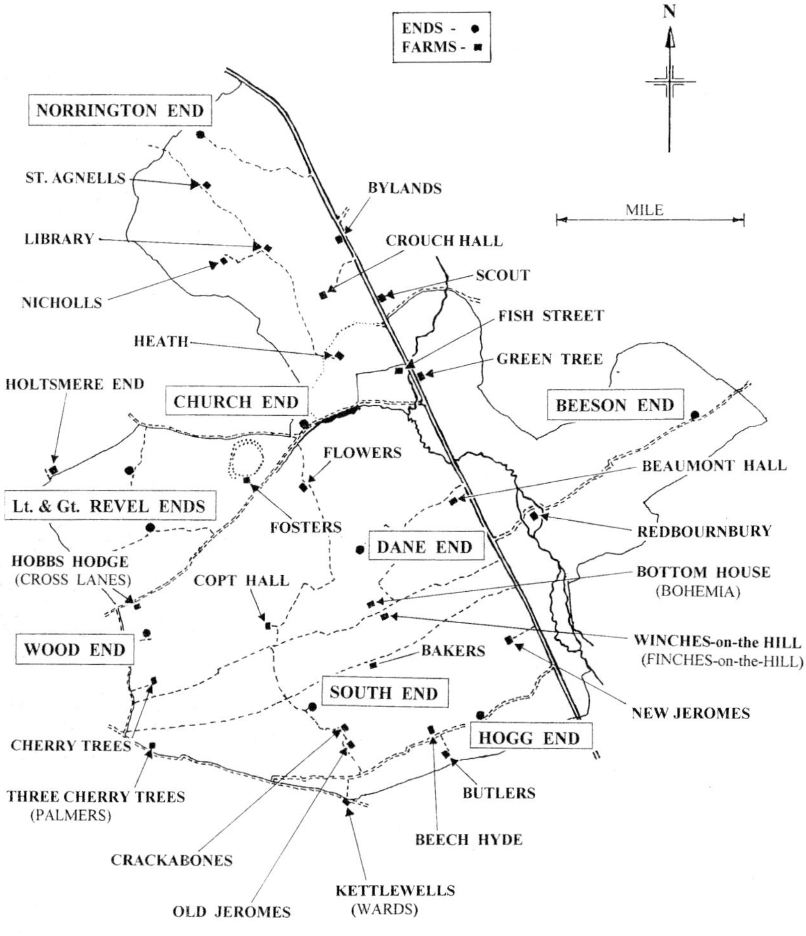

Fig: 6.3 – The ENDS & FARMS of REDBOURN

REDBOURN FARMS

Other farms and their suggested origins are as follows:- (locations see *Fig: 6.3*)
Again most medieval origins come from "The Place Names of Hertfordshire"

BAKERS - A family name as early as 1294, and also in the 1455 Rental.

BEAUMONT HALL - 'Bemond' in 1455, it developed through various spellings to its present form. William Beaumont bought it in 1637 attracted, it is thought, by the chance of it having his own name.[18] *Fig: 6.4* shows that the house had gone by 1767 with an avenue leading up to where it had been, adjacent to the farm buildings. Today's house stands to one side of the avenue.

Fig: 6.4 - Beaumont Hall - 1767

BEECH HYDE - The Beech family were well known in Redbourn from early times. Alternatively, one of the Domesday beech woods for pigs may have provided the name, possibly linked with nearby 'Hogg End'. 'Hyde', or Hide comes from a land area of about 120 acres; its area in 1841 was not far off this (85 acres). See also page 90.

BOTTOM HOUSE – was an alternative name for both Dane End and Kettlewells from 1637 and 1759 respectively.[18] The 1898 Ordnance Survey locates it as an individual farm near Dane End; later maps give this as **BOHEMIA** farm, but that name appears earlier, from 1753 until well into the 20th century.[19]

Fig: 6.5 – Bohemia Farm, c.1920's

BUTLERS - John Aygnel unsuccessfully claimed to be the Abbot's Butler (see chapter 3). Perhaps this was his farm? John Botiler appears earlier in 1307; by 1455 we find 'Botelers messuage and in 1569 - 'Butlers'.[20]

BYLANDS - Is quite a modern farm, which used to stand nearly opposite the present house of that name; the earliest record I can find is 1832.[22]

CHERRY TREES - There were two Cherry Trees farms, sometimes referred to as 'Upper' and 'Lower'. The growing of cherries became popular from the 18th century, but a "Cherycroftfyeld" existed as early as 1590.[23] Upper Cherry Trees farmhouse appears to be Tudor; Lower Cherry Trees, earlier called "PALMERS", then the "Three Cherry Trees", no longer exists.

CHURCH - A Court mentions it in 1516 [24] There is no evidence to suggest that it was the Vicar's Glebe land. In later times it was part of Heath farm.

COPT HALL - Its name suggests the house was of the medieval 'Hall' type. The earliest reference I can find is 1552.[25]

CRACKABONE - A cottage called "Crakebones" appears in the 1455. Doctor Moor mentions a Crakebone family from Essex of similar date.[26] It was sold in 1885 and probably demolished soon afterwards.[27]

CROSS LANES – A later name for Hobbs Hodge.

CROUCH HALL - Robert atte Crouche appears in 1318. Perhaps the medieval 'Hall' house is that referred to in 1519:- *"Crowch Croft, in which, as some say there was anceintly a messuage"*.[28] A later house is referred to in c.1859 when it was described as *"newly erected"*.[29]

FINCHES-ON-THE-HILL - The Finch family were in the 1344 Taxation list. They held the nearby Dene End farm, but the full name only appears from 1665.[30] More frequently it is just called "Hill" farm, appearing as such in 1638.[31] An alternative name from 1767 was "Winches-on-the-Hill".[32]

FISH STREET - Thomas Fyssh a landholder in 1455. Almost certainly the site of the Priory chapels (chapter 5). Now called "Launey House"

FLOWERS - William Flower had a tenement in Redbourn Street in 1455, but the farm of that name only appears from 1609.[33]

FOSTERS - The Forester family of 1287 may have had some connection with the farm name. After the second World War it was used as a holiday centre for people from Bethnal Green before becoming a hotel in the 1960's.[34]

FOWLERS - Richard Fouler was a smallholder in 1455, the farm appears in documents up to 1789.[35]

GREEN TREE - It has been suggested that there was a cult who believed that the stake, associated with St Amphibalus, sprouted into a tree whose bark had healing properties.[36] Records appear between 1609 and 1771.[37]

HEATH - This may have been where Thomas Bedel built his house in spite of opposition from the people of Flamstead, (page 37), it is an obvious encroachment into the early Heath. The earliest date I can find is 1660, which may also be when the oldest part of the present house was built.[38] *(Fig: 6.6)*

Fig: 6.6 – The Heath

HILL - Geoffrey ate Hulle is seen in 1294.. see also Finches-on-the-Hill

HOBBS HODGE - A small farm known from 1519 to about 1789, from 1739 also known as Cross Lanes Farm.[39]

JEROMES – In 1455 the Precentor of the Abbey held land called "Jerommes", and members of the Jerome family appear a few years later.[40] A survey of 1853 differentiates between OLD and NEW JEROMES.[41]

KETTLEWELLS – It was called "WARDS" when bought in 1572 by Nicholas Kettlewell, and renamed when he built a new house there.[42] His old Tudor house was removed to another site in 1983 - see *Fig: 6.7.* See also BOTTOM HOUSE.

LYBURY – Probably made by the amalgamation of strips in "Lye" Common Field. The name may have originated from Hugh at Lee, 1524, or from 'leah',. meaning a clearing

Fig: 6.7 – Kettlewells Farm before removal to another site

MENOLDS-ON-THE-HILL - Or Menolfs-on-the Hill is found between 1516 and 1760 - it appears to be an early name for LITTLE REVEL END.[43]

NICHOLLS - William, the son of Nicholas Nicholls is found in 1307.

PALMERS A Phe. Palmere (Phebe?) is seen in the 1344 taxation list. The farm first appears in 1424, see also "Cherry Trees".

REDBOURNBURY - Site of the Abbey Chamberlain's Grange. 'Bury' comes from the defensive nature of its site - surrounded by water. The name appears from 1471, but parts of the house date from the 14th century.[44]

ST. AGNELLS - See under Manors.

SCOUT - Although not in Redbourn parish until recent years, it appears in the registers between 1640 and 1705.

Other farm names appear from time to time in documents, these are mostly of smallholdings such as The Bowl, Balams, The Cock, Old House or Tassell Hall. Some briefly bear their current owner's name, such as "Bishops" (Bottom House) or "Andersons" (Beeson End), Whites and Wrights, are both unlocated. Other farms, although outside the parish, occasionally appear in Redbourn documents, such as Flamsteadbury, Harpendenbury, Hatching Green and Holtsmere End.

MEDIEVAL VILLAGE BUILDINGS

Archaeological evidence shows that buildings of the early medieval period were better than the crude brushwood huts sometimes suggested. By c.1300 some houses were timber-framed, but still with earth floors, open hearths and a lack of glazed windows. By about the mid 14th century two-story houses appeared, developing into the substantial timber framed houses of the Yeoman farmers by the 16th century. However, these improved structural techniques did not filter down to the peasant houses until a century or so later.[45]

One of the oldest farmhouses researched in the parish is Beech Hyde; remaining features show that it was of the 'Aisled-Hall' type, from about the 14th or 15th century [46] (*Fig: 6.8*) Smoke blackened roof timbers showed that its hall had an open fire. Many other Redbourn farmhouses probably date from the 15th or 16th centuries, but have not been as thoroughly researched. Evidence of lesser houses, such as those of shopkeepers, craftsmen, etc., is scant, but some Redbourn inns are said to date from medieval times.

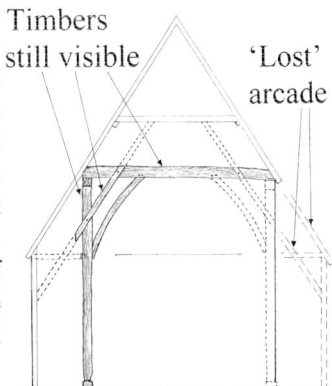

Timbers still visible   'Lost' arcade

Fig: 6.8 - Beech Hyde –Section showing Arcades

Redbournbury Grange was in a class of its own, being a stone built house. It appears to have been an administration centre and court house for the Abbey Chamberlain, rather than his residence.[47] It had a central fire in its hall, with a louvred vent in the roof for the smoke to escape. Its stone construction has been dated to about 1400, but repairs recorded during the time of Abbot John de la Moote (1396-1401) indicate an earlier origin.[48]:-

> He - *"spent a lot of money on thoroughly repairing the Chamberlain's grange at the manor of Redburne. It lay in ruins, and he rebuilt the stone walls and laid a new stone floor - an excellent job"*

The 1455 Rental shows different types of properties, indicated principally by the amount of land attached. Quite large discrepancies can be seen between the poorer and the better homes. The land areas varied from 15 acres (half virgate) to 3¾ acres (half a ferlingate). Lesser houses, like cottages, probably only had about 1 acre or so. Rents were roughly in proportion to areas, ie.:-

Messuage and 15 acres	average rent	6s.8d
Messuage and 11¾ "	insufficient data	
Messuage and 7½ "	average rent	4s.10d
Messuage and 3¾ "	" "	2s.10d
Messuage area not given	" "	2s.6d
Tenements area not given	" "	10d
Cottages area not given	" "	2d

A messuage was a homestead with the site that it occupied, most were farms. Tenements were almost exclusively in Redbourn Street, (the High Street) or Church End, probably occupied by tradesmen and craftsmen, some perhaps being inns. However, there were three messuages in the High Street, which were more highly rented than the tenements, their occupants being recognisable people of higher status. In total there were 50 messuages, 24 tenements and 11 cottages.

REDBOURN MILLS

The Domesday Mills, and the medieval events that took place at each, have been told in chapters 3. Both mills must have originated as wooden structures in Saxon times, but with many improvements and rebuildings during the Medieval period. The main mill at Redbournbury would have mostly ground the corn from the Abbot's demesne farm. The other mill, much nearer the village, was more convenient for use by the villagers. It was first known as "Bettespool Mill", the "Malt Mill" in 1511, "Redbourn Mill" and "Little Mill" alternating from the mid 17th century and finally, what appears to be a nickname - "Do-Little", from the mid 19th century.[49] See chapter 10 for their later history. (*Figs: 6.9 & 6.10*)

Fig: 6.9 - Redbournbury Mill - c.1900   *Fig: 6.10 – Do-Little Mill, c.1920*

In chapter 3 it was seen how peasants were forbidden to have hand mills to grind their own small quantities of corn, but in 1522 one Redbourn man set up in opposition to the Abbot by building his own 'Horse-powered' Mill. William Wiston failed to keep his enterprise a secret from the Abbot, and was soon brought to court.[50] As a result of the case, he was ordered to destroy his mill and have his corn ground only at the Abbot's mills. His operation, while it lasted, appears to have been successful as other tenants and even people from outside the parish used his mill. The court fined them all, but the biggest fine was meted out to Edward Abraham who had initially *"counselled"* Wiston to set up his mill.

COMMON FIELDS

The villagers held small strips of land in the Open, or Common fields of the manor. It is now difficult to find out where these were, as nearly all had been amalgamated into larger fields, or 'Closes', by the time of the earliest maps. However, they often retain a name that identifies their former use, such as - "Lye Common field", "Ryecroft Common", "Southfield Common" etc., while a *"piece"* or *"parcel"* of land, usually means a strip in part of an open field.

A number of Redbourn fields can be identified as having been part of one of the large common fields; particularly in the area east of Lybury lane. *Fig: 6.11* has been compiled from the evidence in several early maps. One feature that can identify an old boundary hedge is its 'reverse S" shape, I have observed a hedge with such a shape in this area. The usual theory is that this shape assisted in turning the heavy ox-ploughs as they neared the end of a strip.

The general scheme was that there would be three or more large common fields around a village, each divided into narrow strips of about 1 acre in size; typically about 220 yards long (1 furlong, or 'furrow long') and about 22 yards (1 chain) wide. Villagers would have held a number of strips in different parts of each field and would have grown only the crops mutually agreed each year.

Where common field patterns survive, the direction of the strips seem very casual, but these were the best practical direction for ploughing and for ease of access by the cumbersome ox-ploughs. Besides the unploughed 'baulks' left to divide each strip from its neighbour, headland strips were left for turning the ploughs.

The following list takes evidence from surveys made in 1609 and 1692, and attempts to group entries into three major fields, placed roughly north, east and south - indeed there is a "Southfield" near South End Farm.[51]

NORTHERN FIELD:-

Beechfield	12 pieces, making 15 acres
Lye Common field	33 pieces, making 59 ½ acres
Redding field	5 pieces, making 6 ¾ acres
Ryecroft Common	12 pieces, making 19 ¾ acres
	Total - 101 acres

EASTERN FIELD:-

Dudley Common	5 pieces, making 14 ¼ acres
Millfield	5 pieces, making 17 ½ acres
Wyatts	2 pieces, making 3 ½ acres
	Total - 35 ¾ acres

SOUTHERN FIELD:-

Broadfield	12 piece, making 32 acres
Grovefield	4 pieces, making 13 ¾ acres
Hatch field, or Hatches	3 pieces, making 3 ¾ acres
South field	9 pieces, making 25 ¼ acres
Spencer field	6 pieces, making 18 ¼ acres
Wood field	6 pieces, making 9 ¼ acres
	Total - 102 ¼ acres

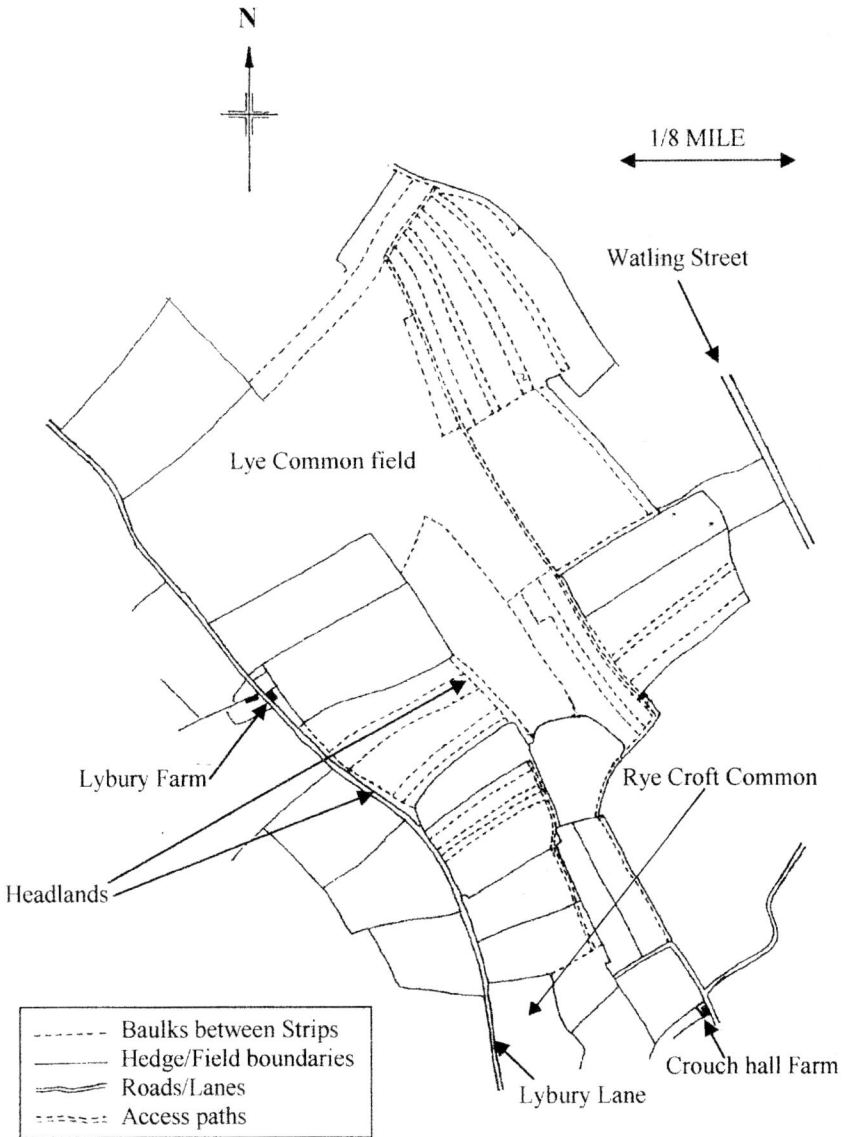

N

1/8 MILE

Watling Street

Lye Common field

Lybury Farm

Rye Croft Common

Headlands

Baulks between Strips
Hedge/Field boundaries
Roads/Lanes
Access paths

Crouch hall Farm

Lybury Lane

Fig:6.11 - Evidence of Common fields to the east of Lybury Lane

LOCATIONS UNKNOWN:-

Camps	2 pieces, making 7 ¾ acres
Cleyshill	2 pieces, making 7 acres
Haycroft	5 pieces, making 4 ¾ acres
Haunchley, or Hemsley	3 pieces, making 3 ¾ acres
Woodfield	6 pieces, making 9 ¼ acres
	Total - 32 ½ acres

The total area is far short of the 480 acres of Domesday - obviously an indication of how far the old system of farming in open field strips had gone out of use by the late 17th century.

In addition I can suggest about 16 acres of common meadow or pasture.

REDBOURN PEOPLE

The most important part of the manor was of course its workforce; not only of labourers, tenants, tradesmen, servants, but also of children, who were employed from an early age. It was chiefly from the efforts of those described in the Domesday survey as 'villeins' and the good management of those in authority at all levels, that the manor was a good economic concern. The number of tenants able to pay quite high rents for their houses is a good indication of this prosperity.

The differences in the rents paid or the lands held is also an indication of a hierarchy among the Abbot's tenants. It can be noted that many of the tenants rented out some of their properties, while occupying the main house themselves.

This suggests two ways of judging the relative wealth of inhabitants from the 1455 Rental, i.e.:-   from the rents they paid, or
                          from the number of properties they owned

HIGHEST RENT PAYERS:-

Robert Fynche	Total Rent £2.17.2 ½d
John Beche	" " £2.15.8 ½d
Thomas Fynche	" " £2.15.2 ¾d

MAJOR PROPERTY OWNERS:-

John Beche   4 messuages and 3 cottages (Rent £2.15.8 ½d)
      (he was also one of the above high rent payers)
John Christmas   4 messuages   (" £1.11.10 ½d)
John Marshall   1 messuage, 3 tenements, 1 cottage (" £1.1.10 ½d)

John Christmas was among the highest property holders, so it is interesting to find him and his family granted manumission (release from servitude) by the Abbot 10 years later. It is probably an indication of his wealth that he was able to pay the substantial amount required to gain his release, described as follows.[52]:-

"On the 28th day of July in the year AD 1465 the Lord Abbot released and set free from all ties of servitude, villeinage or bondage, Thomas Crystmes the elder of Redborne and Thomas Cristmes, John Cristmes and William Cristmes, his sons, Helena and Agnes, daughters of Thomas the elder, with all progeny....etc."

The Rental also shows the appearance of non-resident tenants - such as John Vykery of London, investing in a country property by way of a mortgage agreement. Two others were "Mistress Cressy" and the Precentor at the Abbey.

As part of their tenancy agreements, all villagers were required to spend a prescribed amount of time working on the Abbot's demesne land, especially at harvest time. Not only was this inconvenient and took them away from their own land, but also must have affected the quality of their (unwilling) work for the abbot. This was not just a local problem. The general solution was to employ a separate, paid, labour force with no conflicting ties to their own land. To gain their release from service, tenants had to pay money in lieu - known as "labour service"; this appeared in the Rental as about one third of their rent. However, occasional 'boon work' was still expected from some - usually a day or so per year, but this too was often also commuted to 2d, 4d, a cock or a hen, every year.

A little known tax appears as "Sheriff's Aid". This was intended as a recompense for the Sheriff's official services to the community, and had been levied since the time of King Henry I. [53] In the Rental it varied from half of farthing. ($^1/_8$th of a penny) to $2^1/_2$d.; the 53 such payments totalled 6s.$7^1/_2$d.

Tenants still had to give a tenth of their crop (or tithe) to the Abbot with a smaller amount to the Vicar (the small or Vicarial tithe of milk, eggs, honey etc.). In the 11th century the Great Tithes went towards clothing the monks, but by the end of the century this had been diverted towards the copying of books in the Abbey Scriptorium.[54] The crops taken as tithe were stored in the Great Barn at Redbournbury (unfortunately destroyed by fire in 1944).[55]

Many of the families in early documents have persisted into later centuries:-

BECHE or BEECH - In 1344 until at least 1841

CARPENTER - In 1455, until the death of the last male heir in 1782

CHRISTMAS - In 1344, manumission in 1565 until at least 1617

FYNCH or **FINCH** – In 1344, descendants still in Redbourn

HEYWARD - In 1344 until at least 1760

MARSHALL - In 1455 until at least 1841

MARTYN or **MARTIN** - In 1455 to at least 1760

PECOK or **PEACOCK** - In 1344 to the present day, perhaps the best known local family in medieval times, both here and at St Michael's

THEWER - In 1455 to at least 1665

WILLS AND INVENTORIES OF REDBOURN PEOPLE

Wills are a useful source of information about the village and its people, but as early wills were written in Latin a considerable amount of time is required to fully research them. Of the 168 Redbourn wills made before 1539, I know the contents of only 66. These give much information about the families, sometimes their homes, as well as showing the things to which they most liked to leave their money. The earliest Redbourn will is that of Isabelle Smyth, which named her husband John as executor and 'Simon the Clerk' (the Vicar?).[56] - *Fig: 6.10*

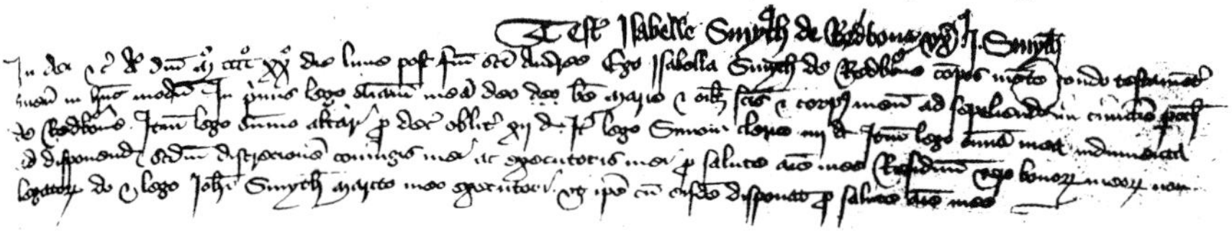

Fig 6.12 - Will of Isabelle Smyth, 1420

Translation of Isabelle's will:-

"Testament of Isabelle Smyth of Redbone, wife of J Smyth
In the name of God Etc., 1420, Monday after the feast day of St Andrew. I Isabella Smyth of Redbone, being of sound mind make my will in this manner. Firstly I bequeath my soul to almighty God, Jesu, St Mary and all Saints, and my body to be buried in the parish churchyard of Redbone. Item I bequeath to the High Altar for tithes forgotten 12d Item I bequeath to Simon the Clerk 4d Item I bequeath all my wearing clothes to be distributed at the discretion of my relatives & executor for the salvation of my soul. The remainder of my goods not bequeathed I give & bequeath to John Smyth, my husband and my executor that he may dispose of them for the salvation of my soul"

The Vicar often appears in wills, either as a witness or as beneficiary of gifts to the church or himself. He may have been at the deathbed, and being one of the few literate people in the village, probably wrote such wills. In the case of William Carpenter, who died in 1497, his youngest son was a 'scrivener', or scribe, and may have been involved in writing down his father's long will.[57]

The poor were mostly looked after by the monasteries in medieval times, thus bequests to their relief were not too frequent - perhaps a little money distributed by the Churchwardens after the burial service. William Carpenter was an exception, leaving a generous 26s.8d. to the poor; Thomas Aylwyn left 3 bushels of malt to *"6 poor men"* in 1510 - presumably for making beer.[58]

After the death of a Copyhold tenant a 'Heriot' had to be paid to the Lord of the Manor before the son could be admitted to the property. A good example of this is shown in a post medieval survey (1665) which gives the value for inheriting a messuage (a house) as one horse and for a toft (land where a house stood) as a sheep, these each being commuted to a payment of £8. [59] Inventories of the 'goods and chattels' of deceased people give interesting insights to the living conditions at that time - the earliest for Redbourn (1533) is shown in *Fig: 6.13*.[60]

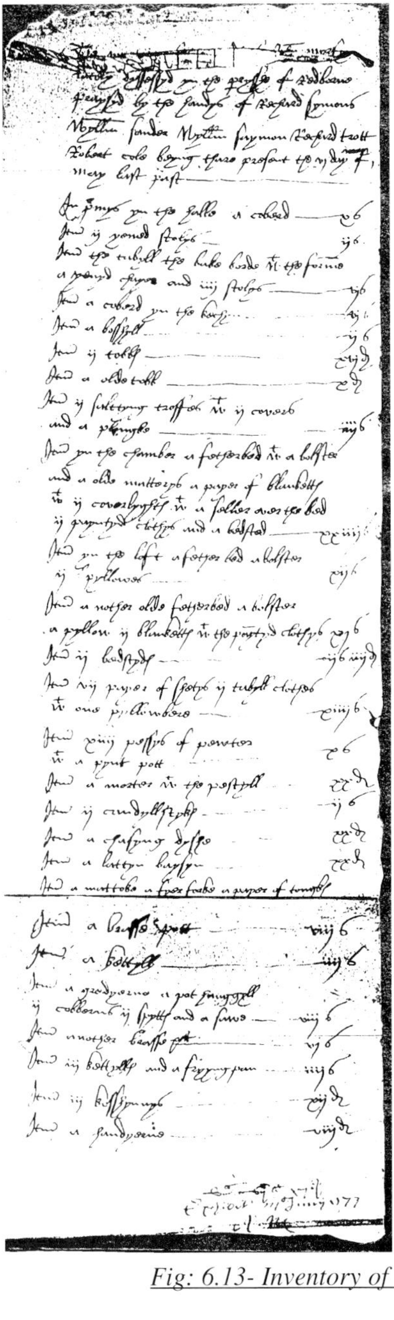

Inventory assessed in the parysshe of Redborne praysed by the handys of Richard Symons Wyllm Sander Wyllm Saymon, Richard Trott,

Robert cole beyng there present the vi[th] day of May last passed

In Primis yn the halle a cubord	x s.
Item ii joined stoles	ij s.
Item the tabyll the buke bord with the forme a jovned chayre and iiij stolys	vj s.
Item a cubord yn the kitchen	vj s.
Item a busshyll	ij s.
Item ii tubbs	xvj d.
Item a olde tubb	x d.
Item ii sauttyng troffes with ii covers and a plangke	iiij s.
Item yn the chamber a fetherbed with bolster and a olde matterys a payer of blankettes with ij coverlyghtes with a seller over the bed ij payntyd clothes and a bedsted	xxiiij s.
Item yn the loft a fether bed a bolster ii pyllowes	xij s.
Item another olde fetherbed a bolster a pillow ij blankettes with the paynted clothys	xj s.
Item ii bedstydes	ijs. iiijd.
Item vij payer of shetys ij tabyl clothes with one pyllowbere	xiiij s.
Item xiiij pessys of pewter with a pint pott	x s.
Item a morter with the pestyll	xx d.
Item ij candyllstykes	ij s.
Item a chafyng dyshe	xx d.
Item a lattyn baysyn	xx s.
Item a mattoke a fier forke A payer of tongkes	xx d.
Item a brasse pott	viij s.
Item a ketyll	iiij s.
Item a gredyerne a pot hanggyll ij cobberrms ij spyttes and a sawe	viij s.
Item another brasse pott	vj s.
Item iij kettylles and a fryyng pan	iiij s.
Item iij kusshyumps	xij d.
Item a hanhyerne	viij d.

(Transcript of Inventry above)

Fig: 6.13- Inventory of …Taylor (alias) Myrson 1533.

THE DISSOLUTION OF THE MONASTRIES

As the lease of the Manor was already in lay hands, and the Priory had become a farm, there would have been no immediate change in local management when the Abbey closed its gates. It is unlikely that the local people would have known Richard Boreman, the Abbot appointed to bring about the smooth surrender of the Abbey, or even to have cared much about what he was doing

Previous Abbots had leased out Abbey property to raise money, including many of Redbourn's assets, a process which had started some 20 years earlier.[61]:-

1518   Great Tithes leased to Ralph Rowlatt of St Albans, with half the great barn at Redbournbury.

1527   An existing lease of the Manor of Lawrence passed from John Stepney to his son (thus a much earlier original lease).

1537   Redbourn Mills leased to William Horne.

1538   The Manor of Redbourn leased to Henry Beech

Presumably the Priory was farmed by the Abbey as no lease is found.

The records of the Court of Augmentations, formed to manage and value all ex-monastic properties, show a different aspect of the village from that of either the Domesday Book or the 1455 Survey. The Court concentrated on valuations, thus giving little information about the extent, location or occupiers of the holdings, even so their records are of great interest - translated, that referring to the Manor of Redbourn, is as follows.[62]:-

Demesne of Redborne	*Rent, Freehold tenants*	*£3.7.11d*
	Rent, Customary tenants	*£42.11.11½d*
	Rent, at will of the Lord	*2.4d*
	Rent, poultry	*2.0d*
	Mills, at farm	*£8.0.0d*
	Tenth portions (Tithes)	*£4.0.0d*
	Pensions	*£1.0.0d*
	Perquisites of Court	*£4.1.6d*
Manor of Redborne	*At farm*	*£15.6.8d*
Rectory of Redborne	*Rectory, at farm*	*£20.0.0d*

Aignells (Manor)

	Rent, Freehold tenants	*5s.6d*
	Rent, Customary tenants	*£4.5.2½d*
	Rent, at will of the Lord	*2s.9d*

(Priory and Manor)   (See Chapter 5)

These valuations do not have much meaning now, except for comparative purposes. Some of the information is difficult to fully understand, however, at a glance it can be seen how varied had been the sources of income to the Abbey.

REFERENCES

1   HRO. Ref. XC6a
2   HRO. Refs. X.C.3A/1 (1514-1634); XI.8 (1635-1642); D/EV.M12-19 (1702-1940)
3   Victoria County History, Vol. 1, p. 365, note 12
4   HRO. Ref. II.A.5 (1629); II.A.19 (1652)
5   Personal letter from the Crown Estates, 12.3.1992, Sale brochure 1930
6   PRO. Ref. E.318/Box 8/294
7   HRO. Refs. II.M.2 (1587); D/EV.M.20-26 (1757-1940)
8   HRO. Sebright Collection refs. 21438-57
9   John Wheathamstead - "Chronica Monasterii S. Albani" Vol. 1, p.190-1
10 As 3, Vol. 1, p.366, note36
11 As 3, Vol. 1, p367, note 72
12 HRO. Ref. 76540
13 As 3, Vol. 1, p.367, note 57 (1527); HRO. Ref. 78511 (1786)
14 HRO. Ref. 78504
15 HRO. Ref. 78511
16 HRO. Refs. 40827 (1545); XI.3 (1560); I.A.83 (c.1600)
17 HRO. Ref. X.C.3a
18 HRO. Ref. III.A.7 & 8
19 HRO. Refs. XI.8, X.C.7c and XI.55
20 Land Tax Assessments and the Gorhambury Estate sale, 1930, St Albans Library
    Y.241.188
21 HRO. Refs. X.C.6a (1455) and XI.2 (1569)
22 HRO. Ref. 81355
23 "Story of Redbourn", published by WEA class at Redbourn, p.30
24 HRO. Ref. X.C.3
25 HRO. Ref. II.H. notes
26 HRO. Ref. II.K. notes
27 HRO. Ref. I.C.12
28 HRO. Ref. X.C.3a
29 HRO. Ref. Miscellaneous 73447
30 HRO. Ref. X.C.16b
31 Inventory of Nicholas Finch, HRO. Ref. A25/3369
32 HRO. Ref. D/EV. P2 (map), D/EV.M39 (schedule)
33 HRO. Ref. X.C.7a
34 Kelly's Directory, 1951
35 HRO. Ref. XI.56
36 "The Abbey Link", No. 47, Autumn 1997, article by Dr. Eileen Roberts "Saint
    Amphibalus re-considered", p 14
37 HRO. Ref. X.C.7a (1609); "Further report of the Charity Commissioners in
    Hertfordshire, 1815-39", p 289
38 HRO. Ref. XI.56
39 HRO. Ref. X.C.3a, SAA.1927 p.60, HRO. Ref. II.B.16a
40 HRO. Ref. II.N.1 and notes

41   HRO. Ref. XI.120
42   HRO. Ref. IV.F notes (1572); XI.55 (1759)
43   HRO. Ref. X.C.3a(1516), XI.56 (1760)
44   J. T. Smith - "Hertfordshire Houses, a selective inventory" 1993, p.145
45   Christopher Dyer – "Everyday Life in Medieval England", 1994
46   J. T. Smith – "English Houses, 1200-1800, The Hertfordshire evidence". 1992, p13
47   As 46, p.18
48   Thomas Walsingham, "Gesta Abbatum", Vol. 3, p.446
49   A. Featherstone - "The Mills of Redbourn" pp.37 & 39
50   HRO. Ref. X.C.3a
51   HRO. Refs. X.C.7a (1609); 41333 (1692)
52   As 9, Vol. 2, p.47
53   Irene Gladwin, "The Sheriff, the man & his office", 1974
54   As 48, Vol.1, pp.54 & 57
55   As 23, p.10
56   HRO. Wills of St Albans Archdeaconry Ref. 1AR7r
57   As 56, 2AR87v
58   As 56, 2AR142r
59   HRO. Ref. X.C.16b
60   As 56, A25/757
61   As 3, Vol. 1, p.370, n.115 (1518); p. 367, n.57 (1527); p.365, n.21 (1537); p.365,
     n.7a
62   Sir William Dugdale "Monasticon Anglicanum", p.253

CHAPTER 7

TRAVELLERS AND TRANSPORT

The key to the development of Redbourn from early times has been the countless travellers along its old Roman road. It took centuries for the villagers in their secluded settlement, some half a mile distant from the road at Church End, to realise the potential opportunities that such travellers offered. When they did start to move nearer, there was the added incentive of the small Priory which had been sited beside the road; this tended to attract even more travellers. It was the "Golden Age of Stage Coaching" that turned their trading, especially catering, into big business, Redbourn becoming known as a "Street of Inns".

Much history leads up to this stage in the story of Redbourn, not least how the care and use of the road developed after the neglect of the Roman road by the Saxons. Only 'Turnpiking' enabled money to be raised to improve the road so that fast stage coaches could operate. This they did in remarkable numbers, happily leading to the employment of many Redbourn people to cater for their needs.

This "Golden Age" suffered a very sudden demise with the coming of faster, more comfortable and convenient travel offered by the main line railways; Redbourn only acquiring a short branch line. With the coming of the motor car (and lorry) traffic returned to the road. However, this time it was not such an advantage - it became excessive, constant and dangerous. Relief has only been obtained with the building of a Motorway and a By-Pass, which have now given us back the freedom of our village street (apart from parking problems).

EARLY ROADS

Prehistoric man probably followed the course of the Ver. A survey of 1650 may indicate part of this early route as - *"the backe waye leading from St Albons to Redborne"*. This length only being from Shafford bridge to the Little Mill.[1]

The road that the Romans built through what is now our village, called "Watling Street", gave their Legions swift access to the north-west, and has since carried millions upon millions of travellers for nearly two millennia. It is a tribute to the Roman planners that it is still a major highway to this day, and basically on Roman foundations.

However, earlier alignments for Watling Street have been put forward (but without supporting archaeological evidence). The Rev Fowler suggesting a line from the north entering the parish along the line of Lybury Lane, while the late Mr Stageman looked with interest at some farm lanes about 250 yards to the west of the present road which would have avoided two crossings of the Ver.[2] The Prior's 'safe road', to avoid his supplies being hi-jacked, is also on this line.

It is often said that the Saxons abhorred anything Roman, including their roads, often siting their villages well away. The early village at Church End is such an example. However, Dr. Oliver Rackham has pointed out that such roads must have remained in use, or within about 5 years they would have become overgrown and after 10 years would have become impenetrable.[3]

Thus travellers along Watling Street in early Medieval times may have been unaware that the village lay just half a mile to the west. All they would have seen were two Saxon Burial mounds on a slight rise near the road and a small chapel for pilgrims to St Albans Abbey (see Chapter 5).

Though the road itself was still used, the wide margins that the Romans provided to make ambush difficult had become overgrown. Because of this travellers were endangered by wild animals as well as - *"robbers, thieves, rogues, banned men and runaways"* Thus Abbot Frederick imposed the condition on three knights, to whom he gave the Manor of Flamstead in the 11th century, that they - *"keep those parts clear alike from noxious beasts and human foes"*.[4]

BRIDGES

Chauncy in his "The Historical Antiquities of Hertfordshire" hints at there being at least one ford between St Albans and Dunstable - *"through the river to Dunstable"*.[5] Whether the Romans provided bridges to cross the Ver is unknown. There were certainly bridges in medieval times, particularly at Bettespool Mill, where the road was embanked to retain the water in the millpond.

In 1609 an unnamed bridge in Redbourn was reported to be *"ruinous despite a collection made for its repair"*.[6] Another bridge, called "Alleebridge" (near the entrance to the former station goods yard), was ordered to be repaired in 1622, in this case the farmer was to be responsible.[7]

The fact that these bridges needed repair quite frequently is an obvious indication that they were wooden, not stone, bridges.

The bridge, at Bettespool, then called "The Little Mill", probably also wooden, was the subject of many court hearings in the St Albans Liberty Sessions between 1638 and 1652, in attempts to get it repaired.[8] The mill owner (a tenant of the Lord of the Manor) was the first to be ordered to carry out repairs, then the Lord of the Manor himself (Sir Thomas Meautys of Gorhambury), and later, Lady Jane Bacon. Even the inhabitants were cited to repair it. Finally the new owner, Nathaniel Walker:-

"hath lately bestowed greate cost in repairing the bridge and that the bridge is very stronge, substantial and fitt for the use of passengers"

By 1890 the County Council were asked to adopt several parish bridges (and thus responsibility for their repair).[9] The Church Council also became involved in 1921 when the ownership of the bridge at the churchyard gate in Hemel Hempstead Road was queried. This was declared a private bridge and therefore Church responsibility.[10] The River Red now runs in a pipe at this point.

ROAD REPAIRS

An Act of Parliament of 1555, made the inhabitants responsible for the upkeep of all the roads in their parish:-

> *"Statute for amending highways, being now very noisome and tedious to travel in and dangerous to all passengers and carriages"*

Every owner of land worth over £50 was to provide carts, materials and labour for 4 days each year, with fines imposed for non-compliance. It specified that every parish should appoint a 'Surveyor' every year to be responsible for the work. This was far from satisfactory. Not only did the Surveyors have no chance to gain adequate experience in just one year, but the 'Statute Labourers' they employed, were either unwilling or treated their 4 days work as a holiday.

The roads presented real hazards to travellers - in summer hard, rutted and dusty; and in winter muddy, slippery and with water filled potholes. The locals also added to the problems by their disregard for road users:-

> The Manor Court in 1622 ordained that - *"Hugh Hurst* (who) *hath layd heapes of dounge (dung) in ye highway, doe carry away the same...under penalty of forfeiture of 10 shillings"* [11]

Occasionally wills contained bequests for the roads. Joan Pecok was generous in her will of 1505, leaving *"one hundred loads of stones for the repair of the highway"*.[12] While Sir Richard Rede left money in his will of 1576 for [13]:-

> *"the reparacion and mending of the High Waye leading from St Albons towards Dunstable, in such fautie (faulty) places as shalbe first and chiefly within the precinctes and lymytes of the parrisshe of Redborne"*

The raw materials used for road repairs are indicated in Joan Peacock's bequest of stones. Flints for this purpose were collected in baskets off the fields, mostly by the women and children, and deposited beside the road (amazingly there is still no shortage of flints in our fields or gardens) The flints were then spread over the roads by the men, filling the potholes first and before forming a layer about 6 inches deep. There was no attempt to camber the surface or to compact the stones - this was left to the wheels of the traffic using the road. The most useful vehicle for this purpose was the lumbering 10 ton carrier's wagons because of their extremely broad wheels, though the effect of the 6 or 8 horses pulling them could not have helped very much.[14]

It can thus be seen that the work of mending roads was far from a skilled job; especially as one way of getting extra labour was to employ men from the

Workhouse. Some the men of the Workhouse were reasonably good at farming jobs, and could be employed by local farmers, others, described in 1818 as *"the worst of the roundsmen"* were put to work *"mending the roads"*.[15]

The 19th century Vestry records give the annual election of men to the post of Surveyor, sometimes called Stonewarden or Waywarden.[16] One solution to spread the load and perhaps get more experience into the job was tried in 1830. This was to appoint a committee of 13 men as Stonewardens, with the Vicar as chairman and including also the Churchwardens and Overseers of the poor.

The Vestry and Parish Council minutes contain many other items of interest concerning roads and bridges, here are a few of them:-

Fig: 7.1 – Roadmen at Redbourn c.1930
The scene in earlier times would have been similar, except for the use of tarmac

1831   A new bridge planned for Chequers lane

1838   The state of Church End required immediate attention, the Stonewardens being ordered to clean the gutters and *"adopt a more efficient means to alter the road so as to have a sufficient drainage and to make it free from absolute nuisance"*

1864   Road proposed for East Common

1879   Hand pump to be provided to sluice the gutters of the High Street

1906   Cobble stone pavements replaced with granite chippings

1905-08 Complaints re clouds of dust stirred up by speeding cars; first solution to water the roads - High Street was tarred in 1908

1908   Agreement to apply a 10 mph speed limit from the Ver bridge to Scout farm (no evidence that this was actually imposed)

TURNPIKE ROADS

The idea of levying tolls from travellers to pay for the maintenance and improvement of roads originated as early as the 17th century, and the first such road in Hertfordshire was operated from 1663.[17]

Watling Street through Redbourn was Turnpiked by the Dunstable and Ponyards Turnpike Trust in 1723 [18](Later the Dunstable and Shafford House Trust) This joined on to, but did not amalgamate with the St Albans Turnpike, which had been built 8 years earlier. The nearest Toll-Gate was at Friar's Wash,

known as Fly's Wash when it was opened in 1838. It did not last for long, going
out of use by 1861, ten years before the Turnpike itself was abandoned.

The toll charges in 1817 were [19]:-

    Chaise and pair of horses   9d
    Chaise or coach and four horses 18d
    Chaise or coach and six horses 24d

    In the same year the number of
vehicles of various types using the
Turnpike was given as 17,284 and
132,000 animals, including saddled
horses.[20]

Fig: 7.2 - Toll Gate in London Road, St
Albans

MILE-POSTS SIGNS AND MAPS

Turnpike Trusts re-introduced the
milepost which was used previously by the Romans. There are four mileposts on
the Turnpike through Redbourn parish, all different - see *Fig:7.3*

Fig: 7.3 - The four Redbourn Milestone - from north to south

    Finger-posts, as the early signposts were called, were introduced in the 16th
century; I know of no really old ones remaining in Redbourn.

    With the modern maps and clear sign posting it is difficult to imagine what
it was like in earlier centuries The only map I can find that showed roads before
the mid 17th century was Gough's map of c.1360.[21] Even the well known map
of Hertfordshire made by John Speed in 1676 did not show roads.

However, about this time John Ogilby appreciated the need for maps made specifically for road users.[22] His strip map showing the route from London to Holyhead is shown on *Fig: 7.4*. The landmarks he shows through the parish are - *"Bemond Hall"*, the village street and the turnings to *"Hempstead"* (Hemel Hempstead) and *"Harding"* (Harpenden).

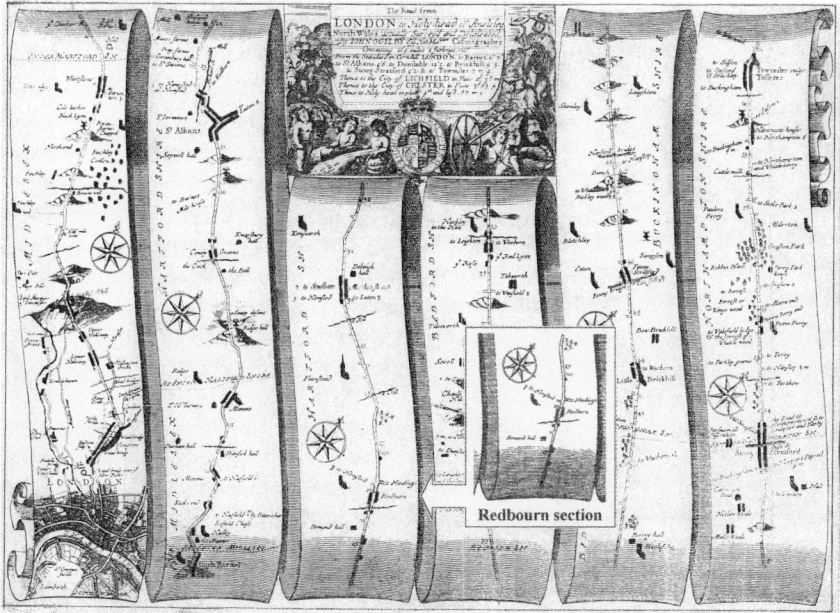

Fig: 7.4 -London to Holyhead drawn by John Ogilby in 1675
(The insert shows the Redbourn section)

County maps made after Ogilby, showed most roads.[33] Prior to the earliest Ordnance Survey maps, such as that by Dury and Andrews in 1766 (reprinted by Hertfordshire Publications in 1980) showed hills and valleys with shading (hatchuring). Later maps adopted the present system of contour lines.

STAGE COACH ERA

Improvements made possible by the Turnpike system (nearly 105,000 miles of main roads were turnpiked by 1838 [23]) made the operation of the fast coaches of the late 18th and early 19th centuries possible. A fairly recent book has collected together timetables of the Stage and Mail Coaches running in 1836.[24] This shows that most of the major cities were served with coaches from London and that there were many cross-country links. Some of the major cities served were as follows, but of these, only the Holyhead coach passed through Redbourn:-

Dover	72 miles in 31 hours
Edinburgh	413 miles in 43 hours
Exeter	168 miles in 18 to 23 hours
Newcastle	278 miles in 31 hours
Norwich	115 miles in 11 to 13 fi hours
Holyhead	268 miles in 27 fi hours
York	200 miles in 24 hours

It is easy to calculate that the average speeds varied between 8 and $9^3/_4$ mph. The fastest service in the country was from London to Birmingham via Oxford which ran at 10.4 mph.[25] The route through Dunstable (and of course Redbourn) was almost as fast, 10 mph. However, in 1830 a record was set of 14' mph over the 109 miles. To achieve this speed, the stopping times were cut to a minimum; breakfast at the Bull in Redbourn normally took 20 minutes, on this occasion only 6 minutes were allowed.[26]

Coaches through Redbourn served most of north-west England, as follows:-

Birmingham	6	coaches, including - "The Greyhound, "Tally-Ho", "The Economist" and (in 1839) "The Swallow"
Daventry	1	"The Daventry Accommodation Coach"
Halifax	1	Royal Mail coach
Holyhead	1	Royal Mail coach
Leicester	1	"The Union"
Liverpool	3	2 Royal Mail coaches
Manchester	6	"The Telegraph", "Red Rover", "Royal Defiance", "Royal Bruce", "Beehive" and Royal Mail coach
Northampton	1	"The "Northampton"
Nottingham	3	"The "Times" and "Commercial"
Shrewsbury	3	"The "Stag", "Wonder" and "Nimrod"
Wellingborough	1	Not named

The Majority of these coaches (including the Royal Mail) were run by the three leading operators - Messrs W. Chaplin, E. Sherman and B. W. Horne. Chaplins, the major concern, owned 64 coaches, 1300 to 1500 horses and many inns, netting an annual income of about a quarter of a million pounds.[27]

The recollection of old inhabitants of the village living in 1879, was that between 80 and 90 coaches passed through the village every day.[28] Looking at the above list we see 26 daily services, each way, making 52, to which must be added several un-scheduled coaches, indicating that the villagers' recollections were not far out.

There were also many other types of vehicle using the roads, from private carriages, carts of the carriers and traders, many of them Redbourn men, to the huge lumbering stage wagons carrying goods of all kinds.

Trade Directories describe the village as having *"an almost constant succession of coaches...*(giving it) *a lively appearance".*[29] Redbourn at that time was thus understandably a prosperous place with many hostelries serving the travellers, the High Street earning its description as a *"Street of Inns."*

With the coming of the railway (as will be seen later) the 'Golden Age of Coaching' came, very rapidly, to an end; even just 3 years after the 1836 list, Pigot's Directory gives only 9 coaches passing through the village.

An important and alarming question concerns the effect of so many passing, horse drawn vehicles, on the village, - what happened to the 'droppings' ? We are not told, but we do know how one person managed to scrape a living by collecting the horse dung. This rather pitiful story was told in the 'Gentleman's Magazine' in 1777, here given in abbreviated form.[30]:-

Mary Lofty was married to a local farmer, by whom she had two children She was abruptly widowed when her husband was thrown from his horse and killed leaving her to manage the farm on her own. After four years she had to give it up because she could not make enough money to provide for her children. The two children married but both died before having issue. Mary took a small cottage and lived by doing gardening or any other work she could find.

At an age of well over 70, a long illness left her enfeebled, but rather than rely on parish charity, she conceived the idea of collecting horse dung to sell to local farmers. She was so assiduous in this that she watched every passing horse and carriage, not going to bed before the last wagon came in and being always up at 3 in the morning.

She at first used a wrapper to collect it in, but from the few pence she made was able to buy a box, which she strapped round her body. Her industry attracted the attention of her neighbours who collected enough money to buy her a wheelbarrow. She lived to an age of over 84 years.

STAGE-COACH TRAVELLING

In 1796 G. M. Woodward wrote of the discomforts of stagecoach travellers passing through Redbourn as follows [31]:-

"Stage coach travellers bound to the north of England usually sup at this village (Redbourn), after which they mix knees, elbows, night-caps, etc., in a firm phalanx, to prevent the joltings of the carriage, and calmly resign themselves to the arms of sleep"

Four passengers could travel 'inside' if they could afford it, but might be crammed between perhaps unsavoury companions. All other passengers, up to eleven, sat precariously on the top of the coach with the Coachman and Guard, while the luggage was crammed into every conceivable space about the coach.

The outside passengers had to face the many dangers of the road, not least the extreme cold of night travel, especially in the winter, arriving with frozen limbs and having to be helped off by the guard or innkeepers. It is no wonder that the coachmen themselves always seemed to favour multi-layed overcoats. Even so, they always laid claim to pride of place in front of the inn fire.

Many of the coaches, but especially the mail coaches, were required to keep to a strict timetable. It is not surprising that when two coaches coincided on the same road that a race would result. Accidents resulting from such rivalry, sometimes led to injury or loss of life to passengers, crew or horses. Such an incident occurred in St Albans in 1819 resulting in the death of a passenger - both drivers were immediately arrested and gaoled. They were kept 'in irons' until their trial, after which they spent a year in prison.[32]

Highway robbery was another danger, especially during night travelling. The introduction of paper money in the late 19th century is said to have put a stop to this.[33] The most famous, or infamous, local highwayman was actually a woman. Kathleen Ferrers lived the life of a Lady at Markyate Cell by day, and was said to have taken to the roads at night on a black horse, with cloak, mask and pistols.[34] Her double life was only discovered when she was mortally wounded during a daring hold-up, she just managed to reach home, but collapsed and died at the entrance to her secret passage into the house. Ever since she has been known as "The Wicked Lady of Markyate Cell".

COACHING INNS

According to figures published for 1756, Redbourn inns had stabling for 206 horses and provided 72 beds for travellers.[33] This compared quite well with other nearby places of comparable size, though naturally St Albans, had far more stabling - for 708 horses and beds for 237 people.

One feature of nearly all stage coach inns was that a cover way was provided so that the coaches could be driven through to a courtyard at the rear. Such ways are a sure 'give-away' in any town, not least Redbourn, where four such examples can be easily spotted in the High Street. They are not necessarily large enough to take stage coaches - that beside the former "Mad Tom in Bedlam" must have catered chiefly for smaller vehicles such as carts.

The chief coach proprietors of course choose the better class inns to stop at along their routes, some even owned inns, but the more 'common' type of travellers would have gone to other, cheaper inns.

Redbourn was on a 'Drove Road' from North Wales. Drovers needed not only accommodation for themselves, but also somewhere to pen their herds. The "Bell and Shears" has a large car park and garden behind suggestive of a site for sheep or cattle pens.[36]

Fig: 7.5 - "The Bull" with its elaborate wrought-iron sign, c.1900

Fig: 7.6 – Breakfast at the Bull by John Pollard, 1815

Fig: 7.7 - "Union" stage coach re-enacting the Leicester to London run in August 2001

Inns provided welcome relief from the discomforts and traumas of stagecoach travel, but it was because of its high reputation for good food that Redbourn was best known. Some travellers were prepared to prolong their journey in order to eat at Redbourn.

"The Bull" was undoubtedly the favourite inn, with a reputation for excellent food, a fact well portrayed in Pollard's painting of 1815 - see *Fig: 7.54.* The picture shows all aspects of the coaching scene - the passengers being served breakfast (complete with a dog begging for food), others are preparing themselves for the journey - one having a shave. The coach drivers make another group, warming themselves in front of the fire, meanwhile the coach is visible through the window, with the guard re-calling passengers with his horn.

The "Bull" must also have been the most prominent inn in the High Street, chiefly on account of its magnificent wrought iron sign which stretched half way across the road see *Fig: 7.5.* This carried not only the Bull sign itself, but had a huge entrance lantern. Sadly this became a danger to later road traffic and was taken down in 1902.[37] On the extreme end was a hook, where a lantern was said to have been hung at night so that travellers could see that they were approaching their destination. A boy was posted outside to keep watch for approaching coaches. He would shout *"up'ards"* or *"down'ards"* according to which way a coach was coming.[38]

HIGH STREET INNS

To gain some idea of the scale of the catering operation in Redbourn, one only has to look at the many inns that existed chiefly in the High Street, and elsewhere in the village in earlier times - see *Fig: 7.6.* Though many inns can be listed, it must be realised that they did not all operate at the same time. Those that existed during the coaching period, about 1760 to 1840, have been starred in the following lists 19 of these were on the main road [39]:-

* **"ANTELOPE"** thought to date from medieval times, closed by 1800
* **"BELL AND SHEARS"** known from at least 1540 and still in use. Amalgamated with the adjacent "Red Lion" in about 1675. Has also been called - "Blue Bell", "Sheres" and possibly "The Swan"
* **"BULL"** earlier the "Black Bull", known from at least 1586, still in use
  "COCK", also "Old Cock", known from at least 1568, closed in c.1810 because the innkeeper, Stephen Raggett, refused to a accept a party of soldiers, so their captain cut down the sign thus terminating the licence
* **"CROWN",** from which Crown Street took its name, known from at least 1717 until about 1889, also ROSE & CROWN between 1633 to 1771
* **"GEORGE"** known from at least 1589 and still in use
* **"GREYHOUND"** existed from about 1630 to 1786 when it was replaced by the "Red House" - See also the "Greyhound" on North Common

* "**LARK**" from at least 1860 to the early 20th century
* "**LION and LAMB**" existed from at least 1779, renamed the "Railway" after the opening of the Nickey line in 1877, closed in c.1966
* "**MAD TOM in BEDLAM**" from at least 1760 to c.1910
* "**OLD MOTHER REDCAP**" from at least 1760 to c.1800
* "**PRINCES HEAD**" once called the "White Lamb", from at least 1786 to c.1910
* "**QUEEN VICTORIA**" may have previously been the "Queen's Head", the later name must date from after 1837, closed c.1956
* "**SARACENS HEAD**" thought to date from medieval times, still in use
* "**WHITE HART**" said to date from the 14th century, closed about 1861
* "**WHITE HORSE**" thought to date from the 14th century, closed c.1837. At a later time it was the home of Dr. Ayre, the village doctor
  "**WOOLPACK**" dating from at least 1635, demolished pre 1707 to make room for the Market House

OTHER INNS ALONG WATLING STREET

* "**BLACKHORSE**" at the corner of Blackhorse Lane, existed at least between 1786 and c.1871
* "**CHEQUERS**" dates from about the 16th century. Still in use
* "**RUNNING HORSES**" was the "Green Man" from at least 1692, to c.1889
* "**PUNCH BOWL**" now the "Spritzers" is known from at least 1633, it was much enlarged in 1901

INNS ELSEWHERE IN THE VILLAGE

*"**ONE BELL**" or the "Bell" in Lamb Lane. Known between 1665 and c.1906, now called the "White Cottage". It may have been the "Bricklayers Arms" mentioned in the 1851 Census return
  "**BLACK CAT**" also in Lamb lane, now a house
*"**CRICKETERS**" known from c.1786 and still in use. May have been the "Three Horse Shoes", if the story on page.164.is true
*"**GREYHOUND**" possibly replaced the inn with the same name in the High Street from about 1768 to c.1910. Once a house called the "THE ASHES"
* "**HOLLY BUSH**" earliest record 1595, in early times "le "Talbot" still popular
  "**JOLLY GARDENER**" once in use both as an inn and a 'Plait School'
    "**SHEEP WASH**" or "Sheep Dip", existed on East Common between at least 1891 and c.1952. It takes its name from the dipping of sheep in the nearby River Red
  "**WAGON AND HORSES**" on Hemel Hempstead Road, known from at least 1803 to c.1910; in 1883 described as a Beer House

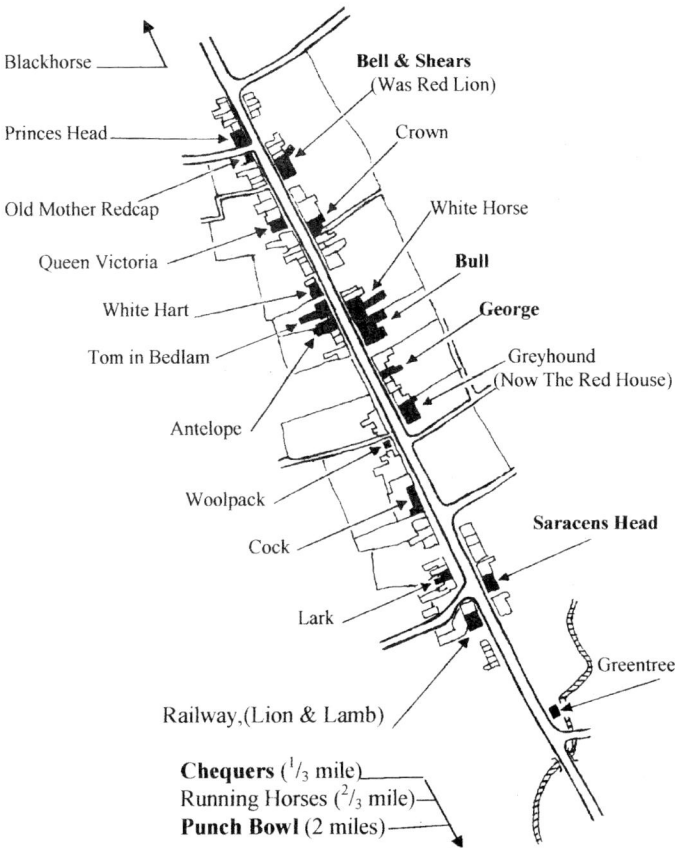

Fig: 7.8 - Map showing the Inns of Redbourn (Not all open at the same time)

INNS WHOSE LOCATIONS ARE NOT KNOWN

There are other named inns that have not been definitely located, some may be
alternative names for inns already listed:-

"BLACK LION", records from 1637, burnt down in 1684

"**CHOPPIN KNIFE**", records from 1692, in 1798 a cottage called the "**SHIP**"

"**FOX**" in 1740 described as near Crouch Lane End; known up to 1828

"**KING HARRY**" said to exist in Medieval times

"**THORLEY ARMS**", in the High Street, only seen in 1871 Census return

"**YEW TREE**"

THE RAILWAY REVOLUTION

Though unsuspected at the time, 1838 was a significant date for many places, including Redbourn. This is when a rail service was started from London, through St Albans to Birmingham - it sounded the death knell of Stage Coaching. Within just four years coaches had ceased to run on this route and in 35 years Royal Mail coaches also ceased running altogether.

This was a disaster for all connected with the business. Many lost their lucrative jobs, but one Redbourn man managed to continue as a coachman by moving to Cambridge where he drove carriages to serve the colleges.[40]

Redbourn had a long wait to get its small branch line. It was first proposed in 1845, starting at Watford, then to St Albans, following the Ver to Redbourn and on to join the LNWR to Dunstable.[41] Fortunately for Verulamium and the Ver valley, this line eventually only went as far as St Albans (Abbey Station).

The route finally adopted ran roughly east west from Hemel Hempstead, through Redbourn and on to Luton. Originally only intended to link 'Hemel' with the main line at Boxmoor, but extended to Luton to help the local Straw Plait industry. This was an error of planning as there was already a Straw Hat factory in Redbourn (see chapter 14), so by popular demand, it was re-routed into Harpenden so as to give a business link to London.

The initial planning of most railways started with 'difficult' public meetings and endless negotiations with landholders on the proposed route. No wonder the line took 15 years to plan and build; the total cost £140,000.[42] It was finally opened on Monday 16th July 1877 by a special train from Hemel Hempstead to Luton and back for a lunch laid on at the Town Hall.

Until the early 1900's the line was busy. Initially 4 passenger trains ran each way daily, rising at its peak to 7 daily return trains. Goods trains also used the line. However, after the First World War trade began to decline, the Railway Company contributing to this by running a bus service between stations.[43]

A steam powered 'Rail Motor' was run from 1905. Being of single carriage length, it only required short platforms making it possible to provide a new 'Halt' (called "Beaumont Halt") near Flowers Farm, serving Church End.[44]

In 1929 this relatively quiet line was used for some experimental running of a vehicle called a "Ro-railer".[45] This consisted of a bus which was fitted with additional rail wheels which enabled it to run either on the road or on railway lines. The only alteration needed to the tracks were special ramps at the entry and exit points to enable it to transfer from one mode to another, taking less than four minutes. There was also a lorry version, but both were unsuccessful.

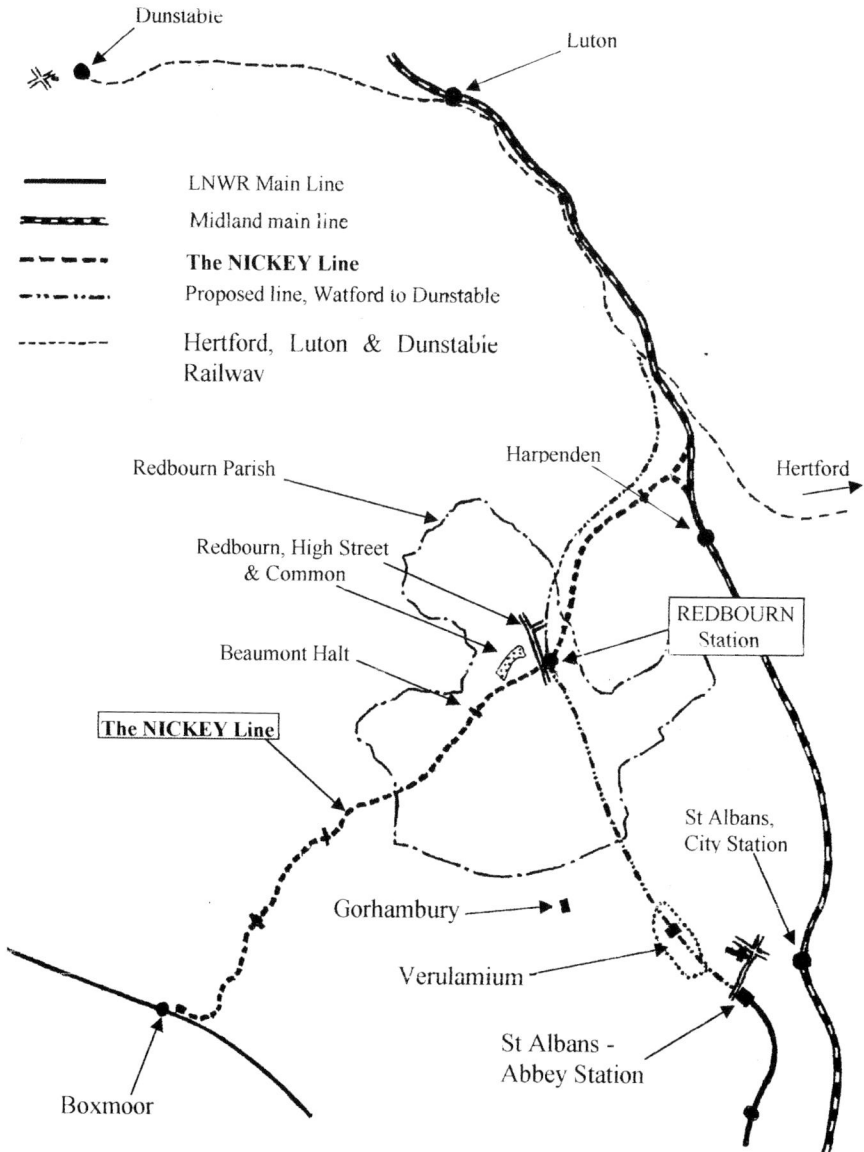

Dunstable

Luton

LNWR Main Line
Midland main line
The NICKEY Line
Proposed line, Watford to Dunstable

Hertford, Luton & Dunstable
Railway

Redbourn Parish

Redbourn, High Street
& Common

Beaumont Halt

The NICKEY Line

Harpenden

Hertford

REDBOURN
Station

St Albans,
City Station

Gorhambury

Verulamium

St Albans -
Abbey Station

Boxmoor

Fig: 7.9 – Proposed railways through Redbourn in the mid 19th century

One particular excursion train endeared itself to villagers - this was the annual Sunday School trip to Southend-on-Sea. The village virtually emptied itself on the day. Mr John Heather took a film of the departure and return in 1949 and after 50 years a showing in the Village Hall never fails to lose its appeal to villagers, especially those who went on such trips themselves as`` children.

Between the two wars trade began to decline though withdrawal of a passenger service was delayed until 1947 and goods traffic stopped in 1963.[46]

However, a new lease of life came in 1968 when Messrs Hemelite re-opened the line from Cupid Green to Harpenden to transport their products, building blocks. After many years of good use, they too were forced to give up the line because of the excessive cost of conversion to electric operation in 1979.

In spite of protests and proposals from preservation groups to use the line, the rails were taken up and the way converted to a footpath for walkers and cyclists. The old station yard at Redbourn was used by a firm of road hauliers, but has now been leased by the Parish Council and made into a picnic site for walkers.

The line is affectionately known as the Nickey (or Nicky) but the actual origin of the name is not definitely known. The following ideas have been put forward:-

> A corruption of 'Funicular' because of its steep gradients - up to 1 in 37
> From the 'Knickerbockers' worn by the Irish navvies who built the line; a type of trousers unknown to the villagers until then
> From the sound made by the engines struggling up the gradients. Two of the engines were nicknamed "Puffing Annie" and "Trickling Emma"
> A reference to St Nicholas church in Harpenden defies explanation

RETURN TO THE ROADS

The decline of the railway seems to have started with the introduction of a bus service by the Railway Company itself between some of its stations. Prior to a swing back to the use of the roads, less than a century after the last Stage Coach ran, it is said that the road was so quiet that birds were able to nest in the middle.

The first regular bus service through the village started in 1908, running from St Albans to Dunstable, see *Fig: 7.11* [47] It took a few years after the war for bus services to become firmly established. National buses gave the better services - Route N4 between St Albans and Dunstable via Redbourn in 1921 and a cross country service from Luton through Harpenden, Redbourn and Markyate to Caddington from 1926.

Redbourn station, c.1920

Pullman coach and tank engine, early 1900's

Railmotor on the Nickey Line, early 1900's

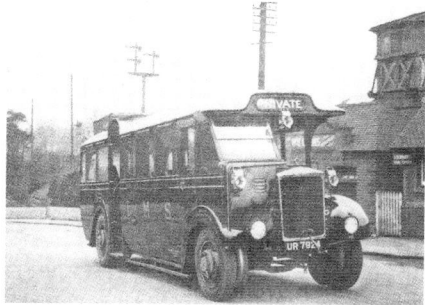

Ro-Railer,1930's - notice the rail wheels

Nickey Excursion for railway enthusiasts, 1956

Drewry diesel, 1970's

Fig: 7.10 - VIEWS OF THE"NICKEY LINE"

The first privately owned car appeared in Redbourn in 1903, owned by Mr Boucher, the local Dentist. His 6 HP "Gladiator" was registered as 'AR.22', its tonneau body was dark green and it had yellow wheels.[48] He changed it within 3 months, but it was not until 1906 that he bought another 'AR' (Hertfordshire) car, another Gladiator (AR.1226). Mr Peake, of Cumberland House also had a Gladiator at about the same time, shown in *Fig: 7.12, (right)*. His daughter Ann, told me that there were hooks in their garage which enabled the top to be lifted off, so the car could be driven out as an open tourer.

Fig: 7.11 - First Motor Bus through Redbourn, c.1910

Fig: 7.12 – The Motor takes over

(Left) Horse drawn carts in the High Street c.1900 (Similar scene shown on the cover)
(Right) Mr Peake's 'Gladiator' at the Harpenden lane ford, early 1900's

The first book of Hertfordshire Registrations, from which I found details of Mr Boucher's car, gives interesting information on motor vehicles with 'AR' registrations between 1903 to 1910. Redbourn owners were as follows:-

AR.137   1904   T. W. Piper - "Excelsior" motorcycle
AR.392   1904   W. Collyer - "Kerry" motorcycle and sidecar
AR.421   1904   W. D. Walker - KC. Motorcycle (Second hand); sold to C. Reed
AR.753   1905   E. T. Dexter - "Vindee Special" motorcycle
AR.976   1906   A. W. Mc.Gregor (The Priory) - "Maurice (Morris?) car

AR.983   1906   W. Collyer - 7HP. "Horley" car, tonneau body
AR.1204   1906   D. E. Mc.Gregor (The Priory) - 5HP "Wolsley" 2 seater
AR.1908   1908   G. A. Dunn (The Aubreys) - 10-15HP "Darracq
AR.1505   1908   The Four Brothers - 15HP "Argyll" delivery van
AR.1544   1908   The Four Brothers - 10-12HP "Herald" petrol van
AR.1871   1909   D. E. Macintosh (Harpendenbury) - 8HP "Renault" car

Fig: 7.13- Motor Rally 'Pit' at the Bull, early 1900's

It seems logical that the favourite inn of the coaching days, "The Bull", should serve a similar function for the motor car - several motor rallies were centred here in the early 1900's, see *Fig: 7.13*. Their vehicles, however, required garages, to look after their needs. Now only a filling station remains. Walkers and Hardings in the High Street, Bylands on the Dunstable Road and Stathams at Church End are all now closed.

THE STATE OF THE ROADS

In 1821 Telford reported that the streets of both Markyate and Redbourn were *"not paved"*; probably meaning that there were no raised edges.[49] However, there were cobbled edges, as these were replaced with granite chippings in 1906.[50]

There were many complaints about the dust thrown up by the *"excessive speeds of cars through the village"* The Parish Council discussed the matter at length, proposing a 10 mph speed limit, but opting to buy a water cart and with a man to operate it.[51] Tarring in 1908, must have greatly relieved matters.[52]

Street lighting, was a job tackled by the Vestry in 1861, soon after the Fish Street Gas Works had been built (see Chapter 14). They bought 10 lights supplied at £1.15.0d. per light.[53]

SERIOUS ROAD ACCIDENTS

The Registers record a few fatalities that occurred in coaching day, such as -

1637 Sara Papit *"a woman, being a stranger, slayne with a fall from her horse in her journey from London"*, buried

1641 *"a footposte from Chester"* buried

1805 A 14 day old child buried - *"who died in a stage wagon"*

With the coming of the motor car and the use of photography, accidents could be recorded in more graphic detail. Though no photographer was on hand to record Redbourn's first motor fatality in 1908, photographs was taken of the scene some time later, see *Fig: 7.13*. However, the 'Herts Advertiser & St Albans Times' devoted 3fi columns to describe the event and subsequent court case in great and grizzly detail. Greatly abbreviated this was as follows:-

A London newspaper proprietor had hired a Rolls Royce with a chauffeur to drive himself and his three daughters for an outing into Hertfordshire. At about 10.45am they approached Redbourn a cyclist suddenly rode out of Chequers Lane and hit the side of the car. He was killed instantly (gruesome details given). It was said that he, Fred Allen, was hurrying to get to his home at Bohemia Farm, riding with his head down.

Fred Allen, who was killed

Fig: 7.14 - Redbourn's first fatal motor accident - Chequers 1908
(A white + marks the spot)

The account described how the chauffeur swerved to avoid the cyclist, but in doing so hit another cyclist approaching from the north. This man had come from Northamptonshire and was on his way to London for an eye operation.

While his wounds were being tendered in the Chequers he missed the money he was carrying to pay for the operation (12 gold Sovereigns), but to his great relief this was recovered by a girl and returned to him.

The chauffeur was arrested and charged with Manslaughter, but at the subsequent Inquest no blame was attached to him. The Jury recommended that *"the hedges be clipped so as to afford a better view from the lane, of traffic approaching along the main road"*.

Reports of later accidents often included photographs showing the resulting damage. The most amazing one occurred on a Sunday in 1932 when a lorry hit Mr Skillman's car as he was turning into Crown Street.[54] The lorry, with its trailer hit the back of Mr Skillman's car, mounted the pavement, damaged a building, tuned a somersault damaged a shop on the opposite side of the road, before finishing up on its side facing the opposite direction. Neither the lorry driver, his mate, or Mr Skillman suffered serious injury - see *Fig: 7.15*

Fig: 7.15 – Amazing Lorry accident in Redbourn High Street, 1932
Left – Overturned lorry, Right – remains of Mr Skillman's car
[Courtesy of the Herts Advertiser]

REDBOURN BY-PASS

First mention of a By-pass appeared in 1935, when a scheme including Markyate was proposed; 4 years later work was due to begin.[55] Unfortunately the start of the war put a stop to all work of that kind. Markyate subsequently got their part of the proposed by-pass, much to the envy of Redbourn villagers, in 1957. It was hoped that the M1 Motorway (opened in 1959) would do the same for Redbourn.

However, accidents, continued to happen, but the one that was the real turning point was in 1974 which resulted in the tragic death of a hairdresser in his shop when a lorry crashed into it [56]. Subsequently it took many public protests and demonstrations, coupled with continuing accidents, before it was finally approved. The by-pass was eventually opened in 1984. The High Street was closed for daylong celebrations - these were certainly justified after half a century waiting for it to happen.

Late in 1996 residents in the Church End area received a terrible shock when they were notified of a Motorway Service Area which was to be built adjacent to their back gardens and the Churchyard. This potentially disastrous plan united the whole village and Parish Council in a concerted protest. This went to a public enquiry, at a cost to the village of £450,000, but it was worth it as the plan was defeated, and everyone breathed again.[57]

AIRCRAFT NOISE

Aircraft seem to have had little impact on the village, that is apart from the noise they make flying overhead. Though Luton is the nearest airport, it was not aircraft from there that initially posed a threat, but it was those from London Heathrow. In 1975 one hundred flights per day were planned to over-fly Redbourn at about 5000 feet.[58] With the passing of that threat, it was aircraft taking off or landing at Luton that disturbed Redbourn. The Redbourn Association set up a noise monitoring station to report and complain of excessive cases. Mostly as a result of their work, but also because of the general use of quieter aircraft, we are not now too often disturbed by noisy aircraft.

REFERENCES

1   Survey of Watermills - Commonwealth, PRO.- E.317/Hertford/23
2   Rev. H. Fowler, Transaction of the \St Albans Architectural & Archaeological Society, 1887, page 41 footnote. Also an unpublished suggestion by Mr Frank Stageman
3   Oliver Rackham - "The History of the Countryside" p.257
4   Victoria County History - Hertfordshire, Vol.1, p.194, note 11
5   William Chauncy - "The Historical Antiquities of Hertfordshire", Vol.2, p.395
6   "Calendar of Assize Records - Hertfordshire Indictments, Elizabeth I", p.37
7   HRO - X.C.3
8   HRO - II.D.8
9   "Orderly Book" containing Vestry Minutes - Redbourn Parish Chest,
10 "Parochial Church Council, Minutes, 1921-1936" in Redbourn Parish Chest
11 HRO - X.C.3
12 HRO - 2.AR.125v
13 PRO - CAREW.20
14 John Copeland - "Roads and their Traffic 1750-1850" p.49
15 As 9 - 1818
16 As 9, various dates
17 Geoffrey N. Wright - "Turnpike Roads", Shire Album No.283
18 Markyate's Past, No. 5 pp.9-14, Richard Hogg, "The Dunstable & Shafford Turnpike Road"
19 As 18 No. 7, p.8
20 Holyhead Road - Reports, 5th report, 1817, HRO
21 As 3, p 267
22 John Ogilby - "Britannia Vol. 1, 1675

23 As 17, p.21
24 "A Directory of Stage Coach Services 1836" compiled Alan Bates 1969
25 Potters Bar Historical Series No. 7 - "The Stage-Coach through Potters Bar" p.10
26 Hertfordshire Countryside Vol.22, No. 104 p.33
27 Ivan Sparkes – "Stagecoaches & Carriages" p.47
28 Herts Advertiser 3rd May 1879 - "Villages of Hertfordshire, II Redbourn"
29 Pigot's Directory 1823
30 "Hertfordshire 1731-1800 as recorded in the Gentleman's Magazine" p.36
31 Hertfordshire Constitutional Magazine, May 1889 p.123 - "Eccentric Excursions by
        G. M. Woodward
32 "Companion into Hertfordshire" W. Branch Johnson, 1952, p.199 . Also-
        Hertfordshire Countryside December 1987, Vol.42, No.344, p.15
33 As 25, p.18
34 "Hertfordshire Village Book", Hertfordshire Federation of Women's Institutes, p.118
35 "English Houses, 1200-1800", J. T. Smith, 1992, p.170
36 This possibility was suggested to me by the late Dennis Robinson
37 HRO, Gerish Collection, folder 3a
38 "Redbourn", May Walker, 1960, p.70
39 **Note**:- Source References for all the inns are too numerous to list, these are kept in my
        own records. However, Mr Ron Such has studied Redbourn inns and holds similar
        information
40 "Hertfordshire Countryside" December 1987, Vol.42, No.344, p.15
41 "The Printed Maps of Hertfordshire, 1577-1900", p.64 and large scale maps HRO refs.
        R.38-41 & 50
42 "The Nicky Line", James and Hedley Cannon, 1977, p.37 Also - "The Harpenden to
        Hemel Hempstead Railway, The Nickey Line " -Sue & Geoff Woodward, 1996, p.33
43 As 42, p.62 and p.99 respectively
44 As 42, p.73 and p.79 respectively
45 As 42, p.76 and p.105 respectively
46 As 42, p.95 and p.135 respectively
47 As 18, No. 4, p.16 – Richard Hogg "The History of Motor Bus Services through
        Markyate"
48 HRO. Register of Motor Cars and Cycles, 1903-10
49 As 21 Telford's 1821 report
50 Redbourn Parish Council minutes, HRO - CP.78/1/2 28th March 1906
51 As 50, 6th May 1907
52 As 50, 1st June 1908
53 Vestry Minutes - Redbourn Parish Chest
54 Herts Advertiser, 1932
55 As 50, 8 March 1935 & 1938
56 As 50, 25 April 1974
57 Numerous articles in all newspapers. The happy conclusion & cost to the village given
        in Herts Advertiser 3 December 1998
58 Common Round, March 1975

CHAPTER 8

REDBOURN PEOPLE AND THEIR HOMES

In chapter 6 it has been noted that the substantial timber framed house that we usually associate with prosperous Yeoman farmers, were common by the end of the medieval period, though it took rather longer for houses of the peasants to develop to anything like the same standard. However, in this chapter I am less concerned about building developments than to introduce the people who occupied, and perhaps built houses in Redbourn.

Not every house can be covered, and some have already been looked at in the preceding chapters such as Farms (chapter 6), Inns (chapter 7)

HOUSES IN REDBOURN

Farmers could afford wooden houses, but stone ones were beyond their means, being only available to the very rich or the Church. In Redbourn, the medieval manor house at Redbournbury was the only example until Sir Richard Rede bought the former Priory and built "Place House" out of its stones.

The houses of the working people of the village would have tended to have been modelled on the timber-framed farmhouses, but on a much smaller and simpler scale. These clustered together at Church End or along the High Street in continuous but irregular lines.

Until later years Labourers' homes would have been thatched. This was of course a fire hazard, and communicating loft spaces made the spread of any fire rapid and disastrous. Two such fires occurred in 1674 when -

> *"Several persons dwelling in the town of Redbourn…sustained great loss by means of two lamentable fires"* [1]

The damage was put at £1948 and as there was no fire insurance, help was sought through the church 'Briefs system'; this appealed for money from other churches in the country (see also in chapter 9). We do not know whether the fires were at Church End or in the High Street. An accurate plot of house ages might give a clue, but a creditable solution would be hard to prove.

Many attractive houses, of a great variety of ages and styles, can be seen around the village. Many hide their antiquity behind later facades. This is particularly so in the case of shops, the Georgian way of hiding a sloping roof behind a brick parapet being popular. The use of brick also enabled old timber framing to be disguised or hidden. Thus it is often only from the inside or their little altered rear elevations that clues can be gained as to their former structure or real antiquity. Where roofs have survived, their unevenness may indicate early warped timbers. Others have been flattened and covered with slates when these became cheap in the nineteenth century.

Besides Church End and the High Street, other old houses can be seen in Fish Street, Shepherds Row, and around the Common.   East Common is particularly photogenic, but when occupied by Irish families fleeing from the potato famine in the 1840's it was scornfully referred to as "Dirt House Row" (or "Dirt Housen").[2] The 1861 census gave it a surprising upgrading to "Mount Pleasant".

High Street house, now removed

Church End

Fish Street

East Common

Fig: 8.1 - VIEWS OF OLD REDBOURN HOUSES

The following are the most historically notable or interesting village houses, see key *Figure 8.2*:-

"THE ARCHERS A fairly modern house, but because of an unconfirmed report of early foundations and a fragment of medieval stonework in its garden, is a possible site for Sir Richard Rede's "Place House" (Chapter 5)

"THE BEESNEST" The earliest record (1657) names it as "The Black Nest", the present name not appearing until 1839.[3] Between 1699 and 1771 it was divided into two, but in later years it was variously described as 3, 4 or 5 cottages - it still has 5 original fireplace positions. In 1885 it was endowed as an Almshouse by the Grinsteads of "The Priory".[4]

"BROCKWAY" Was the "White Horse". Sold in 1892, as *"an old fashioned residence*, and bought by the occupier, Dr. Ayre, who renamed it using his middle name (his Mother's maiden name?)[5] He had previously lived in a cottage before leaving the village after the death of his wife.

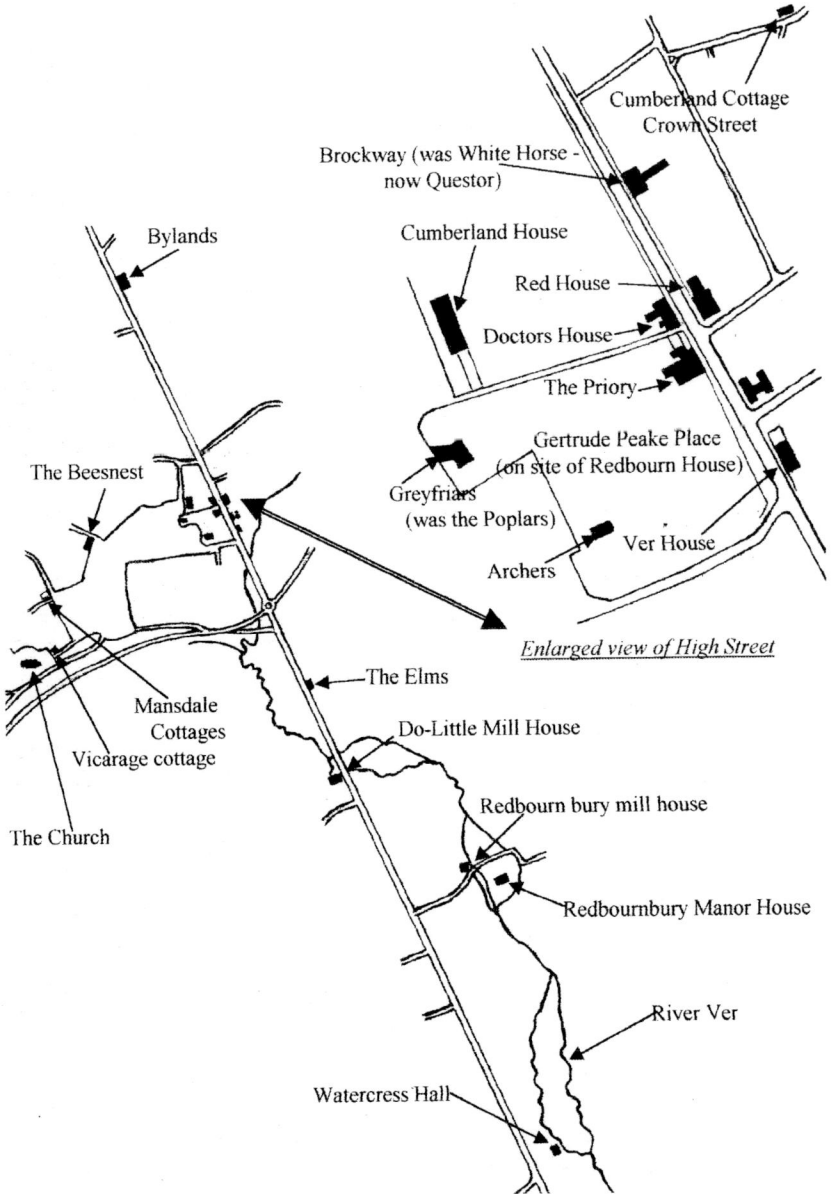

Cumberland Cottage
Crown Street

Brockway (was White Horse -
now Questor)

Cumberland House

Red House

Doctors House

The Priory

Gertrude Peake Place
(on site of Redbourn House)

Greyfriars
(was the Poplars)

Ver House

Archers

Enlarged view of High Street

Bylands

The Beesnest

The Elms

Mansdale
Cottages

Vicarage cottage

Do-Little Mill House

Redbourn bury mill house

The Church

Redbournbury Manor House

River Ver

Watercress Hall

Fig: 8.2 – Key map of houses listed in the text

"BYLANDS" A fairly modern house which only came within the parish with the most recent boundary change. Occupied by Colonel Christian Frederick George William de Falbe, son of the Danish Ambassador in London who lived at Luton Hoo. He was naturalised in 1903 and served with distinction in the army. In the village he was prominent in local affairs and was Vicar's Warden from 1922. In 1924 he was tragically killed in a railway accident in France; his wife and maid surviving. His body was brought back to Redbourn for burial, the funeral being attended by many national and political figures.[6] Among the wreaths was one from the Queen of Denmark and another from the railway company in whose train he had been travelling. The Lady Chapel screen was erected to his memory by his widow.[7]

Fig: 8.3 - Col. & Mrs de Falbe on their wedding day

CUMBERLAND HOUSE [8] "1743" etched on a brick found in the house, nicely dates it to the time that the Duke of Cumberland was victorious at the battle of Culloden. An old lady, who died in 1828, recalled seeing the Duke marching his foot guards through the village on his way to meet the Pretender at Derby before later defeating him at Culloden.

This house was not the Duke's residence, he used it as a hunting lodge in which to entertain guests invited to hunt with him from his kennels on Dunstable Downs. The house had stabling for 120 horses - the first floor being a banqueting hall with a large cooking stove to supply the guests' needs. The main entrance was from the High Street, not from the Common, as it is today. It has been suggested that the Duke used his position as Controller of the Royal Dockyards to obtain timber for the roof.

A subsequent owner became involved in a lengthy Chancery suit (possibly due to the foreclosure of a mortgage) and the house was bought by John Hodgkiss, who lived in Wales. He let the house to various people, including Lord Boyle, and from 1869 to William Thompson White. John Cussans was once entertained by Mr white, who gave him information that he later used in his "History of Hertfordshire". After White's death in 1881, his widow stayed on, getting her gardener Harry Miller, to meet the agent at the Bull whenever the rent was due. When the lease ran out she enquired the price of the house, and gave a cheque - the whole deal being completed the same day.

In 1890 she erected a glazed oak screen in the tower arch of St Marys in memory of her husband.[9]

The next owner was Robert Cecil Peake, a mining engineer from Staffordshire. It was probably his colliery experience that enabled him to install a generator to supply electricity to the house - the first electric lighting in Redbourn. He entered enthusiastically into local affairs becoming President or Chairman of most village organisations, school manager and churchwarden; he also served as Justice of the Peace at St Albans for 37 years. He died at Cumberland House in 1933 and the family commemorated him and his wife, Anna Margaret Hester, with a stained glass window in the Lady Chapel of St Mary's.

Ivy Covered west side

One of four Adam Fireplaces

Ivy covered east side

Hall & Stairs, recent photograph

Fig: 8.4 - VIEWS OF CUMBERLAND HOUSE
(3 Taken by Robert Cecil Peake)

The two Peake daughters, Gertrude and Anne, followed in their father's footsteps by serving the village in many different ways. Gertrude served on both the Parish and Rural District councils. Her passionate interest was in nursing and hospitals, serving in such work during both World Wars. In 1928 she founded a branch of the Women's Institute in the village, an event acknowledged by their gift of the tower clock to St Mary's The memorial that would probably have pleased her most is the home built in the High Street for old people, called "Gertrude Peake Place", see *Fig: 8.5*

Fig: 8.5 - "Gertrude Peake Place", soon after it was built
(Ann Skillman Collection)

Her sister, Anne was particularly interested in church work and its history - a fact for which I am personally grateful as she for passed on much useful information to me. The sisters moved out of Cumberland House to live for a time in "Heath" farm, later building a new house in the grounds called "Heybrigge" (now replaced by modern houses).

A ghost of a maid, said to have been bricked up in a cellar, is said to haunt the house. She is known as the "White Lady". Mr Peake called off his investigation of the cellar because he decided it was too damp.

Lady Wise was the next owner of Cumberland House, she carried out extensive alterations. The next owner, Mr Burton, sold it in 1952 to The Central Electricity Generating Board (later Northmet) This seems rather appropriate as it was the first house in the village to have been electrified. Until its closure in 1998, the house, with modern control centres alongside, controlled the supply of electricity to the whole of the North Thames area.

CUMBERLAND COTTAGE. Frederick Evans Hall (*Fig: 8.6*), married a daughter of the Whites of Cumberland House, giving the reason for its name. The earliest record I can find is 1910.[10] When it was sold in 1932 it was described as - *"a gentleman's small freehold country estate"* and the land as - *"ripe for immediate development".*[11] Indeed, it was developed as housing - now Harpenden Lane and Ver Road. Land extending to Waterend Lane was developed in the 1970's by a later owner, Mr Gordon Hoskins, see chapter 13.[12]

Fig: 8.6 - Mr. F. E. Hall

DOCTOR TOTTON'S HOUSE, is so named after the last of several doctors who lived here. Dr. Jurian Totton practised in Redbourn for 38 years (1924-26), a fact commemorated by a stained glass window in St Mary's.

His name is also linked with the passageway beside the house - "Totton's Alley" (more anciently called - "The Ruins"). The modern development behind the house has also been named "Totton Mews"

The best known of the previous doctors thought to have lived here was Dr. Henry Stephens, the inventor of "Stephens Blue- Black ink - see chapter 10. The older, southern part of the house, was earlier occupied by a school master well known for making quill pens - a nice link with Stephens ink.[13]

"THE ELMS" In a sale brochure of 1823 "**Elm Cottage**", was described as - *"a neat Brick-built dwelling house, having 4 best bedrooms and 4 secondary"*. It included many outbuildings, garden, orchard, adjoining meadows and other land, totalling 25 acres. It was bought by Thomas Pugh, Curate of Flamstead, but who also took Services at Redbourn.[14]

"GREYFRIARS" (was "The Poplars") Pevsner described it as *"a gabled timber-framed cottage"*.[15] Such a construction suggests an early origin; but it only appears from the 1861 Census, being then occupied by Edward Enfield - *"late manager of His Majesty's Mint"*.

The Vicar, William Serocold Wade was the next occupant, moving here after marrying his second wife, Isabella Pugh (her father lived at The Elms) Mr Wade made himself unpopular by blocking up a right of way to the Ruins passage through his garden. He had to face an ugly uprising of villagers headed by the publican of the "Prince's Head".[16] He must have won the day as the exit into the Ruins passage remains blocked up.

After the First World War an architect, called Huxley, lived in the house making extensive alterations. He renamed it **"Greyfriars"**, perhaps trying to connect it with Redbourn Priory - if so he was confused because Greyfriars were Franciscans - not Benedictines as were the monks of the Priory.

"LAVENDER COTTAGE" Tucked away behind the High Street and backing on to the "Archers", this pleasant little cottage is sadly overlooked. It was one of the Bowes-Lyon properties sold in 1892.

"MANSDALE COTTAGES" The only thatched private house in the village, also one of the most attractive. In the Bowes-Lyon sale of 1892 it was described as *"4 brick and plaster cottages"*. The earliest record I can find is in the Land Tax Assessment of 1753.

Fig: 8.7 – Mansdale cottages,c.1920

THE MILL HOUSES The houses belonging to both Redbourn Watermills are very roughly contemporary.

That at "**Do-little Mill**" is perhaps a little older than Redbournbury; as it can be dated to 1603 and was probably built by Roger Pemberton of St Albans.[17] It was built on the opposite side of the road to the mill, a fact that saved it from demolition with the mill for road widening. **Redbournbury Mill House** was built as part of the mill and was already existing when the mill was rebuilt in 1694, it could date from 1650 or earlier.[18] We could also include the **Silk Mill house** on the Common, this dates from 1857. Today it is our Village Museum.[19]

"**PLACE HOUSE**" was built by Sir Richard Rede from materials salvaged from the Priory when he came to the village in 1558.[20] Its possible location is discussed in chapter 5, but no in-situ evidence remains today.

Sir Richard started life as a lawyer at the Court of Admiralty, becoming Master of Chancery and Chancellor of Ireland when he was only 30. Under King Henry he visited London churches to remove "*Popish Imagery*". Under Queen Mary he took part in the trial of the Bishops. With such a background it must be wondered if he influenced the removal of the Holy Rood from St Mary's, which was still in place when he came to the village.

Fig: 8.8 – Brasses of Sir Richard Rede and his wife Anne, in St Mary's Church

Besides the Priory, he also purchased the Manor of Redbourn and was the only Lord of the Manor to actually live in the village. However, the right to appoint a Vicar to the living was one privilege that Richard never obtained.

He also owned properties in London and 8 counties. His lengthy will is a study on its own, having 208 lines of closely written Elizabethan script.[21]

He and his wife Anne lie in a vault under the Lady Chapel. The Latin inscription on top of his tomb, now under the Lady Chapel Altar, reads :-

> *Richard Rede, knight and Anne his wife were buried under*
> *this in the month of September 1560; this is true"*

However, this is **not true** because Sir Richard did not die until 1576.

The tomb was not disturbed until 1783 when Thomas Baskerfield took it down in order to make the Lady Chapel into a room for the Parish Vestry meetings During the work he looked down into the vault and reported that the two skeletons were perfectly preserved, but soon crumbled to dust.[22]

THE PRIORY" A suggested date of c.1750 fits well with its architectural style, described by Pevsner as *"a completely urban early 18th century house which might as well stand in Grosvenor Square".*[23]

The first known occupant was Thomas Baskerfield who lived in Redbourn from at least 1786. He was an artist and antiquarian whose works will be described in chapter 12. When he took out fire insurance on the house in 1794, he gave a Bloomsbury address, indicating that the Priory was his 'country residence'.[24] The policy was with Sun Fire Office for £550. Baskerfield became captain of a local volunteer force, formed to combat a possible Napoleonic invasion and headed his troops at a ceremony to present 'colours' at Gorhambury in 1804. [25] The colours were presented by Harriet, Lord Grimston's daughter. Baskerfield later wrote to Grimston asking permission to pay court to Harriet; but was rejected, chiefly on the grounds of the disparity in their ages. The fact that Harriet never married might be an

Fig: 8.9 - "The Priory

indication of a possible reciprocation of feelings, while Thomas left it quite late in life before marrying Sophia.

He died in1816 and was buried beside his parents in a vault under the High Altar in the church. His widow, lived to the age of 91, dying in 1846. She left money for the Sunday School, the poor and the upkeep of the vault and memorials tablets commemorating all the family.[26]

The next owner was Captain de Vere Brown; who also held the "Cock" with a malt mill at the rear.[27] Subsequent owners were related to the Bowes Lyon family. Firstly Joseph Grimstead, a brother of Lady Charlotte Glamis, who was described as living on the Common, which could mean "the Priory", as its land extended from the High Street to the Common.

It then passed to Hugh Charles Bettesworth Trevanion, by marriage to Frances, a daughter of Lady Glamis, they died within years of each other. A sale catalogue of 1903 lists Frances' *"Valuable Antique Furniture"* The 479 articles for sale make interesting, and with their prices, mouth watering reading. Here is a short selection, the total sale fetched £513 [28]:-

9 Volumes of Shakespeare	*2s.*
Mahogany Chippendale Secretaire	*15s*
Mahogany Chippendale Reading Table	*14s*
Single Brougham	*£14*
Pony Phaeton	*£2.5.0d*
4 wheel Dog Cart	*£8*

Like Sophia, the Grimsteads and Trevanions were long living families:-

Charlotte Grimstead	died 1848	aged 81 years		
Thomas Grimstead	" 1884	" 81 "		
Frances Grimstead	" 1893	" 70 "		
Hugh Trevanion	" 1901	" 72 "		
Frances Trevanion	" 1903	" 70 "		

The next owner was Arthur William Mc. Gregor, one of the early car owners of Redbourn, buying two in 1906 - see page 119. The house was also occupied at some time by the brother of the Maharajah of Sarawak.

In 1945 it was converted into flats for workers in the newly established Brooke Bond factory and in recent years it has become commercial offices.

Hearsay has it that an underground passage ran from the cellar of the house to the Church, but this I consider unlikely, as explained on page 70.

"REDBOURN HOUSE" This was certainly the most impressive and important house in the village, but in the end no one could afford to restore it, and in spite of being classified as 'Historic', demolition followed in the 1960's. However, its front portico was preserved and stands beside the Museum of St Albans - see *Fig: 8.10.* The old site of "Redbourn House" is now occupied by "Gertrude Peake Place", -see *Fig: 8.5* Early members of the ancient family who originally built a house here can be traced back to the 1455 Rental; which names two members - William Carpenter and his son John. William's will gives some idea of his wealth by listing his Properties in Redbourn, Flamstead, Harpenden,

Fig: 8.10 - The Portico, now at the Museum of St Albans

Hemel Hempstead and Wheathampstead.[29]   His   many   benefactions
amounted to the large sum (in those days) of £33 in addition to gifts for
building work in St Mary's (chapter 4), ten surrounding churches and a
bequest to the shrine of St Alban.

As with most men of his time he was much concerned to provide for his
place in the after life. At his funeral torches and candles were placed around
his hearse and 9 marks paid for an *"honest priest"* to sing masses for his
soul. Prayers were repeated twice annually in a *"Dirge or Mass"* sung by
3 priests and 4 clerks. This was paid for from the income of land rented to
-*"8 honest persons"*, and covered the cost of the bells, bread, ale and cheese
for those attending, and 8 pence to the Churchwardens for their trouble.

He extended coverage by having a 'Tental of Masses' (30 Masses) said at
Dunstable and Northampton, leaving money also for acceptance into the
Abbey Chapter - presumably this ensuring him a place on their 'prayer list'.

His family were well provided for with gifts of money and property. His
home at Retherfeld End (now Revel End), remained the family residence
until at least 1640. John his son and heir also held - *"a messuage and
curtilage with a barne, newly built* (in 1517), *lying in Redbourne Street".*[30]
It was probably on this site that the Georgian mansion named "Redbourn
House" was built in the early 18th century.

For five generations the eldest sons of the family were called George, at one
time three sons with that name lived in the village. This must have been
most confusing, but is even more so to historians trying to decide which
George, is referred to in a document.

An example of this arises when a George Carpenter (father or son?)
obtained permission in 1742 from the Earl of Verulam, to plant trees across
the Common. These elms made a magnificent avenue, which still exists to
this day, but with different trees. A great gale in 1916 wreaked havoc with
the originals, but in later years the gaps were replanted until the deadly
'Dutch Elm Decease' destroyed all the remaining elms, necessitating further
replanting. Most of these have matured into trees, but not yet approaching
the magnificence of the original elms.

The last George Carpenter died in 1782 and is commemorated by a
memorial tablet in the church (*Fig: 8.11*) recording that he was - *"the last
male heir of an ancient and respectable family long resident in this parish"*
The name of Carpenter died in the village with this George, but his daughter
opened a new, more prestigious, chapter.

The story starts when George Carpenter experienced leaks in his roof, which was flat and covered with lead;. because of this he had to employ a plumber (skilled in lead working) to carry out repairs. This was John Walsh, a London plumber, who came and lodged in the house, bringing his teenage daughter, Mary Elizabeth, with him. Despite the great disparity in their ages, he was nearly 70 and she only 18, they struck up a friendship and soon decided to marry.[31]

Fig: 8.11 – Memorial to George Carpenter

Fig: 8.12 – Redbourn House, c.1890

The outcome of their union was the birth of a daughter, 3 months after George's death, named Mary Elizabeth Lousia Rodney Carpenter. She, like her mother, made a good marriage - to Thomas Lyon-Bowes, later the 11th Earl of Strathmore. They were thus the Great, Great, Great, Grandparents of Queen Elizabeth the Queen Mother - giving Redbourn the Royal connection of which we are quietly proud - see Family Tree, page 136.

The couple's son, George Thomas, married Charlotte Grimstead, and lived in "Redbourn House". They owned much property in the parish, as shown by the sale of the estate in 1892, some 11 years after Charlotte's death. This included 57 Houses and cottages, 1 farm, 1 factory and 26 plots of land.[32] That part of the Bowes Lyon family tree which shows the above relationships is shown overleaf.

Several occupants of the house followed, one Mr Magor, incurred local anger put into a poem by Mr Fred Allen.[33]:-

> *"Who when he has a job or two*
> *Sets Redbourn working men askew*
> *And sends off for the Hempstead crew*
> *Why Magordew"*

CARPENTER / BOWES-LYON FAMILY TREE

George CARPENTER = **Mary Elizabeth (Walsh)**
of "Redbourn House" | Plumber's daughter
1713-1782 | b.1762

Thomas LYON-BOWES = **Mary Elizabeth Rodney (Carpenter)**
11th Earl of Strathmore | (1783-1811)
(1773-1846)

Thomas LYON-BOWES = **Charlotte (Grimstead)**
Lord Glamis (1801-1834) | Lady Glamis (1798-1881)

Claude LYON-BOWES = **Frances Dora (Smith)**
13th Earl of Strathmore |
1824-1904

Claude BOWES-LYON = **Nina Cecilia**
Lord Glamis (1855-1944) | **(Cavendish)**
b.1862

KING GEORGE VI = **QUEEN ELIZABETH**
1895-1952   (The Queen Mother)

Mr Magor was followed in 1899 by F. Montague-Douglas Scott, one of the Duke of Buccleugh's family.[34] His very musical wife (*Fig: 8.13*) trained local vocal and instrumental talents who, supplemented by a few instrumentalists from outside the village, gave concerts, sometimes in her spacious garden. Geoffrey Bowes -Lyon was the last of that family to occupy the house.(between 1924 and 1935) He ran an antiques business from there, using a car for this business (Rolls Royce?) with the family crest painted on its side.[35]

Fig: 8.13 - Mrs Scott

"THE RED HOUSE"   Was built on the site of one of Redbourn's two "Greyhound" inns, for Rebecca Goulds in 1786.[36] In 1865 it became the home of Lady Charlotte Glamis when she found "Redbourn House" too large and expensive. She had a single story extension built on the north side to house her pictures and a very large mirror.

After her death it was put up for sale in 1892, by which time it Rev. W. A. Pope occupied it as the Vicarage - *"at the extremely low rental of £45 pa."* The sale catalogue mentions the fine Dining room, 20 feet high - *"formerly used as a picture gallery"* (as built by Charlotte for her pictures), Drawing room, Library, etc., and 10 large bedrooms. There was also stabling and a coach house for 5 or 6 carriages.

At the auction it was bought by Mr T. Connor of Harpendenbury and

Fig: 8.14 - The "Red House"
(Picture gallery on the left)

renamed "Delaneal House" and within two years Mr Pope moved into the new Vicarage at Church End. Since 1978 it has been in commercial hands and an additional floor has been installed in Charlotte's former picture gallery, but without spoiling the appearance from the outside.

REDBOURNBURY MANOR HOUSE As has been seen earlier (page 89), is the oldest house in the parish.

"VER HOUSE" Built by William Burchmore, for his two sisters, in the first half of the 19th century.[37] Later occupied by John Sansom, the watercress grower, and given its present name for obvious reasons.

VICARAGE COTTAGE This little cottage, once part of the Vicar's Glebe, for a time it was a butcher's shop.[38]

Fig: 8.15 - Ver House

"WATERCRESS HALL" In 1841 Census Return William Payne, Cress man, occupied "Water Cress Cottage", then part of Redbournbury Farm. Subsequent returns give it as "Water Cress Hall", but by 1891 the occupant was William Lee, Game Keeper. By 1910 it, with its *"Cress ditches"*, was in the hands of Thomas Sansom, watercress grower.[39]

MISS MAY WALKER

Before leaving the subject of Redbourn people and their houses, mention must be made of a remarkable lady - May Walker. She was the daughter of a coach builder whose premises, in the motoring age, became 'Walkers Garage'; its forecourt clock has been retained in front of recently built houses. This was just one of her father's activities. Between the wars he built many houses in the village, chiefly in Crouch Hall Lane, Crouch Hall Gardens and Bettespool Meadows. May told me how they used to purchase old used bricks, from as far away as Wales, and when there was enough, another house or two would be built.

Fig:8.16 – Miss May Walker
Left – Photographing The Moor
Right – On motorbike with a passenger in wickerwork sidecar, c.1914

May Walker carried on the business, but she too was involved with other activities. She had a passion for motorbikes, and may even have been involved in testing them. The bike she is seen with in *fig: 8.12* is a huge machine for a lady to tackle; the cane-work sidecar is particularly interesting. Other interests were in drawing, photography and local history; her book called "Redbourn" was published as a limited edition. Sadly she was killed in a motor accident just after approving the final draft at the printers. It is from this book that I have drawn many references for this chapter.

REFERENCES

1   Gerish collection in the HRO.
2   May Walker "Redbourn", p.50, also Census Return for 1851
3   HRO. Ref.73446
4   HRO. Ref. D/EV/1552.B2
5   As 2, p.61
6   St Albans Times 22nd March 1924
7   HRO. Faculties DSA.2/1/8/53,54 and 67
8   3 sources have been used - May Walker, "Redbourn" pp.47-8;   "The Story of Redbourn, p.90;   Mrs Jane Bird "The History of Cumberland House" 1988 (College Assignment)
9   Parish Registers, HRO. Ref. Register Book 1/4
10 HRO. Land Value Act, 1910 books ref. IR2.59/1
11 Sale document, 12.Oct.1932, Rumball and Edwards, loaned by Mrs Mary Nelder
12 P Thompson "It happened in a Hertfordshire village" 1976
13 As 2, p.66
14 HRO. Ref. 73438
15 Nikolaus Pevsner "The Buildings of England, Hertfordshire", 1977, p.277
16 As 2, p.48
17 HRO. Ref. X.C.7a; Also - Alan Featherstone "The Mills of Redbourn", pp.51-2
18 PRO. ref. E.317. Herts/23 "Survey of Watermills - Commonwealth"
19 HRO. Ref. D/EB.1873.T.3
20 Emden "Biographical Register of the University of Oxford", p.481
21 PRO. Carew 20, ref PROB 11/58
22 British Library ADD.MS.9063 fol.248b
23 As 15, p.277
24 Guildhall Library - Records of the Sun Fire Office, No. 624597
25 Nora king - "The Grimstons of Gorhambury", pp.89-91
26 Extract among the Charity Commissioners documents in the Parish Chest
27 As 2, p.67
28 HRO. Ref. D/EB.1552.B.8
29 HRO, Will, 2AR.97
30 HRO. Ref. X.C.3a
31 As 2, p.58
32 Sale Brochure, 1892, Redbourn Village Museum ref. RDBVM.87.830
33 As 2, p.59
34 As 2, p.59
35 Information collected by me, but original source not recorded
36 As 2, p.60
37 As 2, p.58
38 As 2, p.53
39 As 1, IR.2, 59/1

CHAPTER 9

THE POOR OF REDBOURN

Before the Dissolution, the care of the poor, sick and aged fell largely to the Monastic houses; locally this was St Albans Abbey and to a lesser extent, Redbourn Priory. At the latter, the monks were encouraged to give any food that was left over from their meals, to the poor at their gates.

After the Dissolution the care of the poor devolved mostly on what could be organised by the Civil/Church authorities, and paid for out of local taxation - the 'Poor Rate'. To some extent the bequests in the wills of the more wealthy residents, helped matters; there were also a few Charities, Guilds and Friendly Societies. But much time and money was spent by local Vestries trying to rid themselves of the responsibility and cost of any unfortunate 'non-native' paupers in their parish, by passing them back to their place of birth.

The foundation of workhouses was an attempt to house the poor more cheaply under one roof, and there to put them to some simple work, or give them menial employment around the parish. The early 19th century records of our Workhouse survive, and have been studied. These give no obvious indication that any cruelty or mistreatment of the inmates occurred, as they did in some parishes - I like to think that Redbourn adopted a humane and caring attitude.

The people and houses so far described were mostly the more prosperous Redbourn inhabitants - a few 'gentry', but mostly large land owners and yeomen farmers. However, the majority of the population did not fall into any of these groups, though many villagers owned some land and seem to have been able to pay their dues and taxes. But there were others who were extremely poor (often called 'paupers'), unable, through age, infirmity or sickness to earn a living wage. These poor residents lived in cottages scattered around the village supported to a large extent by the rest of the population, while others were totally kept by the parish in the Workhouse. This was situated in Church End; whether by design or accident far away from the rich, mostly living on the other side of the Common.

Before looking at the way 'officialdom' managed the poor, other forms of help must be considered. Little is known about the generosity of people during their lives, but perhaps benefactions left in their wills represent the <u>culmination</u> of their giving.

WILLS

Before the Dissolution there was not so much need for bequests to the poor, because of monastic support. I can find only two such bequests in this period [1]:-

     1510 Thomas Aylwyn - left 3 bushels of malt to 6 poor men
     1514 Robert Roys - left 20 pence to the poor attending his burial and the
          same at his *"month's mynde"*

In the years after the Dissolution similar bequests appear, such as:-

1551   Robert Martyn - *"to the poor man's box 8d"*

1553   Alban Fynche - to the poor people of *"the strete and Church End 6s.8d*

1554   William Fynche - to the poor in Redbourn 20s.

1558   Edward Abraham - to *the poor at my burial 46s.4d, 6 dozen (loaves) of bread, and 2 kilderkynnes of beer; and at my month's minde 40s. and the same quantities of bread and beer*

1568   Edward Carpenter - to *the poor people there, 3s.4d*

CHARITIES

The above wills were all 'once off', or at the most, 'twice off' payments, but in 1576 Sir Richard Rede attempted to provide for the poor in the long term. His bequest, remarkably, still exists, though now absorbed in the paperwork of the 20th century 'Redbourn Charities'. His lengthy will, amongst bequests to many different good causes, including these specifically to the poor of Redbourn [2]:-

A once off payment to the poor after his burial of £10,

1 groat (4d) each to 12 of the poorest people in Redbourn

£2 to *"poor maydens in their Mariage Daye"* (5s each)

Out of £10 rent from land in his Manor of Redbourn, £2 for *"bread, freeze and canvas"* to the poorest of the parish on Good Friday

However, the latter was nearly lost because tenants of the lands stopped paying their rents to the charity, but some parishioners were so concerned that they banded together and took the matter to court. A brief account of the action is written on a large board hanging in the vestry.[3] *(Fig. 9.1)* This names Richard Peacock of Revel End and Timothy Axtell of Butlers, assisted by *"one Weston, a chimney-sweeper, who was their solicitor"*. Weston won the case for them and a payment of £100, with which they bought land on "Dudley Hill", thereafter referred to as the "Poor's Land".

Dudley Hill was farmed by various tenants until 1884, when it was decided to let it out to villagers as allotments - this increased its income dramatically from £22.10.0d to £35.15.0d per annum.[4] During the First World War a searchlight was positioned there.[5]

Fig: 9.1 - Board in the Church about the Sir Richard Rede Charity

In 1962 it was sold to the Crown Commissioners for £1,282 and the money incorporated into "Redbourn Parochial Charities".[6]

Later Charities can be summarised as follows:-

1631 EDWARD SMITH of Sandridge, left £200 to John Brocket of Wheathamstead, for land in Sandridge. And from the annual rent from this £10 was to be divided amongst the poor of Wheathamstead, Harpenden, Sandridge, Hemel Hempstead and Redbourn.[7] After the deduction of taxes, Redbourn's share was £1.12s.0d received annually until the early 19th century

c.1650 REDBOURN MILLS Eight pounds, previously paid to the Crown, was allocated to the poor of Brickhill, £5 from Redbournbury Mill and £3 from Redbourn Little Mill.[8] Payments are recorded until c.1731

THOMAS CARPENTER a citizen of London, left his manor of Woodhall in Hemel Hempstead to his nephew George Carpenter. Out of this, George was to give £10 annually to Mr Collett, master of a school in Redbourn *"for the use of poor scholars there - so long as the school shall continue"*.[9] Shortly before his death in 1782, George Carpenter stopped payments because of a disagreement with the master. In 1801 the Vestry talked about reclaiming back payments, which the Charity Commissioners thought they had a chance of getting, but nothing came of it.

1756 JOHN OGILVIE of Edmonton married into the Carpenter family and left a £10 charity to the poor of Redbourn to be given in bread on the first Sunday after the 24th June each year out of rents on Bohemia Farm.[10] From 1788 the rents were withheld and could not be recovered.

18-19C. REVEL END FARM. A Charity board in the upper vestry refers to annual payments of 5s to poor families of the parish, out of this farm.[11]

1837 MRS MARY PEACOCK left £100 in 3% Consolidated Bank Annuities to the Minister and Churchwardens.[12] As trustees they were required, after maintaining the family tombs, to use the surplus dividends to give 2s.6d. each to 12 poor *"aged Widows, the sick and most necessitous families"*

1846 SOPHIA BASKERFIELD left £200 in 3% Consolidated Bank Annuities in trust, £4 out of the dividends to support the Sunday Schools in the church, or if there was not one to another Sunday School in the parish, or else to poor people not receiving Relief.[13]

1869 TOMSON AND HOW In 1868 "Netheridge Down" was bought in trust by William How of Hammonds End from John Christopher Tomson, late of St Agnells farm.[14] Is now allotments known as "Tassell Hall"

1871 MISS ELIZABETH KINGSTON left £18 in 3% Annuities, the dividends *"to lay out in the furnishing of bread, blankets, coals and wine for poor people in Redbourn"* to be distributed on 10th October.[15]

1889 REDBOURN PAROCHIAL CHARITIES. This was a scheme to amalgamate and regulate all the remaining Redbourn charities.[16]

1904 LADY FRANCES TREVANION, late of "The Priory", left the annual income of £12 to be used as follows:- £2.2s.0d to the Vicar on the 25th May each year if he conducts a service in memory of her husband, Hugh [17] After paying for any repairs to the family vault, the balance was to be distributed to the oldest inhabitants who attended the service.

The Vestry minutes recorded in 1907 - *"A very satisfactory division of the late Frances Trevanion's gift took place; after the usual memorial service, 58 deserving poor of the parish participated in the gift, receiving 2s.6d each* . An attempt was made to revive this service by Rev. Ian Robson and was so well attended that more cash had to be sent for from the Holly Bush.

1909 SHERWOOD AND HOW. Mrs How, who used to live at The Heath, gave a field called "Netheridge Down" (see Tomson and How, above) and £50 of 3fi % India Stock to buy coals annually for the poor.[18] She also gave double the amount for the upkeep of the family vault in the Churchyard.

1917/26 WOOLLAM CHARITY. Charles Woollam, who ran the Silk Mill (see chap 13), gave a piece of land called "The Brache" as allotments, the rents being given to the poor.[19] His widow enhanced this gift in 1926, by building a group of 4 Almshouses on part of the land.[20] Then in 1961-2 the land behind these was sold to the Rural District Council for development, part of the land being reserved for further old people's bungalows - the old and new make the present square, collectively called "Woollams".[21]

1964 REDBOURN CHARITIES All the charities administered by the 1889 Redbourn Parochial Charities, together with those given subsequently, were amalgamated under the above title in 1964.[22] The new scheme was introduced saying how the poor of Redbourn could be

Fig: 9.2 - "Woollams" Alms Houses

helped with gifts, useful articles, comforts and weekly allowances.[23] The Vicar was an ex-officio trustee, but that this was not a church charity, thus members of any religious denomination could benefit.

FRIENDLY SOCIETIES

In the 18th century, Friendly Societies began to gain in popularity. In a way these were a throwback to the Medieval Guilds and Brotherhoods, in that they were intended to benefit and look after their members. Typical is that for the "Holly Bush", its rules beginning.[24]:-

> "..the objects shall be, by voluntary contributions of the members, to raise a sufficient fund for the relief and maintenance of the members in sickness and infirmity"

By 1793 friendly societies had to be registered with a Clerk of the Peace, those registered in Redbourn were as follows.[25]:-

        1794 The Saracens Head
        1800 The White Horse
        1808 The George
        1809 The Tom-in-Bedlam, also repeated in 1836 and 1838
        1816 The Lion and Lamb
        1863 The Holly Bush

After the Dissolution of the Monasteries individual parishes were made responsible for the care of their poor. Private giving of alms was an offence but could still take place in the form of bequests in wills and collections taken in Church [27] At the latter a club room was built adjacent to the inn, this building still exists, now used mostly for social functions. *(see Fig: 9.3)* Similar organisations were run by the church. In the late 1880's there were two "Clothing Clubs", one for adults the other for children; the latter was variously called a Shoe, Clothing or School Club. The annual amounts paid out were usually of about £150, and among the named subscribers was the Earl of Verulam.[26]

PARISH MANAGEMENT OF THE POOR

After the Dissolution of the Monasteries, individual parishes were made responsible for the care of their poor. Private giving of alms was an offence, but could still take place in the form of bequests in wills and collections in church.[27]

Of the many Acts of Parliament relating to poor, that of 1601 was the most comprehensive, and though intended as a temporary measure, it

Fig: 9.3 - The "Hollybush" Club Room

remained as the basis of poor administration for about two centuries.[28] A prime object was to put the able bodied poor to work, even pauper children.

The problem remained of those who, because of age, infirmity or sickness, were unable to work. Money for their relief was entrusted to locally elected "Collectors of the Poor", later called "Overseers of the Poor", a title which remained in use until 1925.[29] These officers initially had the power to coerce parishioners to be generous, but later a rate was set, based on land holdings, called "The Poor Rate".

SETTLEMENT

The most invidious part of the poor laws related to which parish was chargeable for their financial support - this depended on where they were allowed to 'settle'. Those who were not native to the parish where they lived, and were unable to support themselves, could be forcibly 'settled' elsewhere by an infamous Act of Parliament dated 1662.[30]

To relieve a parish of the burden of supporting such a family, a legal order could be obtained to have them returned to the parish of their birth, apparently oblivious to their ability to survive such a journey on foot. In forty years the Redbourn Registers of burials record 5 such deaths:-

1617	*"a poore boy, brought by passe to be conveyed to Chippin Ungar"*
1620	*"Stephen Ashley travayled with a passe, given at Islington to go to Lancton in ye county of Leycester, heere dyed and was buryed"*
1646	*"a stranger brought with a passe"*
1655	*"John Jones, a poore boy that came with a pase"*
1657	*"Margaret Harisonne, a vagrant taken up near London and pasing to Stiventon in Northhampton sheere"*

Evidence of attempts at re-settlements to or from the parish can be found in the Sessions records as follows.[31]:-

1674	William *Broadneck to be settled at Redbourn, Caddington discharged"*
1726	*"Order allowing the appeal of Redbourn against a warrant removing William Cook and Sarah his wife from Harpenden. He had been a servant with Edward Hawkins of Redbourn, a farmer"*
1729	*"Order dismissing the appeal of Redbourn against a warrant removing Henry Palmer and Elizabeth his wife and daughter from Kings Langley"*
1778	*"Ann Brickmore, in the House of Correction (prison), for returning to Redbourn from whence she had been removed, without bringing a certificate"*
1784	*"Order allowing an appeal of Great Gaddesden against a warrant removing John Ringsale and Mary his wife from Redbourn"*
1828	"Redbourn against the removal of Sophia Kempster, widow and her three children, from Caddington - Dismissed"

Part of the Act of Re-settlement referred to hardened vagrants who before being ejected from the parish could be whipped. One such case was reported at Redbourn in 1676.[32]:-

> *"George Snoden, a sturdy vagrant beggar of a low personage, black haired, goeth stooping, making use of a crutch, aged about 19 years, was openly whipped at Redbourne according to law for a wandering rogue, and is assigned to pass forthwith from parish to parish by the Constables...the next way to Stowsley (Stokesley) in Yorkshire, where he confesseth he was borne or dwelt last by one whole year...the Constables of every town he shall come (to) are required to allow him necessary relief for the passage and to help him with lodging."*

MAINTENANCE

An alternative, more humane, method of looking after these 'displaced persons' was to demand payments for their maintenance from the parish of their birth. Many such Maintenance payments appear for Redbourn, some were paid out, but most are of amounts received for paupers living in Redbourn. Perhaps this indicates a humane attitude by our Vestry - or perhaps this was more profitable than getting rid of them by obtaining court orders for their removal?

Between 1798 and 1815 payments were received from the parishes of [33]:-
>Chelmsford 1798-1807
>Hatfield 1802-3
>Offley 1803-7
>Datchworth 1804-7
>Mimms 1807-8
>Cheynes 1808-9
>Watford 1809
>Clerkenwell 1809-10
>Ridge 1813-14

A few payments to other parishes are recorded:-
>1800 to Quainton, for a bastard child
>1808 and 1815 to Abbots Langley, the former for a woman with two children whose husband had been deported
>1823-4 to Frome in Somerset as described below

The following account of the latter case has been deduced from a long series of letters, showing the care taken by the Vestry to not pay out unjustified amounts.

The family concerned were the Strattons; most probably the same family of Paper Makers who ran the Redbourn Paper Mill between 1753-84 - see chapter 13.

The first we hear of the matter is a copy of a reply given by a Churchwarden,

Mr George Lee Cane, of Beaumont Hall, to an unsigned and undated letter from Frome. His letter shows that some Relief had already been given to the Stratton family, who were said to be *"in a very deplorable and afflicted situation"*. However, he sent another £2 in good faith, but with the request that the matter of why relief was needed should be looked into, and asking whether it was illness that prevented their Removal (back to Redbourn). This letter was delivered by a reliable man, Mr Giblett

Several more unsigned letters were received, to these Mr Cane countered by saying that he did not approve *"of relieving paupers by anonymous letters"*. However, he said that he was willing to pay some reasonable amount, but that they should *"pass them home"* so that they could be put in our Workhouse. At this stage, Mr Giblett reported that there seemed to be something wrong at Frome, because the Strattons were already receiving some pension money.

At last a letter arrived with the signature of Mr Harris - Overseer of the Poor of Frome. He firmly stated that there was no deception and that he was getting Mr Giblett to visit the family to see for himself. He said that Stratton's pension had ceased at his death, that one boy was on low income as an apprentice to a shoemaker and that one of the girls *"would soon be an idiot in addition to her being a cripple"*. He went on to say that he did not personally approve of the Law of Removal, and that it was not the policy of their parish.

Mr Giblett confirmed that he had seen the family and that matters were as stated. Presumably the 5 shillings per week was then paid by Mr Cane.

The last letter from the Overseer of Frome ends the case, but rather shows up Mr Cane, our Churchwarden, in an uncaring light. Another case later in the same year tends to confirm that he favoured the removal of paupers, rather than paying maintenance. This concerned William Carter, from Chesham, who had been taken ill at Redbourn. Cane demanded early action from Chesham as to how to *"dispose of him"* and even threatened to have him removed himself if they did not take action.

The five shillings per week paid to widow Stratton seems to conform to the following list of payments that I have deduced from our Workhouse records: -

For men, or for 'Bastard' children	1s. to 2s.
For Widows and women without children	1s. 6d to 3s.
For women with 1 child	3s.
For women with 2 children	4s. 6d
For women with 3 or more children	6s.

THE REDBOURN WORKHOUSE

Knatchbull's Act of Parliament, dated 1723, recommended parishes to set up 'workhouses'.[34] Here their poor people could be housed together, as this was thought to be cheaper than paying pensions to people scattered in cottages around a village. Such an arrangement also enabled the inmates to be more easily employed in making things for sale or for being sent out to do manual work.

A "Church House" is mentioned from 1486, but in 1706 it was referred to as - *"Certain Alms Houses called 'The Church House' "*.[35] Forty years later the burial of *"a child from the workhouse"* shows that Knatchbull's Act had been followed, but may have been no more than a rebuilding of Church House, with its present 'Mansard Roof'. *(see Fig: 9.4)*

Fig: 9.4 - The old Workhouse at Church End (The Plaque is arrowed)
The plaque, shown in *Fig: 9.4,* records a later repair or rebuilding:-

This Work House **REBUILT**	
Anno Domini 1790	
Edwd. Dollin	Churchwardens
Willm. Harris	
Jno. Aslin	Overseers
Willm. Kent	

In his report on the "State of the Poor in England", in 1795, Sir Frederic Morton Eden confirmed that the Workhouse had been in use for many years and gave many interesting facts about the poor of Redbourn.[36]

Eden refers to the inmates as being 'farmed' and its master as the 'farmer'. This meant his salary was supplemented by what money his charges could be made to earn. His salary also had to be used to maintain them in clothes and food. Such an arrangement was obviously open to abuse by masters trying to maximise their salaries by cutting back on food and clothing.

However, Eden detailed the meals that were provided in the workhouse, these seemed fairly reasonable for that time, if they were truly as stated. Indeed, in giving similar information for the St Albans house, he said encouragingly that every person was *"allowed to eat till he is satisfied"*.[37]

The meals said to have been provided at Redbourn were as follows:-
> *"Breakfast, every day - Broth or gruel.*
> *Dinner, Sunday, Wednesday and Friday - Meat pudding, etc*
> *Monday and Thursday - Cold meat*
> *Tuesday and Saturday - Bread, cheese and beer*
> *Supper, every day - Bread, cheese and small beer"*

If this was indeed a truthful picture it seems to have contrasted with some other workhouses where masters of a mean and cruel disposition were appointed in order to discourage entrants and thus cut down on parish expenditure.[38] Another indication of a humane attitude here was that extra money was sometimes given when conditions deteriorated. Such instances occurred in 1794 when an extra £3 per month was allowed *"on account of the late dear season"*; and in 1800 when 6d extra per week was given to families with 2 or more children.[39]

Eden reported that in 1795 there were 30 inmates in the house and 22 housed elsewhere as 'out pensioners'. Workhouse Accounts do not distinguish between residents and non-residents; the totals between 1809 and 1820, being between 50 and 60, must include both categories.

Information between 1800 and 1836 is set out in a large book containing both the Workhouse Accounts and the minutes of the Vestry meetings.*(Fig: 9.5)* It is from this extremely interesting volume that most of my information has been compiled. (detail references are not given) From these, sometimes confusing records, it is difficult to arrive at a sensible statement of the finances for the house, however, some idea of the scale of the operation can be gained from the following figures:-

Expenses; for meat, bread etc (1800 - 1809) -	£320 to £894 pa.
Maintenance payments (1800 - 1811) -	£104 to £360 pa.
Maintenance payments to other parishes (1808 – 1815) -	£3 to £22 pa.
Salaries of the Master (1801-16) -	£26 to £62pa.
1817	£40 pa.
1819-32	3s. 6d. to 4s. 6d. per head per week
1833-4	£50 pa.
Salaries of the Doctor - 1812-19	£12 to £35 pa.
1820-34	£45 to £50 pa.

WORKHOUSE MASTERS

The workhouse master who Eden referred to as the 'Farmer' was not named, but by 1801 we hear of Luke Brickland of Hemel Hempstead, appointed at the same salary of £26.[40] His conditions as laid down by the Vestry were:-

> *"To live and inspect into the poor of the Workhouse and to keep them neat and clean and see that they go to work.   And   likewise...to find himself and family with tea, sugar and butter..."*

Thus he was not expected to feed them, only himself and family, but was still

Fig: 9.5 – Workhouse/Vestry book from 1800 (Left), page of payments (Right)

to 'farm' them out to work - their wages coming into the parish coffers. The Vestry themselves were to purchase - *"a sufficient quantity of Good Beef, Potatoes, Rice and other provisions for immediate consumption"*. It was also arranged that selected men should assemble every Friday morning to cut up, weigh the food and then deliver it to the Workhouse.

In 1803 there was a change in both the Master and the organisation of the house. Daniel Bull was to be paid £37-10s. per month, but out of this he was expected to *"furnish them with every thing that may be wanted and necessary for them to have, and keep them clean and decent"*. He also had to pay their weekly allowances out of his salary, including the paupers who lived elsewhere in the village.

In 1806 there was drama in the Vestry meeting. After agreeing to let Bull continue to be Master at a salary of £50 per month, a lower offer of £46.13.4d. was made by John Lines. This was an offer they could not refuse, so Lines was duly appointed at that salary. It would be interesting to know how much rivalry there was between the two men, both of whom were members of the Vestry, before and after the incident. Lines only stayed in the post for 3 years, after which Daniel Bull was re-instated, but at a much increased salary of £62. However, yet another applicant put up for Master in 1814, this was Thomas Farey, again at a lower salary - £56. The next year Bull was back yet again at £58 per month.

After a brief two years Thomas Potter, the next Master, drew up a completely new system of payment, which was accepted by the Vestry. Briefly the new system was to pay 4s.6d. per head per week for everyone living in the house, instead of a monthly or yearly salary. A stocktaking system also involved valuing everything in the house, including the clothes worn by the inmates. It was further required that Potter should teach the children *"in reading, spelling and the church catechism"* and to see that everyone who was able, went to church on Sunday.

By mid 1820 another Master was appointed, under the same system, this was William Stone. He held the post longer than anyone else, occupying the house for 12 years; even Bull had only logged 9, non-consecutive, years. At last the method of management had stabilised.

Major changes to the Workhouse itself began in 1833, and coincided with the election of the Curate, William Serocold Wade, as chairman of the Vestry meetings. The first thing he did was to advertise for an Assistant Overseer, Workhouse Master and Vestry Clerk, the applicant being expected to do all three jobs, and to be a married man *"without the encumbrance of a family"*.

A committee was set up to vet applicants; but the man they recommended turned out to be a bad choice as he quit the job after only 4 months. This was Charles Woods, he was succeeded by Thomas Collins of Rickmansworth, who was appointed at the same salary, £50 pa. However, the committee's new choice was still not a good one - after just 5 months they admitted that, though he was:-

> *"a highly respectable man... he has not hitherto shewn himself capable of keeping the parish accounts and documents as vestry clerk and that however they may feel well inclined towards him they are bound to declare that he is unable to fulfil his contract"*

The next, and final, appointment seems to have been a good man at last. James Greenwood undertook other jobs for the parish, as well as the three advertised a year earlier; becoming a Constable, Stonewarden as well as being trusted to bargain with local bakers over the price of bread for the workhouse.

DOCTORS TO THE POOR

The earliest we know of medical provision for the poor, is the case of *"Joseph Arnold's daughter"* in 1809.[41] The doctor in this case was Mr Kingston of St Albans who set, or re-set, the girl's broken arm at parish expense. Three years later the Vestry had woken up to the desirability of engaging a medical man, with a regular salary, to look after the sick paupers of the village.

Thus in 1812 Mr George Huston agreed to - *"...doctor all the poor in the parish that should happen as casualties as being parishioners, and them that are sent by the officers, as they may think are not able to pay for themselves"*

His salary was £12 per annum, and additionally he was allowed 14 shillings for each *"lying in"*, and expenses if he had to travel outside the parish. Huston's contract was renewed annually for the next five years, by which time it had increased to £35, with an additional 10s.6d. for midwifery cases beyond 4 miles.

The next Doctor to the Poor was Redbourn's most famous medical man - Henry Stephens (see chapter 9 for more details). His contract with the poor started in 1820, initially at a salary of £50, but after two years it was unaccountably dropped to £45. His terms were laid down in great detail, particularly with respect to journeys outside the parish, including any visit to London to procure admission of a patient to hospital there.

Stephens was followed by Thomas Trentham Irish, initially for the same £45 salary, but this was later reduced to only £40. His last contract before the closure of the Workhouse was recorded in 1835.

END OF THE WORKHOUSE ERA

In 1834 a major national change in the workhouse system began to take place. By Act of Parliament, the small village workhouses were to be gradually amalgamated into larger 'Union Workhouses'.[42] These 'Union Houses' were to be governed by Guardians under the Poor Law Commissioners.

The process began locally with the drawing in of all paupers to the village workhouse. No additional pensions were allowed and labourers living outside either had to find their own work or else to enter the house. The only exceptions to this rule were *"those of weak or imbecile mind"*. A court order was required by potential entrants, as a deterrent to easy entry.

The conditions within the house were also tightened up - segregation of the sexes was insisted upon, inmates being confined to their own "wards" or "yards" Allowances were subtlely adjusted so as to make it more worthwhile to seek work elsewhere.

At Redbourn the process began in earnest with the adoption by the Vestry of *"the plan pursued at Sandridge"*. This involved certain internal alterations to the house, presumably to do with segregation; remarkably both parishes spent the same amount (£200) and both had to raise a loan.[43]

Particulars of Sale, of a

Freehold Building
And Premises,

LATELY OCCUPIED AS

Redbourn
WORK HOUSE,

WHICH WILL BE SOLD BY AUCTION, BY

MR. RUMBALL,

AT THE BULL INN. REDBOURN,

On Wednesday, September 27th, 1837

At Three o'Clock in the Afternoon,

By order of the Board of Guardians of the St. Alban's Union, in One Lot.

This ESTATE is situate adjoining Redbourn Church Yard, the

WORK HOUSE

Is almost entirely Brick Built, and is Tiled, it is in good repair, and contains 8 long Garretts; 7 Chambers and a Store Room on the first floor; and on the ground floor, a Parlor, Kitchen, Brewhouse, (in which is a large Oven,) Pantrys, and a large Apartment used as Men's Dining Room. There are Two Yards, in which are a Range of Sheds, a Boarded and thatched Barn, a Wood House, and a Pump of Water; there is also a good Garden, with a small running stream at the end of it.

The main Building is of such dimensions, and so built, that it can with very little difficulty and expence be converted into about 8 Cottages with Out Buildings and Gardens, or it is well adapted for any sort of Manufactory, and in a Neighbourhood where there is no other Manufactory, and therefore where hands could be readily obtained.

May be viewed at any time by applying on the Premises. Particulars may be had at the Place of Sale ; of R. G. Lowe, Esq. Solicitor; and of Mr. Rumball, Land Surveyor and Auctioneer, and Agent to the Sun Fire and Life Offices, St. Albans.

☞ The Conditions will be produced and read at the Sale, being the same as those under which several Sales of Property have been made in the same Union.

Langley, Letter-press and Lithographic Printer, High Street, St. Albans.

Fig: 9.6 - Sale notice for Redbourn Workhouse, 1837

By 1836 a great reduction in the number of Paupers in local houses had taken place and centralisation began. Redbourn workhouse was closed and its inmates transferred to St Stephens workhouse in St Albans; while *"the able bodied and worst description of paupers"* were sent to Sandridge. The final stage came with the opening of Oysterhills workhouse at St Albans in 1838.[44]

In the autumn of 1836 application was made to the Commissioners for permission to sell the Redbourn workhouse and 18 cottages at Wood End, Holtsmere End, Library Lane, South End, Crackabones, Hog End and near the Punchbowl. These had been used to accommodate the poor. *(see Fig: 9.6)*

The sale notice gives the only picture of the inside of the house- *Fig: 9.6.*[45]:-

> *On the ground floor, a Parlour, Kitchen, Brewhouse (in which is a large oven) Pantrys, and a large apartment used as Men's Dining Room. There are two Yards, in which are a range of sheds, a boarded, thatched Barn, a Wood House and a pump of water; there is also a good Garden with a small running stream at the end of it"*

The sale notice went on to suggest that the building could be converted into about 8 cottages or adapted *"for some sort of manufactory"*. Thankfully the latter idea was not taken up and thus, instead of it being made into a factory, we now have an attractive row of cottages. The house was bought by James Greenwood and William Weir, acting on behalf of Joseph Abbot, the landlord of the Hollybush, on the opposite side of the road. Some collusion must be suspected as Greenwood was the last Master of Redbourn Workhouse and Weir Master of Sandridge Workhouse and later the first Master of Oysterhills. The sale of the Workhouse enabled the parish debt of £200 to Mr Cane to be paid off with a bit to spare.

This was not the end of village involvement with their poor, money still had to be raised by means of the Poor Rates to maintain those at Oysterhills - for example in 1838 £20 was required for 75 paupers there. The Vestry was not always too happy about the demands made on it by the Board of Guardians, but they agreed to pay the £72 demanded in 1841 for the enlargement and alteration of the Union Workhouse. In 1894 they protested that *"continued increased expenditure...more than exhausts the relief which we expected to get from the extra contribution made by the Government to the County Council"*

REFERENCES

1   Wills of the Old Archdeaconry of St. Albans, kept in the HRO.
2   PRO, ref. PROB.11/58
3   Further Report of the Charity Commissioners 1815-39" p.289
4   Book of Receipts and Disbursements, ref. RC/11

5   As 4, Accounts 1884, ref. RC/12
6   Parish Magazine February 1964
7   As 3, pp.290-1
8   Alan Featherstone "The Mills of Redbourn", pp.17-8, with references
9   As 3, pp.291-2
10   As 3, p.292
11   As 3, p.292
12   As 4, Mary Peacock Charity, ref. RC/1
13   As 4, Sophia Baskerfield Charity, ref. RC/2
14   As 4, ref. RC/3
15   As 4, ref. RC/4
16   As 4, ref. RC/6
17   May Walker - "Redbourn", p.44
18   As 4, ref. RC/12
19   As 17, p.45
20   As 4, ref. RC/8
21   Parish Magazine February 1963
22   As 4, ref. RC/9
23   Parish Magazine July 1964
24   St Albans Library ref. Y.222, pamphlet 17
25   Printed books of Session records of the Liberty of St Albans, Vol. IV, pp.44-142
     Except for the "Hollybush"
26   Parish and School accounts and reports - those I have seen are held by Mr Cyril
     Harling
27   The Local Historian's Encyclopaedia (Ed) John Richardson ref. K5
28   As 27 ref. K.10
29   As 27 ref. B.179
30   As 27 ref. K.11
31   Printed books of Session records of St Albans, Vols. II to IX
32   As 31 Vol. I, p.266
33   Parish Chest - "Orderly Book and Workhouse Accounts"
34   As 27, ref K.14
35   Victoria County History, Vol. 1, P.370, note 133
36   Sir F. M. Eden - "The State of the Poor" pp.206-7
37   As 36, p.206
38   As 36, p.73+
39   As 36, p.207
40   As 33
41   As 33
42   John G. C. Cox - "St Albans & West Herts News of 1890", pp.195 & 236
43   R. G. Auckland - "Sandridge Workhouse", p.13
44   As 43, p.16
45   Sale leaflet, 1837, and details of sale by Mr Rumball, given to me by Mrs J. Mary
     Moyse

CHAPTER 10

VILLAGE TRADES AND OCCUPATIONS

This chapter could rightly start in Mesolithic times with the known manufacture of flint tools just to the west of the High Street (see chapter 1). Undoubtedly the earliest occupation still practised is farming, which dates back at least to the Iron Age farmers of "The Aubreys". From farming, men with individual skills in trades such as blacksmithing, carpentry, the care and management of animals, etc., developed.

It is difficult to do more than guess when early trades were first followed. Written mentions do not generally appear until the 16th century Church Registers. The 17th century Militia Lists are also useful, but it is not until the Trade Directories and Census Returns of the 19th century that a picture of the whole parish can be seen.

It is obviously not possible to discuss, or even list all the occupations known from the above sources, but an attempt will be made to cover the common trades as well as others, which are of more than passing interest.

FARMING

The first farmers in Redbourn were the men who built "The Aubreys" Iron Age site, but it was over a thousand years before a village settlement emerged out of the many isolated farm clearings, or 'Ends', by late Saxon times. (see chapter 1)

By the time of the Domesday Book a well established farming community flourished under the Lordship of the Abbot of St Albans. By c.1344 we learn the names of the chief tenants from a taxation list for the Abbot (Chapter 3). While a 1455 Rental gives a further update and much more information about their farms and valuations (Chapter 6) No other comprehensive list of tenants is seen until a survey of 1609 gives almost complete information about each farm and its farmer.

The title 'farmer' does not appear in writing until a will of 1634; prior to this they are called 'Husbandmen' or 'Yeomen'.[1] The latter being freehold tenants who were almost of gentleman status, except that they still worked with their hands; people like the Beeches, Finches, Hawkins and Peacocks etc., in farms like Nicholls, Beason End, Wood End etc.[2]

Early documents concentrated on the value and extent of the holdings rather than on the farmers themselves or those who worked for them. It is not until the advent of the Census Returns of the 19th century that we obtain a complete picture of the people of the village and learn what their occupations actually were.

A Trade Directory of 1823/4, stated that Redbourn market sold - *"considerable numbers of sheep and other cattle"*. The number of Cowmen, Herdsmen, and Shepherds (12 shepherds in 1861) indicate that there were significant herds of cattle and sheep.

Dairy farming first appears in the 1881 Census with George Webb at the Dairy farm on the Common; it survives elsewhere to day, as "Redbourn Dairy"

The effect of the Industrial Revolution can be glimpsed in the existence of a steam ploughing team in the village from 1871 with Edwin Brown as both manager and engineer. Edwin Brown took his engines beyond the village, once getting into trouble for obstructing the road with *"an engine and two large machines"* at Sandridge *where* they had stopped to take on water.[3] Edwin Brown did not get all the village custom, in 1878 G. Edwards of Luton did *"Steam cultivation"*.[4] Steam was also used for thrashing and later for rolling roads surfaces. In modern times an interest in steam has preserved many such engines, even using them to demonstrate the old techniques.

WATERCRESS GROWING

It is not known when watercress (Nasturtium officinale) first grew locally; it could have existed naturally with the reeds of Redbourn and been eaten by Stone Age men.

To successfully grow watercress a plentiful supply of spring water of constant temperature is needed; such conditions are found along the Ver and many other Hertfordshire rivers. For successful commercial cultivation a good transport system to the best markets, such as London, is also essential. The main road, Watling Street, and later the railway system, provided ideal transport for local growers. However, with competition from the beds in Hampshire, which had a longer growing season and equally good transport to London, the local beds lost business and declined.

Fig: 10.1 Watercress Beds in Waterend Lane
Notice the baskets in which the cress was sent to market

Fig: 10.2 Thomas Sansom
Watercress Grower

The earliest known Redbourn grower was William Payne who lived at "Watercress Hall", beside the Ver to the south of the village. He lived here from at least 1862 to 1890, styling himself as "Master Watercress Grower".[5] A later and perhaps better known grower was Thomas Sansom. He lived in "Ver House" in the High Street and came from a family of watercress growers whose members had other beds at Boxmoor, Rickmansworth and Welwyn.[6]

In more recent times the beds were cultivated by the late Walter Vise who lived at "Do-Little Mill House". He contributed an article to the 1960 Common Round stating that Redbourn was one of the first places to send watercress to the London wholesale markets. He recalled the Londoner's love of winkles and watercress for Sunday tea and the familiar London street cry of - *"Any watercress today ma'am?"*

TRAVELLERS AND CATERERS

From the time when the Romans built Watling Street this area has been associated with a great number of travellers and pilgrims. In Medieval times villagers recognised their opportunity to cash-in on these opportunities and began the move away from the old village at Church End, to today's High Street.

Much later, during the stage-coaching era, and probably long before that, the village hostelries were particularly well known for providing good food. The many inns catering for all kinds of travellers have already been mentioned in chapter 7 and the records are littered with names of Inn Holders, Publicans, Victuallers and the occasional Tap Keeper.

There were also many other men taking part in providing or operating coaches, such as - Coach proprietors, Coachmen, Guards, Hostlers (Ostlers), Grooms, Farriers, Saddlers, Harness-makers, Horse trainers etc. Then there were men who built and repaired the vehicles Coachmakers, Blacksmiths, Carpenters, Wheelwrights (Wheelers). All these appear in the records from the 16th century, but were obviously already well established trades by then.

Fig: 10.3 - Three generations of Blacksmith
Left to Right - Will, Bill & Joe Sibley

Fig: 10.4 - Bill Sibley at work

The last of these trades to die out has been that of the Blacksmith. Bill Sibley was the last of a long line of village blacksmiths, succeeding both his Father and Grandfather in the trade. As a village trade they were beginning to die out in the late 19th century. Bill Sibley gave up his forge in 1960.[7]

The coming of the railways saw the sudden demise of stage coaching in this country and the loss of many trades and occupations connected with it. A few men were able to find employment with the new railway companies, particularly when the 'Nickey' branch line was built in 1877 (Chapter 7). The Census Returns show that George Ashley was the first Station Master at Redbourn until at least the end of the century. Also living in the village in 1891 were - 5 Engine Drivers, 4 Porters, a Signalman and 4 Railway Labourers. A man described himself as a "Gauger" in the Registers - perhaps another name for a Plate Layer, of which there were 5 in 1891.

The transition from coaching to the motor age is seen in the Walker's garage business in the High street. In 1910 W. Walker was a "Wheelwright", but five years later he and his sons are described as "coach and motor body builders".[8] A nice reminder of the old garage, is the recently restored forecourt clock.

BUILDERS

It was not until the early crude buildings of the common people started to be replaced by small timber-framed houses, copying those of the yeomen farmers, that the skills of the carpenter were required. The Carpenter family of Redbourn House (chapter 8) obviously owed their name to an ancestor who plied this trade.

Sawyers were essential to convert trees into suitable timber for the carpenters. The earliest to be seen in the records date from the 1768 Militia List; by 1861 there were 10 in the Census Return. An essential tool of their trade (besides the saw) was a saw-pit. These could be dug anywhere to suit either the work in hand or the site of timber to be felled. The site of several of these in the parish are known from field names and traces of pits which have been found. Some that I have come across are :-

> Sawpit wood, near St Agnells
> Upper Sawpit field
> Lower Sawpit field
> Sawpit Orchard
> Sawpit field, near Butlers Farm
> Sawpit Wick, near Nicholls Farm

The early use of bricks for building is usually associated with Tudor times, but they were not used for the houses of the common people until much later. A Brick Maker is recorded in 1831 and 1841. He may have used the small field at Redbournbury called "Brick Kiln Mead". This was obviously a small scale operation, and none of its bricks have been identified in the adjacent farm or mill.

The earliest bricklayer I can find was John Sparkes, the elder, who died in 1668.[9] By the 1891 Census there were 12 bricklayers living in the village.

Though glass has been used to glaze windows from Roman times it was only commonly seen in ecclesiastical buildings, or in a few of the larger houses. In humbler dwellings window openings only had semi-opaque coverings or were completely open but with shutters to keep out the worst weather. The earliest records I know are of "*P Seaben 1758*", etched on a window pane in St Mary's Church and "John Reading, glazier" in the 1762 Militia List.

The actual name "Builder" does not appear until Walter Kent took his son to church for baptism in 1815.

Fig: 10.5 - Walker's builders at work on Crouch Hall Gardens

MILLS AND MILLERS

The history of the two Watermills have been described in chapters 2 and 6. The present mill at Redbournbury was built initially by Samuel Clover in 1694, and has since been much altered, chiefly in the 18th and 19th centuries.[10] Its machinery dates from the late 19th century and the installation of a steam engine, to supplement water power, was tried between c.1899 and 1916.

In the mid 20th century it was run by Ivy Hawkins, who came from a long line of millers, taking over from her father, Henry, in 1932. A Times article gave her unwanted notoriety as the only Lady Miller in the country. She was well known locally especially for the occasion when she nearly lost her life. She had gone inside the wheel to tighten some nuts when it began to turn, she became trapped between a spoke and the axle support, remaining thus for about an hour.

Fig: 10.6 - Ivy Hawkins at work in Redbournbury Mill   *Fig: 10.7 – Ivy in her 20's*

After a serious fire in 1987 the mill has been completely restored with a grant from English Heritage, by the present owners, the James family. They have repeated history by installing an auxiliary diesel engine, siting it where the earlier steam engine had been.

The other Redbourn Watermill, initially called "Bettespool Mill", (Later Little or Do-Little Mill) went through a similar chequered history of rebuilding. Between 1666 and 1706 it did not exist at all, having been demolished and its land used as a small holding. A new mill was built by Thomas Dagnall, and soon after converted for Paper making (see next section). After a fire, it reverted to grinding corn until final closure came, and despite a desperate attempt to modernise by installing a water-turbine, milling ceased in c.1928.

Fig: 10.8 – Redbourn Little Mill (LHS), Mill House and Pond (RHS), c.1920

The Dagnall family, who were well known millers and millwrights in Hertfordshire, besides operating the "Little Mill" for nearly 50 years, also built a Windmill - in "Windmill Field" nearly opposite the "Punchbowl". It existed roughly between 1718 and 1753 and would most probably have been of the 'Post' type in which the whole mill was rotated to face into the wind on a sturdy vertical post. Its fate after such a short life is not known, but could have been from a number of natural causes or just that it was removed to another location for economic reasons.

PAPERMAKERS

For just 30 years paper was made at the Little Mill, during which time it was called "Redbourn Paper Mill".[11] In 1753 it was leased to John Vowell, a stationer from London, with its *"going gears and implements"* and converted to the making of paper. For this the millstones were not required, instead, a Rag-Stamper had to be installed to produce a pulp similar to wallpaper paste, which was suitable for making paper. – see *Fig: 10.9*

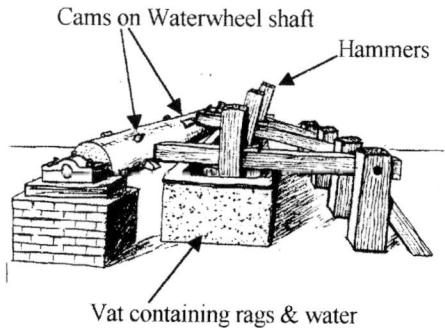

Cams on Waterwheel shaft

Hammers

Vat containing rags & water

Fig: 10.9 - A Typical Rag-Stamper

The Militia lists between 1753 and 1783 gave the names of many of the paper makers working here, but among them the Stratton family predominates. As manager, Hugh Stratton took out a fire insurance on the property and its contents, with the Sun Fire Office, for a total of £400.[12] After a fire in 1783, a payment was made for *"his loss"* of £230 covering the insurance value of the mill and it's contents, but not a separate drying shed or the mill house across the road, which were presumably left undamaged.

No attempt was made to restore the mill to its previous use, instead it was rebuilt as a corn mill. Some of the insurance money was used for this purpose, Hugh Stratton keeping £100 as compensation for his loss of paper and equipment. His employees would have found work in the paper mills in the nearby Gade valley.

MALTING AND BREWING

Barley was first malted and fermented for ale about 6000 years ago; the Romans knew the process but preferred to import wine from Italy. It was the Saxons who popularised the drinking of ale. In the Monastries brewing was carried on by the Cellerar, quite a vital man at the Abbey, especially when important visitors came.

Barley was the chief ingredient, but other cereals or potatoes were also used.[13] After malting, or heating in a kiln, the barley was ground or milled and added to water, together with sugar and yeast. Grinding of the barley was carried out at Redbourn Little Mill, called the "Malt Mill" at least between 1511 and 1669.[14]

The following is a list of references that I have found to Redbourn Malthouses:-

> 1602 - A malt house of three bays (nearly 50 feet long) owned by John Haward and Rowlatt; the latter name suggests that this may have been at Beason End, where Ralph Rowlatt of St Albans held property.[15]
>
> 1609-1611 - References to a Malthouse adjacent to Revel End farm.[16]
>
> 1636 - A malthouse was part of the Bell and Shears, but by 1692 it was referred to as *"a cottage, heretofore a malthouse"*.[17]
>
> 1665 - A malthouse near Beaumont Hall Farm.[18]
>
> 1665-1674 - A malthouse built with a house and barn on a former orchard behind the "Woolsack" inn.[19]
>
> 1692-1799 - Another, built by Richard Sparks near Fish Street Farm [20] was still referred to as *"Sparke's Malthouse"* over 100 years later.[21]

An essential part of a malthouse was a spacious floor on which the barley could be spread out to germinate, Haward's 3 bay building is a good example. By comparison, the area required for a brewery, especially for a small operator, was quite small and thus often gets overlooked in documents. The earliest Brewer noted is Thomas Whitehead in 1611.[22] Another is Thomas Beech, who took out fire insurance on his property, part of the Cock Inn, in 1718.[23]

It is logical that at the height of the stage-coaching era in the 19th century we should see several breweries in Redbourn, mostly attached to High Street inns:-

> 1854 - James Hawkes and Robert Home, brewers, the latter at the "Bull".[24]
>
> 1859 - J. Puddephat named as a Redbourn brewer.[25]
>
> 1866-1878 - Redbourn Brewery was run by Thomas and John Edwards.[26]

Benjamin Bennett took over from the Edwards' in 1881 - see Brewery cart in the "Bull" yard, *Fig 10.10*. Sixteen years later he auctioned it together with 10 inns [27] Mc. Mullins bought the "Bull" but were not interested in brewing there; the other inns were also bought by brewers, illustrating the common practice of the 'tied system' of ensuring outlets for their own beers.

Fig: 10.10 – Bennetts Brewery 1897

The 1897 sale document gives a description of the property. Behind the inn there was a *"spacious yard"*, with stabling for 10 horses,*(A)* coach house *(B)* and outbuildings. Brew House *(C)* for *"a Five-Quarter Plant"*, Boiler house,*(D)* Mill room, Storerooms,*(E)* Cooperage (for casks), Tun room and Cellars. A Malting *(F)* contained a kiln, and large barn, the plan shown on *Fig: 10.11* shows the location of these brewing facilities. The inn itself is also listed as having an entrance hall, large bar, bar parlour, private sitting room, lofty billiard room *(G)* 32' x 22', eight bedrooms and other domestic and service rooms Brewing had become big business, but there was - still room for the small man such as those brewing and selling beer from their own houses. These were known as Beer Shops and were usually unlicensed, several are mentioned in Redbourn some later becoming named inns.

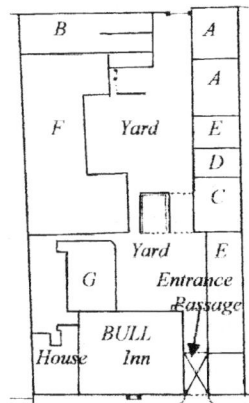

Fig: 10.11 - Plan of the "Bull"

     Perhaps the best known beer shop was that held by James Smith the official Rat-Catcher of the Gorhambury Estate.[28] He bought beer and started to retail it from his home until brought before the magistrates for selling without a licence.

However, the Earl, his employer, intervened and showed him how to apply for a licence. This was granted and the "Three Horseshoes" sign went up; the 1861 Census shows him at *"The Horses, beer shop"*. His daughter married George Thorogood who was landlord in 1871, by which time it had become "The Cricketers". Strangely there was a James Smith who was rat/mole catcher to Lord Salisbury at Hatfield in about 1855.[29]

Fig: 10.12 - the "Cricketers Inn"

MEDICAL PEOPLE

In Monastic times it was mostly the monks who possessed the medical skill to mix herbal potions to treat the sick, and to nurse them back to health in their Infirmaries. They not only nursed sick monks, but also visited beyond the Abbey walls to care for the local people. When sick monks were recovering they would be sent to recuperate at the Priory; thus the Prior or his assistants must have possessed some medical or nursing skills.

     Medical people also existed outside the monasteries with a hierarchy headed by the top university degree of 'Doctor of Medicine' from the 14th century. 'Physician' may have been the title under which they practised and they were

Chartered from 1518. Physicians did not normally operate, but left Surgeons to carry out all but major cases. 'Surgeons' were thus the craftsmen, who from 1540 were members of the Guild of Barbers, gaining their own charter in 1800. Lowest in the chain, but just as ancient, were the 'Apothecaries', being members of the Grocers Guild from 1345. They dispensed drugs, gained the right to prescribe in 1542 and gained their own charter from 1618.

The earliest records of **Doctors** or **Surgeons** appear in the Militia Lists – Joseph Law, 1758-68 and John Hawkins, 1772-86. The latter was probably the grandson of George, the apothecary. About this time Harriet Grimston, of Gorhambury, made a recipe to cure the Ague and claimed that people living in St Albans and Redbourn had been cured.[30]

In 1809 Mr Kingston, a surgeon of St Albans was called in to cure Joseph Arnold's daughter, whose arm had been incorrectly set, resulting in her becoming a cripple.[31] This incident may have had the effect of alerting the Vestry to the desirability of having medical assistance in the parish, dedicated (or paid) to look after the poor or any others who became sick.

For this purpose they contracted with George Huston to be doctor to the poor people of the parish, agreeing to pay him £12 pa. and 14 shillings for each *"lying of a woman"* (i.e. midwifery). This was in 1812, the following year his salary was increased to £35 and he continued to serve the Vestry until about 1818.

About this time, Henry Stephens, an up and coming young doctor appeared on the Redbourn scene. He had come to the village at the age of 5 when his father took over as landlord of the Bull inn.[32] After being apprenticed to Dr. Wingfield of Markyate, he studied medicine at Guys and St Thomas's hospitals in London, qualifying in 1816. In his student days he shared lodgings with John Keats, the poet, and is said to have suggested an alteration to a line in his long poem "Endymion", changing it from - *"a thing of beauty is a constant joy"* to the often quoted - *"a thing of beauty is a joy for ever."* In 1820 he was offered the same post as Huston, but at the increased salary of £50. For this he agreed to attend the poor of the parish within a 10 mile radius *"including midwifery, surgical operations, fractures and other accidents or injuries"* He once diagnosed a woman seriously ill with a hernia and, after overcoming much reluctance from her family, carried out a successful operation (without the use of chloroform); he later wrote his procedure as a Treatise.

Fig: 10.13 - Henry Stephens

Besides being a fine Doctor, Stephens also acted a Vet for the Gorhambury Hounds and received a picture as thanks for his treatment of them. He was fond of horses, holding a contract to supply teams for one stage of the Royal Mail coaches.. A local resident commented on his fine horsemanship as follows:-

"It was a sight to see him ride up the street; we all used to come out and look at him, a fine rider he was"

While living at Redbourn he is thought to have occupied the house just to the north of "The Ruins" passage. It is said that his Mother continued to live there after he moved to London, and if news got around that he was visiting her, a queue would form, obliging him to use her kitchen as a surgery.

It was said that his methods were in advance of common practice and his surgical skills much before their time. These abilities attracted the attention of Sir Ashley Cooper, physician/surgeon to the King, who lived at Hemel Hempstead. He thought that Stephen's talents were wasted in Redbourn and persuaded him to move to London. This he did in 1828, where certainly these talents were put to better use in research, writing, lecturing etc.

Writing must have alerted him to the unsatisfactory nature of available materials; and led him to develop an improved ink. The manufacture of "Stephens Blue-Black Ink", became a family affair, eventually being taken over by his son Charles, later known as "Inky Stephens".

Its waterproof qualities were proved by the legibility of salvaged documents from shipwrecks.[33] It is interesting to note that the small house attached to his former Redbourn home is said to have earlier been occupied by a well known maker of quill pens - a nice connection with ink! [34] He also patented various pens and inkstands, as well as developing wood stains, which were used in the Great Exhibition of 1851.

Henry Stephens died suddenly on Farringdon Station in 1864, age 68.[35]

Thomas Trentham Irish, occupied the same house that Stephens is thought to have lived in; but had a new door put in one of the front rooms so that it could be used as a surgery.[36]

It was always the practice that inoculations were not included in the doctor's salaries. The reason is apparent in 1833 when Dr. Irish was contracted to vaccinate the poor at 2 shillings a head, quite an expense on the parish. Irish continued as Doctor to the poor until the workhouse closed. A succession of doctors followed, one was Joseph Brockway Ayre, from 1850 until his wife's death in 1861. In 1892 the house which is thought to have been Henry Stephen's, came up for sale; then occupied by Dr. Disney, the sale document particularly mentioned *"a newly erected surgery"*.[37]

In more recent times many villagers still remember Dr. Jurion Totton who served here for 38 years from 1924, living in the same house as Disney, and commemorated by a stained glass window in St Marys church. More recently Dr. Lindsey Miller served from 1952 to 1992, and Dr Turnbull for a similar period.

The earliest village **apothecary** I can find was George Hawkins who died in 1722.[38] Henry Pitkin, a 'Druggist', had a shop in the High Street in 1839, followed by, James Harrison, 'Druggist and Chemist', in 1850.[39] Our present Chemist most probably occupies the same shop.

Of our modern Chemists undoubtedly the best known and loved was the late George Wilson. He served the village from 1937 to 1978 and lifted the spirits of many depressed customers with his cheerful banter.[40] Strangely there was a doctor with exactly the same name in 1890 Kellys Directory, probably no relation to George.

It has for long been the women who have provided the nursing skill, at first in the home and later in hospitals. **Nurses**, Midwives etc are largely unmentioned in records until the Census returns, which lists Night Nurses, Monthly Nurses, Nurse Maids. Of roughly the same period as George Wilson, District Nurse Trudgett, affectionately known as 'Trudge' served the village. She was awarded the MBE in 1954 for her work here, which included delivering 2500 babies.[41]

In medieval times, Redbourn became a refuge for monks trying to escape the Black Death (chapter 5). There is no record of deaths among either the villagers or monks at that time. Other plagues can be deduced from the Burial Registers.

In 1574 sixty people died, 3 times the normal death rate, some households suffered up to five losses. Just 28 years before the Great Plague in London - "*A mayd, being a stranger from the Black Lyon*" died, and within 3 months there were another 16 deaths, all from "*the Plague*", another victim also coming from the Black Lion. In the same year that Dr. Irish carried out inoculations in the village (1833) there had been 13 deaths from Cholera.

Before the end of the 18th century Redbourn had its own isolation hospital. This was run by Rebecca Brandreth, who had lost two brothers in childhood, one from Smallpox at the age of 15. Rebecca died in 1799 at a ripe old age. This hospital is remembered in 1811 as - "*two cottages at Frogmore, lately used as a Pest House*".[42] Frogmore was on the other side of the Moor near Church End.

A century later the matter came up again when it was proposed to have an isolation hospital in the village. This immediately proved to be a sensitive matter and the cause of great concern to villagers. In 1908 the siting for a Smallpox Hospital was discussed by the Council, possible sites being at Crouch Hall Farm, "Fillpockets Field" (near Wood End), and "Old Woman's Field" (near New Jeromes?).[43] Another position at Bylands was viewed with alarm by the Council.

The solution came the following year with the gift of land by Mr Dunn at Cherry Trees Farm, but with strict instructions that [44] - *"no smallpox patients are to be brought through the High Street, across the Common, or via Church End"*. Its first Matron was Miss E. M. Banner. It was sold as a private residence by the Ministry of Health in 1952. *Figs: 10.14 and 10.15* show its plan and present appearance.[45]

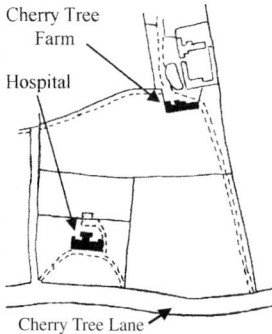

Fig: 10.14 - Outline Plan of Smallpox Hospital, 1936

Fig: 10.15 – Present appearance of former Isolation Hospital

In spite of all this experience, Redbourn was very short-sighted as regards the need for sanitation and a good water supply. Mr White, of Cumberland House" wrote a long letter to the Herts Advertiser in 1861 arguing against a new sewerage system for the parish. He pointed out that all the cases of fever had been brought into the village from elsewhere. Concluding that a sewerage system was *"the greatest delusion which it is possible to imagine"*, advocating instead a scavenging system which he said would pay for itself.

His views resulted in all plans being put 'on hold' for many years; even when the St Albans Rural Sanitary Authority proposed the laying of sewers in 1873, the Vestry only appointed a sub-committee. The Herts Advertiser reported in 1879 that this committee said that such a system was not needed; expense being the key word. The same attitude was taken towards the piped supply of fresh water. Writing from memory in 1965, "Greensward" commented on this long running affair.[46]

> *"For years the sanitary conditions in Redbourn were appalling - how the Parish Council fought against it, to them it was a waste of money. What was wrong with the sail carts collecting refuse in the middle of the night? Our forefathers were satisfied with these conditions, and what was good enough for them was good enough for us!" At last common sense prevailed, as German bombers were overhead, Redbourn was in the middle of having a sewage system installed"*

Plans for a Mains Drainage system were approved in 1937.[47]

Until 1745 the **barbers** controlled the 'craft of surgery' which included **dentistry**, with the Act of that year the two were separated, but each retained the right to extract teeth and this remained so until.1878 when an Act of Parliament instituted a register of Dentists under the General Medical Council.

Almost certainly, James Miles, who was a barber until his death in 1692, was also our local extractor of teeth.[48] Frederick George Boucher who has already been mentioned as the owner of the first car in Redbourn; was also village dentist. He lived here at least between 1899 and 1915 and became much involved in local affairs, being an active member of the Parish Council and for a time its chairman.

LAW KEEPERS AND BREAKERS

Saxon Abbot Leofstan granted Flamstead to Turnot, a knight, and his two companions, provided that they protected the manor from *"numerous robbers and hurtful beasts"*.[49] In 1401 this condition was still in force, now applying to Watling Street from Redbourn to Markyate. I can only find one recorded case of Highway Robbery near Redbourn, this was in 1585 when Richard Hudson a labourer of Stevenage, assaulted John Bannister and stole 50 shillings from him.[50]

Murder has touched Redbourn many times, perhaps the first being that of the Vicar, discussed in chapter 4. In 1538 a gang came before a St Albans Justice of the Peace for the murder of John Lion.[51] They consisted of a man and his wife, a single woman and Thomas Langford, the chief suspect. Before the crime they had visited 11 places in the county, but never stopped more than a few days in any of them. Then they came to *"my Lady of Norfolk's place"* at Redbourn (Possibly Redbournbury).

They then went to *"the alehouse at the upper end of the town"* (perhaps the Red Lion). When they left there, the two women were sent ahead to find lodging and to beg on their way - this sounds like their normal practice, conveniently leaving the men, unhindered, to rob and steal, and perhaps murder, on their way.

They rather gave themselves away when it was later told that a man, John Lion was dead, one of them said - *what a pity that he was murdered"*. The most poignant evidence was blood on Langford's shirt, which he tried to blame on a nose bleed. We do not know the outcome of the case, but it would seem highly likely that Langford and possibly his companion ended up on the gallows.

Thirty-five years later, William Fynche and his wife were more fortunate, after being indicted for murdering Dorothy Forde and robbing her of a gown, petticoat, linen, a purse and two gold rings - they were found not guilty [52] There were many cases of assault, some apparently quite minor such as when Feanna French had struck William Countys in the Churchyard in 1616.[53]

In 1799 a rather complicated incident of threatened assault occurred within the Workhouse.[54] A woman had been collecting stones for road repairs with two male inmates. The men connived together to overcharge the Master by two loads, but kept their scheme from the woman; refusing to share with her when she found out. After reporting them to the Workhouse Master, one of the men threatened to *"knock her brains out against the copper"* or the throw her in the pond. Next day she became ill after eating her broth and suspected that she had been poisoned. The truth came out when a serving girl confessed to adding something to the broth that one of the men had given her. The outcome was unfortunately not recorded.

The the murder of Sarah Seabrooke in c.1920 was described by Geoff Webb as *"one of the saddest happenings in Redbourn history"* [55] She was bludgeoned to death by a petty thief with a hammer. The murderer, a boy, deposited the hammer in a well,where it was later found.

Fig: 10.16. - Funeral Cortège for Mrs Sarah Seabrooke, murdered c.1920

Cases of theft were fairly common, some more dramatic than others, like that of the cross stolen from the Priory in 1215. Some were quite audacious, like the gang who stole 12 oxen from London Colney in 1269 and got as far as Redbourn before they were caught. All but one managed to escape, this unfortunate being left to suffer capital punishment for them all.[56] Another rustler of 19 sheep from Caddington in 1597 was "allowed Clergy" and avoided punishment.[57] But a few years later the theft of 5 hens incurred whipping.[58]

Many petty crimes were carried out because of abject poverty. Such as poor Mary Mead, who stole rags from her employer, a Bleacher of rags for the paper industry, in 1796.[59] Perhaps the rags that Mary was sorting were better than her own or her children's clothes?

In 1855 Benjamin Taylor, who worked for Mr Webb at Beaumont Hall, was rather unnecessarily taken to court over a misunderstanding.[60] He had taken his normal allocation of wheat to the Little Mill to have it ground, thinking that a fellow worker had cleared it with Mr Webb. The Farm Steward's wife reported him to the police and the case had to go to court. Mr Webb said the message had not reached him; he gave Taylor a good character, saying he had worked for him for about 20 years. Taylor was acquitted.

Other cases of theft in the mid 19th century illustrate English Justice at work.[61] James Abbot, for stealing a "pottle of peas" had the option of a half crown fine or seven days in gaol. For poaching an eel from the river near Fish Street Farm, James Feary was fined two pounds with 13s.6d costs.

Thomas Thorogood was more seriously involved, having said he had 'found' some lead in Waterend Lane. He sent it to a St Albans warehouse by donkey cart and negotiated its sale to someone in "The Lark" for five shillings, but settled for 3s.3d. and a pot of beer. It actually came from the roof of Redbourn House.

The **Constables** were responsible at local level for the apprehension of felons, but well off property owners sought to add their weight, and money, to the recovery of property. This is shown by a board hanging in Wardown Museum, Luton, giving details of a - *"Society for the Security of persons and property in the parishes of Redbourn, Harpenden, St Michaels, Kensworth and Flamstead"*. dated 1801 this gives a long list of rewards for information, ranging from £15 for livestock, to 10s. for vegetables etc. The Earl of Verulam was the chief subscriber

Constables were basically untrained and unpaid men, elected on an annual basis, by the Parish Vestry. The earliest name I can find was William Fynche - could this be the same man accused of murder 12 years earlier? [62]

Their duties extended far beyond arresting felons and keeping public order in the village and its ale houses. They had to report anyone not attending church, help parish officers in the relief of the poor as well as dealing with vagrants (see case on page 146). In the latter part of the 19th century they had to submit lists of men eligible for service in the militia as well as to help with their training.

Sometimes the work was dangerous, as Constable Trott found in 1620. [63] He was called from his bed in the night because of fighting between some men in the High Street, and in spite of calling other men to help him - *"he received ten several wounds by means whereof he lost the use of some of his lymmes"* He subsequently said he had spent most of his "estate" trying to cure himself and asked the court for a life pension and was granted 20s.

In 1820 the Vestry meeting received a most unusual request from the Constable and the Overseer. They had 'affected entry' into the house of William Barnard Bacon, for some unstated reason, and sought the support of the Vestry for their action; they were wisely advised to seek legal advice

If someone was arrested they had to be detained in the local lock-up or cage. After 1707 this was in the Market House which had been built on the site of the "Woolpack" inn in the High Street.. [64] During the 20th century there was a small Police Station at the corner of Fish Street with a lock-up; in recent times it was demolished to widen the access to Fish Street Corner *Fig. 10.17.*

Fig: 10.17 - Police Station, corner house on left, Police cart in right foreground

The Census Returns give the names of the Redbourn Constables from 1841. In 1891 there were two Sergeants. An unusual resident was recorded in the same year - *"John Croome, Superintendent Detective Sergeant 1st class, Chief Officer of the Metropolitan Police, now employed as Superintendent Officer of the premises of the Civil Service Co-operative Society"*

FIRES AND FIREMEN

When Redbournbury Mill burned down at the end of the 13th century there was no fire engine or firemen, the same was the case when the great fires of 1674 ravaged the village. On those occasions all able-bodied people would have turned out to try to extinguish the flames with buckets filled from the Ver. However, things may have changed by 1783 when Redbourn Paper Mill suffered a serious fire (page 163), it was insured with the Sun Fire Office, who may have been able to provide some sort of fire-fighting equipment.

Sun policies had also been taken out on the Cock, Rose and Crown, Bull and the Swan, with all these properties it may just have been viable to provide a fire engine in the village.

Other companies insuring village properties then or later were - Bristol, County, Norwich Union, Phoenix (*Fig: 10.18*), Protector, Royal and the Union. They all had metal fire marks to identify the houses they insured; it is often said that if an engine turned up at a fire and the house did not have their company's mark on it, they would refuse to help.

By 1835 the need for a privately owned engine was no longer necessary, the parish had its own fire engine.[65] In that year it must already have been of some age, as the Vestry sent it to London for repair. It was housed in the old Market house until this was sold in 1855, we do not know where it was kept after this.

The indications are that fire fighting after this may have been neglected - no mention appears until 1906 when Mr Hyde, the captain, was ordered to call practices and to have all firemen's houses marked, including his own house which doubled as the Fire Station.[66]   More progress was made the following year when a new brigade was formed, still with Mr Hyde as captain, the men being equipped with hatchets, boots, caps and (presumably) uniforms.

Fig:10.18 - Phoenix fire policy for Fish Street Chapel, 1891

This new crew demanded a new engine, but this was slow in materialising - in 1912 an engine to serve the local parishes was proposed; then in 1914 other proposals were minuted :-

> "*A truck to be procured to place the fire engine on for travelling & so that it could be worked on or off the truck*" also to - "*have the pump repaired that is attached to the water cart so that the pump that is used as a fire engine may be kept for fire purposes only*"

Similar indecision affected choice of a site for a Fire Station. In 1946 it was proposed to purchase the old cottages standing in front of the Village Hall for the RDC for £150. Today's fire station was proposed and built soon after 1949.

MAKERS OF CLOTHES

From primeval times women were the chief makers of clothes. Later centuries saw a great diversity and complication of garments, requiring specialist skills to make, this saw the trades such as Tailoring increasingly practised.

Tailors appear in Redbourn records from 1586, and by the 19th century there was a constant 7 to 9 in the Census Returns. One of the latter was much more than just a tailor in village life: this was Moses Moody. His tailoring took him around the local farms where he could make more money than in the village itself. He was also the Parish Clerk, sometime Constable and I guess just about every other public job on offer in Redbourn. He was both respected, (and, by the children,) revered and even feared (see also chapter 12).

The Census Returns are a good source of information on the trades associated with the making of clothes, which range from Dressmakers, Milliners and Bonnet makers to Cordwainers (making shoes) to Glovers.

Other trades that were essential to the making of clothes, such as weavers, cloth makers, straw plaiters, lacemakers, tanners etc. The latter must have sold their skins to the many boot and shoe makers of the village, (a maximum of 29 in 1871). The tannery was at the bottom end of the High Street and existed from at least 1595 until the late 19th century.

SHOPKEEPERS

As might be expected, shopkeepers have always been very prevalent, especially along the busy High Street. In early days houses would have been converted by having shutters that let down outside to form tables on which to display wares. The earliest shopkeeper I have found is a Grocer (1596). There would have been many others selling various wares, but there is no the space for a full list.

The High Street is the primary shopping area, but shops also existed in other parts of the village. From early times in Church End of course, but also elsewhere in the village, (a nice reminder on East Common being "The Old Bakery").

DOMESTIC SERVANTS

The Census Returns give us quite a good idea of what servants were employed by Redbourn people in the latter half of the 19th century, the total number varied between 67 and 90. As would be expected, the larger houses in the village were the best 'served' with live-in domestic staff. The prosperity of the farmers in the period is indicated by the number of servants they employed, even small farms like Bakers, Flowers or Fosters generally kept at least one servant, but rarely a cook. On the other hand the inns, which you would expect to need quite a bit of domestic assistance, rarely employed live-in servants, probably because staff, like barmen or barmaids, could come in on a daily basis.

The servants listed by the Census fall under many descriptions, from Butler to Page or House Boy and females from Housekeepers, Governess' to the humble Kitchen Maid. We have to look at the larger houses in the village to see the major area of employment; the four largest houses were staffed as follows:-

REDBOURN HOUSE No member of the Bowes Lyon family was ever in residence at the day that a Census being taken; in 1851 Lady Glamis was away, having left the house in the care of two trusted servants. By 1871 the house was occupied by the Hon. Ferninia Stourton with 7 others living with her, all of independent means, including a Roman Catholic Priest. She kept an equal number of live-in servants to occupants:-

Butler	House Maid
House Keeper	Nursery Maid
Governess	Kitchen Maid
Nurse	Maid

Twenty years later Mr Magor, an East Indian Merchant, was in residence, the eleven occupants included quite a small staff:-

Cook	Kitchen Maid
2 House Maids	

CUMBERLAND HOUSE In 1891 Robert Peake, a mining engineer, had taken up residence only the previous year with his wife, 3 daughters and 2 sons. Their staff in that year comprised:-

Cook	Kitchen Maid
Sick Nurse	House Maid
Groom	

THE PRIORY Living here in 1851, Martha Vere Brown was described as "Landed proprietor and Fund Holder", there were four other independent adults and 4 children who were served by 6 servants:-

Housekeeper	Monthly Nurse
House Servant	Man Servant
Cook	A "Gardening man"

THE VICARAGE - Was always well staffed. Mr Wade, who had become Vicar in 1850, employed:-

| Cook | Parlour Maid |
| Nurse | House Maid |

Over the next 20 years we see changes in his requirements. The first sign was the appearance of a Coachman, obviously his horse riding days were over. Three years before his death he only needed a Cook and a Coachman

OTHER TRADES AND OCCUPATIONS

The occupations listed in the Registers, Census Returns and Trade Directories are too numerous to mention here, I can only list a few that I think might interest, or perhaps surprise readers, and give the dates when they first appear:-

1762	Footman		1870	Chiropodist
1768	Exerciseman		1877	Machine Maker
1786	Whittler		1881	Chemical Merchant
1828	Wire Weaver			Newsletter Carrier
1830	Chair Maker			Fancy Bag Maker
1837	Type Founder		1886	Boiler Maker
1840	Sieve Bottomer			Coffee Taverner
1851	Tinplate Worker		1887	Billiard Maker
	Chelsea Pensioner			Barge Lighterman
	Blind Maker			Fiddler
	Well Digger			Glue Size Maker
	Umbrella/Parasol Maker	1891	Iron-founder	
1853	Clerk in Parliament			Marine Store Dealer
1861	Judge			Gold Jeweller
	Rope Maker			
	Photographic Artist			

FAIRS AND MARKETS

In 1638 King Charles granted the right to hold weekly markets and three fairs each year in Redbourn.[67] The markets were to be held each Tuesday and the fairs on the Wednesday after Easter, 20th July and St Luke's day (18th October). Higglers (market dealers), Chapmen (dealers) and Hawkers were known from about this time, the village also being called " *a small but bustling market town*"

For such market activities a covered centre for the officials to operate from was needed, but it took a further 70 years before a 'Market House' was provided. This was erected where the old "Woolpack" inn used to stand before 1707, the land being given by William Grimston to be held in trust by villagers.[68] The market was held further down the High Street where it widens just before Fish Street corner; this gave rise to a saying that if anything was lop-sided it was - *"like Redbourn Market, all on one side"*

The fairs lasted a week, each day being allocated to different trading:-
Sundays - Racehorses
Monday - Hunters
Tuesday - Cart Horses
Wednesday - Cattle
Thursday - Sheep
The hooks where the animals were tied up can still be seen in the wall of "Cumberland House".

By 1906 the sale of animals was of minor importance as indicated by it being then called a *"Pleasure Fair"*, giving way in modern times to the Fun-Fairs which we see occasionally today. These events, are still under the control of the Parish Council, who have sadly had to discontinue the annual Guy Fawkes firework displays.

REFERENCES

1   Will of William Squirge, HRO. Ref. 8AR262r
2   John Richardson - "The Local Historian's Encyclopedia",ref. B.49
3   St Albans Liberty Petty Sessions, 4th May 1872
4   A receipt given to me by Mrs Edwards, ref. AFN.6-18
5   GPO. and Kelly's Directories
6   Victoria County History, Hertfordshire, Vol. IV, p.272
7   "Hertfordshire Countryside" No. 43, p.348
8   As 5
9   HRO. Will, Ref 9AR92r
10 & 11   References in this section are as quoted in my book "The Mills of Redbourn"
12 Sun Fire Office records in the Guildhall library - MS.11936, Vol.101, p.391 and MS.14932, Vol. 12
13 Maurice Lovett - "Brewing and breweries", Shire Album 72
14 My book "The Mills of Redbourn" p. 39
15 HRO. X.C6d, Survey, 1615, sheet 16
16 As 15, sheet 6
17 HRO. X.C16b, Survey, 1665, sheet 22-23 and Miscellaneous 41333, Survey 1692, sheet 53
18 HRO. X.C16b, Survey, 1665, sheet 7
19 As 18, sheet 22
20 HRO. Miscellaneous 41333, Survey 1692, sheet 54
21 HRO. XI.56, Quit rents 1799
22 HRO. Will, ref.8AR17v
23 Guild Hall Library ref. 11374
24 & 25   Helen Poole (Compiler) "Here for the Beer", A Gazetteer of the brewers of Hertfordshire, Watford Museum, p.40
26 Lease dated 3.5.1881, Copy in Redbourn Village Museum, ref. RDBVM.87.355
27 Sale document 1897, copy in my collection

28 May Walker - "Redbourn", 1960, p.75
29 From correspondence between Robin Harcourt Williams, (Librarian & Archivist to the Marquis of Salisbury) and myself, in 1993
30 Norah King - "The Grimstons of Gorhambury" 1983, p.77
31 Orderly Book of Redbourn Vestry meetings from 1800, in St Mary's Parish Chest
32 Most information in this section from - Martha Walsh - "The Life of Henry Stephens FRCS
33 & 34 As 28, p.66
35 Copy of Death Certificate - HRO. ref. Miscellaneous 73581
36 HRO. ref. D/EB.1873.T.10
37 Redbourn Village Museum ref. RDBVM.87.829
38 HRO. Will, ref. 159AW25
39 Kelly's Directory 1890
40 Information given by his widow, Hilda Wilson
41 "Common Round" June 1969
42 Moulton Collection, HRO. ref. 44501
43 Redbourn Parish Council records, HRO. ref. CP78.1/2, 1909 meeting
44 As 43, Parish meeting in 1908
45 St Albans RDC, Agreement 1936, copy kept at "Kyngston House", St Albans
46 "Common Round" (parish magazine) November 1965
47 As 43, CP78.1/3, Parish Council meeting 1937 & CP78./28/2 (Plans)
48 HRO. Will, ref. 129AW30
49 Victoria County History, Vol.1, p194, notes 3 & 11
50 Calendar of Assize Records, Hertfordshire Indictments, Elizabeth I, p.372
51 Letters & Papers 29 HEN VIII, No. 243
52 As 50, p.126
53 W E Tate - "The Parish Chest", p.99, a Presentment from the St Albans Archdeaconry
54 Liberty of St Albans, Session Rolls, Vol. IV, p.61
55 Geoff Webb, "Redbourn Memories", p.70 and Greensward "Common Round" May 1965
56 John Trokelowe - "Chronica et Annales" Rolls series 1866, p23-4
57 As 50, p.831
58 As 50, p.1006
59 As 54, vol.4, p.51
60 Liberty of St Albans, Sessions book 1849-56
61 These three cases are from the "130 years ago" series in the Herts Advertiser, 1990
62 HRO. Court Rolls for the Manor of Redbourn, 1595-8, ref. D/EX.640.M.21
63 As 54, Vol. V, p.37
64 HRO. document ref. D/EX.138.T.13
65 Book containing 'Vestry Orders' from 1800, kept in the Parish Chest
66 As 46 Parish Council minutes various
67 HRO. ref. II.A.6
68 HRO. ref. II.J.23

CHAPTER 11

INDUSTRIES OF REDBOURN

In the last chapter I considered occupations carried out by just a few people, but where large groups are involved, usually working in a purpose made building, this becomes an Industry and thus the subject of this chapter. Another difference is that their products, instead of being basically for very local use, could be distributed much more widely, even nationally.

The provision of large buildings where people could work together to manufacture commodities, is basically a 19th century development. Often local people already practising similar skills, could be employed; a good example is the many hat and bonnet makers who already used straw plait made by nearly every family in the village. It took Lady Charlotte Bowes Lyon to realise the need of a local outlet for their finished plait, so she built a small factory off the High Street, devoted to the making of Straw Hats. Thus giving not only a convenient outlet for the products of the busy plaiters, but also giving employment to the many other villagers.

STRAW PLAITERS AND HAT MAKERS

Straw Plaiting was a 'Cottage Industry' that was carried out in almost every home in Redbourn during the 18th and 19th centuries. Its origins in this country are said to date from when James I, settled some French plaiters, who Mary Queen of Scots had befriended, at Luton Hoo. From there it spread throughout the adjacent counties of Hertfordshire, Buckinghamshire, Essex and Bedfordshire. However, there is another suggestion that the craft was brought over earlier by Flemish refugees in the 16th century.[1]

In 1804, Arthur Young, in his "A general view of Agriculture in the county of Hertfordshire " describes straw plaiting thus:-

"... Redbourn is the place where the manufacture is most prevalent; where some women earn "£1.1s. a week,... some clever little girls 15s. Farmers complain of it as doing mischief, for it makes the poor saucy, and no servants can be procured, or any field work done......But good earnings are a most happy circumstance which I wish to see universal"

Other quotations are not hard to find, such as Pigot's Directory of 1823 :-

Redbourn - *"from its thoroughfare, situation and the manufacture of straw plait, the principal support of its inhabitants arises"*

Edwin Grey, a Harpenden resident, wrote about village life at the turn of the 20th century, recalling how straw plaiting, even then, dominated family life, many women and girls doing it, even some men and boys taking part after their days work elsewhere.[2]

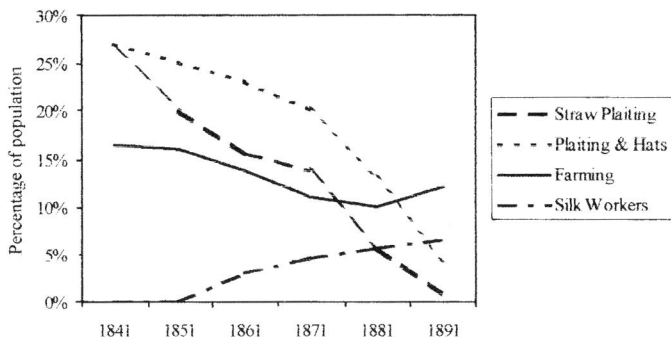

Fig: 11.1 - Employment numbers as percentage of population, 1841 to 1891

The making of hats, from lengths of plait, also developed initially as a cottage industry, before giving way to industrial concerns set up in villages to support factories in towns, such as Luton. Mention by Shakespeare of maidens wearing *"platted hives of straw"* and *"sheav'd hats"* as early as 1597 can be found.[3] Also Samuel Pepys when staying at Hatfield in 1667 commented that women in his party donned straw hats which - *"are much worn in this country and did become them mightily, especially my wife"*

The early Census Returns show that a large proportion of the population were engaged in either Straw Plaiting or Hat Making, see *Fig: 11.1*. In 1841 51% of the Redbourn women were Plaiters; Hat Makers do not appear in such high proportions. The returns also highlight the youth of the majority of workers, most of whom were female. The figures below are taken from the 1851 Census:-

Age Groups	Straw Plaiters		Hat makers
Up to 10 years	49 females	22 males	1 female
11-20 years	112 "	7 "	45 "
21-30 "	84 "	1 "	24 "
31-45 "	63 "	1 "	7 "
46 and over	64 "	0 "	7 "

(NB. Other workers such as Dealers, Cutters etc., are not included)

Of those under 10 years of age, six were girls of 5 years and five were boys of the same age. However, as will be seen, the majority group were girls in their teen age; perhaps at about 20 many got married and either moved away or gave up plaiting for a regularly paid job. The oldest plaiter was a lady of 81 years.

Straw plaiting was a skill that required training and lots of practice before good quality saleable plait could be produced. As Grey suggested, it was a constant occupation for most women and children, continuing while they were walking, talking and even courting. About 70 yards of plait were required to make one hat and it has been calculated that a woman could make about three and a half miles of plait in a year (enough for nearly 90 hats).

Nimble fingers were essential for plaiting, this is why women and children, rather than men, did the work - there were exceptions, such as two men over 30 at Redbourn. It has been said that children as young as two years old were taught to plait, but in the 1851 figures five was the minimum seen. However, they were sent to learn the skill at a 'Plait School' from a very earlier age.

At least three such schools existed in the village, one in Mount Pleasant, another in the High Street and the third in "The Jolly Gardener", probably about the same time (see Chapter 14). They were expected to receive some basic education as well as learning to plait. This did not necessarily happen, as some plait teachers were illiterate and others were said not even to be able to plait.

The men folk acted mostly as suppliers and preparers of the straw. They obtained the right type of long-stalked straw, often specially grown by farmers around the edge of their fields. It was cut into lengths of about 9 inches, known as 'splints', these were then split into narrow widths suitable for plaiting, using a "splitter" - see *Fig:11.2*. It was then bleached and rolled flat ready for use. One Redbourn man invented an *"elaborate and unusual Straw Sorter"* to separate and mechanically sort straws into sizes.[4] This was refined by others and appeared in various forms but essentially unchanged in principle - see *Fig 11.3*

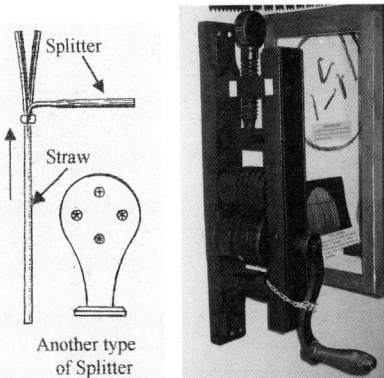

Fig: 11.2 – Types of Splitter (Left), Straw
Mill in the Museum (Right)

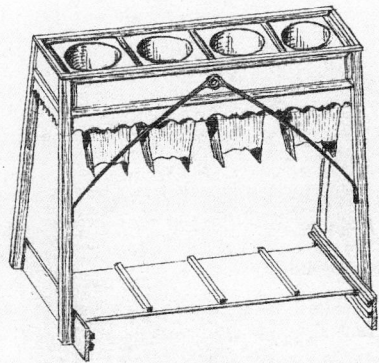

Fig: 11.3 - Straw Sorter, similar to that
invented at Redbourn

The Census Returns give a useful picture of the occupation and industry of Straw Plaiting and Hat Making in the latter half of the 19th century, however from the graph, *Fig: 11.1*, it is obvious that numbers are in decline by the first Census in 1841. This reflects a national trend, starting in the previous century, when imports from Europe, chiefly France, caused serious competition. After a temporary respite given by the Napoleonic wars, cheap imports from China in the 1870's and Japan in the 1890's caused the final collapse; leaving only a few elderly women still plaiting straw by the first World War. The graph shows that only 19 Redbourn Straw Plaiters were left in 1891 and the 1914/15 Kelly's Directory stated that plaiting was still carried on in the village.

Not quite the same effect is reflected in the fortunes of the hat industry; they took advantage of imports of cheaper plait, the numbers remained nearly constant between 1861 and 1881, but starting a fall by the 1891 Census. Hat makers who changed to other materials like felt were able to survive.

Hat makers at Redbourn are first seen in the 1851 Census, as - "Bonnet Sewers" or "Straw Bonnet Sewers"; there were 85, one of whom made "Brazilian Hats". This work was obviously more skilled and was mostly practised by girls between 15 and 30. Most would have sold their products at the market, while others worked for local hat factories in Luton or St Albans.

It was not long before the hat manufacturers realised that there was a potential skilled labour force existing in many villages and that this could be tapped by building satellite factories. In Redbourn, one was planned by Lady Charlotte Bowes-Lyon of "Redbourn House" in 1861.[5] This was built and leased to Messrs Vyse & Co., of Luton for £50 pa.[6]

REDBOURN.

TENDERS.

The following tenders for building a factory at Redbourn, for Lady Glamis, to be occupied by Messrs. Vyse, straw hat manufacturers, were received at the "Bull Inn," Redbourn, on Tuesday, the 10th inst:—

Mr. Groom, Hemel Hempstead £667 0 0
Mr. Obee, Markyate-street 662 0 0
Mr. Thorogood, Redbourn 627 0 0
Mr. Dunham, St. Alban's....... 620 0 0

We have not learned whether they have been decided on.

Fig:11.4 – Tenders for the factory,
(Herts Advertiser 10th September 1861)

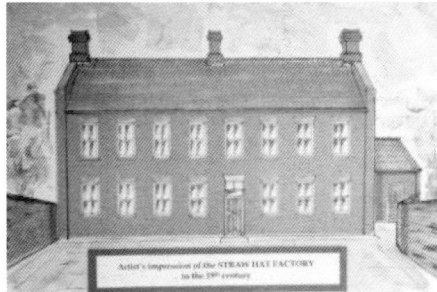

Fig: 11.5 – Artist's impression of Redbourn Straw Hat Factory (in Redbourn Museum)

The factory was sold to the sitting tenant in 1893 for £700.[7] The sale brochure describes the factory thus:-"On the upper floor - two large workrooms; on the ground floor - Blocking house, Drying room, Kitchen with furnace and sink, Spacious passage, Large warehouse and 2 WC's; Brick and slated Barn and Wash house with copper and pump" Its large windows back and front, were essential for the fine work of sewing plait to make many different types of hat.

The workers employed in this factory can be identified in the Census Returns, as - Blockers, Drawers, Pressers, Stiffeners, Sewers, Makers or just as Workers. No doubt many of the village hat makers came to work in the factory, while others learnt these skills at the factory to become Machinists, Finishers or Trimmers. The factory stayed in operation until at least 1906 but had to close soon after, because of a national decline in the trade as has been explained.

The factory appears to have been unused for some years before it was purchased by the Parish Council in 1921 for £100 more than Messrs Vyse paid for it in 1893.[8] In spite of the many alterations and additions which make it such a useful venue for its present day village activities, as the Village Hall, the old Hat factory part can still be easily recognised by the large windows of its first floor.

In 1948 the row of old cottages which cut it off from the High Street (except for a narrow passage) were demolished to give access for car parking. Photographs of these indicate that they may have been of 17th or 18th century date; (*Fig: 11.5*) May Walker in her book "Redbourn" commented sadly.[9]-

"It was a pity they were not restored instead of being demolished. They were hardly suitable for modern housing needs but would have been picturesque examples of early domestic architecture if restored "

Fig: 11.6 - Spiral stairs to the projection room, soon after 1921

Fig: 11.7 – Old cottages demolished to make room for the car park, c.1948

SILK THROWERS

Silk Throwing is a process which turns raw silk, from the silk worm cocoons, into a yarn suitable for weaving and similar uses, by twisting and winding individual threads together, several times. The process started in China about 1600 BC. but did not reach Europe until the 15th century and this country by 1721.[10]

Early Mills were mostly converted Watermills, but with the advent of steam a more even and constant power source, more suitable for this delicate process, was available.

John Woollam converted the St Albans Abbey corn mill for making and weaving silk in 1804.[11] He also converted other mills, including an unsuccessful paupers mill at Hatfield. But steam power gave a more even and constant power source than a waterwheel, and was more suitable for this delicate process of silk throwing. So he turned to Redbourn and built a completely purpose made, steam-powered mill beside the Common in 1857.[12]

His silk mill consisted of a series of single story buildings with large windows to let in light for the delicate work involved. The position of engine house, with its tall chimney, can be seen from *Fig: 11.6*. Also visible is the bell which summoned workers in the mornings and is now displayed in the Museum. During the First War it also acted as a warning of Zeppelin raids.[13]

The process of silk throwing was carried out in the Redbourn mill, but I can find no evidence of weaving also being done here. However, the 1871Census lists 50 'weavers' but this is an obvious misuse of the name by one of the Enumerators as the others correctly used 'Winders', Throwsters' (and later 'Silksters) for workers at the mill.

From c.1867 John's son Charles ran both the St Albans and Redbourn mills, but employed a manager for the latter who lived in a house on the site – see two story building attached to the factory, *Fig: 11.9*

Fig: 11.8 - Silk Mill Buildings from the east
Notice the large windows & chimney

Fig: 11.9 – Aerial view - new Brooke Bond buildings top left

As with Straw Plaiting, children were employed in the Silk Mill from an early age. This often caused problems with their education because their contribution to the family income was thought to be more useful than paying a penny a day to go to school. A compromise was eventually reached whereby they were supposed to attend school for at least 3 hours on alternate days.[14] Even so these 'part-timers' usually left school as soon as they could to work full time in the mill. It is interesting to note that in 1881 the same family was involved with each side of these arguments. Charles Harvey was the Boys School Head, while Elizabeth and Henry Harvey were joint foremen at the Mill.

The age when children were permitted to work at the mill (part time) was initially set at 8 years but required a doctor's certificate saying [15]:-

> "....he has the ordinary strength and appearance of a child of at least eight years of age, and I (the Doctor) believe the real age of the child to be at least 8 years."

Keen eyesight and small nimble fingers were required for the delicate work of handling the very fine silk threads involved; thus the reason that children and young girls predominated the workforce at the mill. The number of workers in the factory in the 1871 was stated to be 100 males (mostly boys) and 40 females, but only 97 are individually listed in the Census Return. This confirms that other workers were recruited from the surrounding villages.

In 1871 and 1881, we see William D. Ashwell living almost next door to the mill, thus very convenient for his job as - *"Engine Driver in the Silk Factory"* . This was the stationary 'engine' used to power the winding machinery of the mill.

Woollam's mills in both St Albans and Redbourn were taken over by John Maygrove & Co. Ltd. at about the turn of the century until closure in 1938.[16] Like the Straw Hat industry, the demise of Silk Throwing was caused by foreign imports and the introduction of materials like Nylon and Rayon in the early 1930's.[17]

Thus the mill was standing unused, but with much of it's machinery remaining, at the outbreak of World War II. This was fortunate for the Brooke Bonds when they decided to disperse their operations away from the vulnerable East End, where one of their factories had been bombed. Thus Extracts Ltd., part of Brooke Bonds, took over the Silk Mill.

They later extended the site on adjacent land by erecting 3 large packing sheds; eventually demolishing the old mill but retaining the house for their managers. After closing the factory in 1996 they refurbished the house as a museum and generously gave it to the village. This opened its doors to the public on May 5th 2000, showing displays on the Priory, village occupations and with a picture gallery of photographs, as well as giving a permanent home to the Millennium Wall Hanging in early 2001.

Brooke Bonds are remembered as a good employer and for their contributions to village life in many ways. One example of this was their idea of using excess heat from the factory to warm water in their static water tank so that it could be used as a small swimming pool for employees.[18] They thoughtfully also invited the local schools to use this facility and many Redbourn children learnt to swim here.

The Woollams also gave a field called "The Brache" for use as allotments. On part of this land Mary Woollam, the widow of Charles, erected a row of almshouses in 1926 (see *Fig: 9.2*). In 1963 further adjacent bungalows for old people were built, known collectively as "Woollams".[19]

HARBOROUGH'S JAMS

In speech made in the Houses of Parliament, William Gladstone in 1880, suggested that the household occupation of jam making could be undertaken on a commercial basis.[20]

Mr Russell Harborough, a grocer of Redbourn, heard of this and put it into practice from his own kitchen. He was so successful that he soon had to expand by building a 49 foot long factory next to his house and employing many local people to help him. In time even this was not large enough, so a modern factory was built on the site, this can still be seen although it has in recent years been much modernised.

Mr Russell Harborough   *Russell Harborough's House & first factory*

Jam in production   *The second factory*

Fig: 11.10 - RUSSELL HARBOROUGH AND HIS FACTORY, EARLY 1900'S

Fig: 11.11 – An early Harborough delivery van

His did not stop at just making jam, but also made marmalade, sweets and seaside rock. During the making of sweets there was some waste because of broken pieces, but a local sweet shop used to take these and sell them in bags as "big mixed", which were very popular with the village children. The new factory was thoroughly mechanised, except for delicate operations such as stalking strawberries. The workers were not only employed in the factory, but also helped pick fields of fruit bought by Russell Harborough for making jam.[21]

THOMAS MERCER LTD.

In 1956 the Harborough Jam factory was taken over by the very long standing firm of Marine Chronometer manufacturers, Thomas Mercer Ltd.[22] Thomas, whose grandfather was a watchmaker in Liverpool, set up his own business in Clerkenwell in 1858 at the age of 36. He moved to St Albans in 1874.

It was when the firm diversified into the filed of Metrology, to make dial gauges and later air gauges, that the latter were made in the old Jam factory. When they moved in, much of the old jam making machinery was still there.

BRUSH MAKERS

Except for its location in the Hemel Hempstead Road, and its name, little is known about the Brush Factory.[23] The Directories list the business between 1899 and 1915, first as Henry Rose & Sons and then as Brushes Ltd, with T. Pennington as owner.

GAS IN REDBOURN

At the inaugural dinner at the Bull of a small Gas Works in Fish Street, in 1861, the following poem was read by the manager of the St Albans Gas Works.[24]:-

"If the dead could but rise, oh, how they would stare
To see us lit up with nothing but air!
They'd watch us with wonder, and think it a trick,
To light Redbourn up without oil or wick:-
If coachman and guards, as we have known some,
Who many years back, morn and noon used to come,
Could see the White Hart, Bull, Lion and Lamb,
All lighted with gas, they'd think it a sham;
Or fear the White Horse would prance at the light -
The Saracen's Head become grey with affright.
But 'tis really a fact which can't be gainsayed
That inflammable gas can now be conveyed
To silk mill, shops, houses, and mansions so neat,
By underground pipes from the works in Fish Street.
We all wish success to the company's labours
Put forth with a view to enlighten their neighbours"

Fig: 11.12 – Manager's house(left) Houses on right are where the Gasometers stood

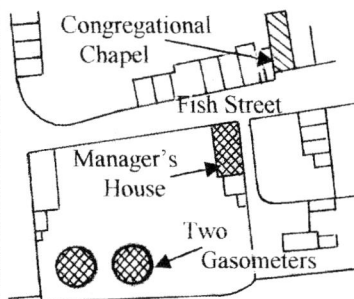

Fig: 11.13 - Plan of Gas Works

The Parish Council was quite far sighted for their day they decided to have the High Street lit by gas from the new gas works.[25] Ten lights were ordered for a total cost of £17.10s. and the following year a further £12 was allocated from the Stone Rates (normally for the repair of roads) for "lighting the town and Common".

Fish Street Chapel, which stood almost opposite the works, had gas lighting installed, as part of a reconstruction programme in 1865 - the cost was £10.6s.1d.[26]

While St Mary's, more remote from the works, did not avail itself of the facility. Instead, a hut was built by the Hemel Hempstead gate to house an Acetylene gas generator, in 1906, see chapter 12.

The Fish Street works went out of business when gas was piped to Redbourn from the St Albans works. It is now piped to us from the North Sea. The site where the two gasometers stood, built on the site of a stagnant pond, is now occupied by new houses.[27.] The works manager's house is still in use and can be recognised by its yellow bricks and its gable end to the road.

REFERENCES

1   Historical details in this section taken from - Jean Davis - "Straw Plait" Shire Album 78, 1981 and - Charles Freeman - "Luton and the Hat Industry" 1976
2   Edwin Grey - "Cottage Life in a Hertfordshire Village" (1977), chapter 2, pp.68-90
3   "Victoria County History - Hertfordshire" Vol. IV, p251
4   As 5, p.253, note22a
5   Information from Mr. Roy Craske, quoting the Herts Advertiser
6   Redbourn Parish Council sale documents dated, 2.10.1893 and 17.10.1893
7   Sale Brochure held by Redbourn Village Museum, ref.RDBVM.87.829
8   As ref. 6, document dated 2.3 1921
9   May Walker - "Redbourn", 1960, p.61
10 Sarah Bush - "The Silk Industry", Shire Album 194
11 W. Branch-Johnson "Hertfordshire", 1970, p.215
12 Gorhambury Manorial Records, HRO. ref. D/EB.1873.B6
13 Redbourn Parish Council records, HRO. ref. CP78.1/2, 1916 meeting
14 Roy Craske - "Redbourn Girls School, 1863-1951", p.2
15 Factories Regulation Act - CAP. XV.6.6.1844
16 W. Branch-Johnson, 1970 - "The Industrial Archaeology of Hertfordshire", p.67
17 As 10, p. 9
18 Hertfordshire Countryside Vol.21, No.96, p.723
19 St Mary's Parish Chest, ref. RC/8 & Article in "Common Round" Feb. 1963, p.11
20 booklet called "Forgotten Paragraphs", issued by Russell Harborough Ltd.
21 Two articles in "Common Round" in 1971 by "Greensward" describing work in the factory
22 Souvenir Brochure for Silver Jubilee of Queen Elizabeth II - history by F. A. Mercer
23 Duties on Land Values in Redbourn (Dacorum)1910, HRO. ref. IR2.59/1
24 Herts Advertiser - "Villages of West Herts, No. II. Redbourn, 3 May 1879
25 Taken from the Vestry Minutes kept in the Parish Chest
26 Record Book of the Fish Street Independent Chapel kept by the Museum, ref. RDBVM.97.050
27 As 9, p68

CHAPTER 12

THE POST MEDIEVAL CHURCH

As has been seen in chapter 3, St Mary's was structurally complete by the end of the 15th century; few external changes have since been made until the new 'Transept Hall' was added in recent years. Internally it has been a different matter many changes have taken place during the last four and a half centuries.

In chapter 8 an attempt was made to 'clothe' village houses with the people who built or lived in them - a similar pattern will be used here. However, in this case it is mostly the incumbents who controlled developments, though several lay people will be mentioned who left 'their stamp' on the building. Thus instead of describing each new work under its own heading, they will be attributed to the incumbent of the time who probably ordered, inspired, or even paid for, the work.

First let me 'set the scene' by trying describe how St Marys might have looked at the beginning of the period, noting some of the later changes.

THE EXTERNAL APPEARANCE

Medieval churches with rough flint walls, are thought to have been plastered and possibly painted. Old photographs show that this was true of St Marys - see *Fig: 12.1;* there are even signs that the plaster was painted. Extensive repairs of the early 20th century compromised by re-plastering so that the flints were not completely covered, enabling their random coursing to be seen.

A 'Hertfordshire Spike' of the 14th or 15th century stood on top of the tower until 1802 - see *Fig: 12.7*

It is more difficult to imagine what the churchyard would have looked like in early days particularly with respect to the trees. The paths may have followed the same courses that we know today, they may even have been ancient when the church was built, owing their origin to the tracks made by early men going to and from the Aubreys.

Fig: 12.1 – Stonework before repair, 1913

THE INTERNAL APPEARANCE

On entering the church the medieval pews, possibly with 'Poppy-Heads' carved with rural figures, were to remain until replaced by 17th century Box Pews and today's 'Chapel' type from 1850.

The Rood Screen, after the removal of the Rood figures and possibly paintings of saints on its panels, would have been much as we know it today, except for a gallery on top and double doors leading into the Chancel. However, the Rood itself remained untouched until at least 1558, as evidenced by the bequest of Edward Abraham of 12d. for the *"Rodelight"*.[1] After its removal the Royal coat-of-arms would have been put in its place.

The stone Altar would have been replaced by a simple wooden table under Queen Elizabeth. In the floor were several brasses of the 15th and 16th centuries, a few of which have survived or are indicated by 'indents' in stones. There was some stained glass but none has survived from medieval times. Lighting probably remained unchanged until oil lamps replaced torches fixed to brackets on the walls; 23 bequests for torches appear in wills between 1497 and 1554.

CHURCH 'GOODS'

Henry's son Edward VI turned his attention to removing all items associated with the Roman Catholic Mass from English churches. He sent Commissioners out to record all items of church property; in 1552 listing the following at Redbourn [2]:-

> "a Challic guylte poz xvij onces   ["a Gilt Chalice, weight 17 ounces"]
> another Challic guylte poz xvj onc d(emi)
> another Challic parcell guylte xj ozffyve Belles in the steple
> a Cope of redd veluet
> another olde Cope
> a vestment of redd veluet
> a vestment of Blew veluet
> a vestment of Whyt Damaske
> iij other olde Vestments
> iij Alter Clothes of Satten Bridges
> a Clothe of the same for the deske
> a Canape Clothe of the same"
>   (None of these items survive today)

Even if any of these *"profane cups"* were not confiscated by Edward, most disappeared during Elizabeth's reign. However, parishes were allowed to keep one chalice and paten, until they could be replaced by [3]:-

> *"a fair and comely communion cup of silver, and a cover of silver...which may serve for the administration of the bread"*

That specification was issued by Archbishop Grindal in 1576; St Mary's Elizabethan cup (with lid or cover) is dated a year later.

THOMAS WILKINSON, Vicar 1556-1577

Thomas Wilkinson came to Redbourn in the same year that Thomas Cranmer was burnt at the stake in Queen Mary's reign; serving 2 years in her reign and a further 19 under Queen Elizabeth.

All we know about his life stems from an unfortunate incident with two parishioners who were not happy him and said some very hard words about his life.[4] They made a feeble excuse about the Communion, i.e. that *"the cakes were not sweet"* (the Communion bread) choosing to attend Harpenden Church. The Vicar's attitude inferred ill will towards them - *"if you will have other bread you shall have bread enough"*. They continued with a damning condemnation of him, saying - *"he is an infamous person and ministereth irreverently, he is also a drunkard and detected of incontinency, besides other causes plenty"*.

The earliest registers date from Wilkinson's time; the actual books have been lost, but he sent copies to the Archdeaconry, known as "Bishop's Transcripts".[5] They record, in Latin, the last burial he performed - that of Sir Richard Rede in 1576; (see chapter 8) his *"per me thoma wylkynson cleric"* own being the first recorded by his successor, on June 3rd 1577

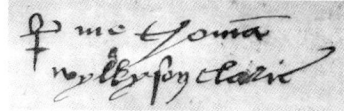

Fig: 12.2 - Thomas Wilkinson 1576

NATHANIEL BAXTER, MA., VICAR 1577-79

Baxter was the first incumbent to be appointed by Sir Nicholas Bacon after obtaining the Advowson of the Vicarage from Ralph Rowlatt.[6] He and subsequent owners of Gorhambury appointed a whole series of Puritan minded clergy. Baxter was certainly firmly in this mould, dating back to his time at Cambridge where he was in contact with Thomas Cartwright a well-known advocate of Calvin's radical doctrines regarding government of the Church and the State and the denying of Royal Supremacy. Baxter and others, including Richard Gawton, who was later to also become Vicar of Redbourn, offered their support to Cartwright when he had to flee to the Netherlands.[7]

Before coming to Redbourn, Baxter had been tutor to Sir Philip Sydney and wrote - "Sir Philip Sydney's Ourania", now an extremely rare book. He continued writing on Puritan based themes until his death in 1633 at Younghall in Ireland where he was Warden, he must, therefore, have lived to a ripe old age.[8]

EDWARD SPENDLOVE, BA. MINISTER 1579-88

In 1579 the Churchwardens reported that there were two clergymen in the parish until Easter when - *"Mr Baxter shall depart and Mr Spendlove to be in full possession...in consideration whereof he must pay Mr Baxter a certen sume of money"*.[9] The reason for this financial arrangement is not explained.

Spendlove was a married man, ordained only 2 years before coming to Redbourn. Both he and the previous vicar had degrees and wrote their Registers in Latin. They were also of a strong Puritan persuasion, indicated by their use of the title 'Minister' and an unwillingness to conform in every respect to Church laws. Spendlove was unwilling at first to wear a Surplice, later saying that he was *"willing to reform his attire as soon as able to provide"*.[10]

He was obviously keen to root out misdemeanours amongst his flock, ordering penances and five excommunications for mothering (or fathering) illegitimate children. A certificate shows the humiliation inflicted by a penance.[11]

> *"She came into the church immediately after the first lesson at Morning Prayer, in a white sheet and stood in the middle aisle until the end of the prayers and preaching, but she used no manner of speech openly in the church".*

An order to do penance for a quite different reason was served on Innocent Robinson, as detailed in a letter to the Archdeacon in 1585.[12]

> *"...for coming into the Church in his 'maide marrians' attire disguisedly and in the time of preaching...unreverently. ...for his levity and contempt, was injoined to do certain penance. That since then [he] hath been taken or retained to serve as a 'solgier' under on Mr. Henry Norris and was charged presently to repair unto the said Captain, so that he could not perform his penance. ...that he did what he did do rather by the persuasion of others than by any motion of his own nature".*

The reason for his *"attire"* is that at the Whitsun Ales (held to raise money for the church) it was a common practice to represent Maid Marian and Robin Hood as part of Morris dancing.[13] A few days later Robert Purslove did perform a penance in church, perhaps for playing the part of Robin Hood at the 'Ales'?

Spendlove himself was in trouble at various times; just four years after coming he was in financial difficulties, complaining that *"if his stipend and living be not augmented, that he shallbe constrained to seek [money] further".*[14] He did in fact obtain quite a prestigious extra job in the Diocese as the Archdeacon's surrogate; this involved presiding over court sessions and examining clergy.[15]

Clergy were required to report any parishioners who had not take communion three time a year; Spendlove made an elaborate excuse for failing to do so, saying that the people - *"come thronginge and pressinge in great numbre comonly with out all good order".*[16] This difficulty is understandable when the figure for the number of communicants is given 4 years later as 420.[17] His final problem, resulting in his resignation, is both interesting and intriguing.

He had been required to provide certain armour (as were all clergy) being charged particularly with supplying.[18]:-

> *"One Corslet complete with vambraces, Traces, and Bourgoret, a Pike armed, an arminge sworde, dagger and girdle, and a man to wear them".*

[A 'corslet' comprised the armour for the body and arms – see *Fig: 12.3*]

However, he wrote to excuse himself from this duty because he had been convicted of an, unstated, crime.[19] The court having given him the option of either suffering *'open punishment'* (the stocks?) or of resigning his Benefice, he wrote –

"I choose rather to forego my benefice, for my profession's sake, than to incur that open infamy, whereupon I humbly crave that I may not be charged with the said furniture".

His departure from Redbourn came with his resignation on the same day that the Armada was sighted off the Lizard. The bishop's instruction for celebrating the victory came too late for Spendlove to take part, however, sermons were provided in places where there was no clergyman.

Fig: 12.3 - Armour of the type required

INTERREGNUM PREACHER - MR WILLIAM DYKE

The Interregnum lasted for 16 months, during some of the time relieved by the presence of Barnabas Saul, named as Curate [20] Lady Anne Bacon was obviously worried about the parish, so she sent a man to preach who she had put in at St Michael's to help their aged, week and non-preaching Vicar.[21] He was Mr. William Dyke. His title 'Mr' gave him away as a Puritan, in fact he had got into trouble for his preaching in Essex and had come to Lady Anne for protection.

He had started a Revival at St Michael's and tried to do the same at Redbourn, but he ran into serious opposition from Mr. Innocent Rede, the son of Sir Richard. Innocent compiled a list of complaints against Dyke; to which Dyke answered .[22] His main excuse was he was trying to stir the people up to pray for *"a Godly and painful labourer"* (as their next Vicar).

He was conversant with happenings at Redbourn, quoting the case of Maid Marian coming into church and causing laughter and kissing at the time of prayer. He was particularly outspoken against the Whitsun Ales, which he said were *"in their origin bad....were shamefully abused, profane, riotous and disorderly, yea, the way unto perdition and Hell".*

He railed against Vicars who did not preach, saying they were - *"dumb dogs, damned spirits who have not the gift to preach"* also having a go at clergy who haunted ale-houses, there playing dice and cards games, which he called *"odious faults".* He even went back to the case of the insufficiently sweet communion cakes in Thomas Wilkinson's time.

Dyke was outspoken about reforms in the church, particularly with respect to signing the cross at baptism, kneeling to receive communion, the 'superstitious observance' of fast days etc. Because of enemies within the church hierarchy, the chief of whom was the Bishop of London, he settled beyond his jurisdiction in Hemel Hempstead, becoming their Vicar in 1595.

HUMPHRY WILDBLODE - Vicar 1589-92

Another minister in the Puritan mould, Mr Wildblood (variously spelt - Wilde Bloude, Wildeblood, Wylblud) was much favoured by Lady Anne Bacon, who commented *"I humbly thank God for the comfortable company of Mr Wyborn and Mr Wylblud"*.[23]

His extreme views lead him into trouble that even Lady Anne could not avert. He would not obey any injunctions and would not attend the Archdeaconry and certainly did not produce the 'corslet furnished' as required by the state.[24] In 1592 he was deprived of the living and though still licensed was not allowed to preach, or be a schoolmaster. He continued to serve Lady Anne, until moving to Pinner, where he ended his days in 1625.

RUDOLPH BRADLEY, Vicar 1592-1602

Described as a *"non-graduate and a preacher"*, Bradley was soon in trouble for not producing his Orders of Induction and license to preach - several times.[25] He showed more responsibility with regard to armour, producing the required Corselet Furnished on at least three occasions, though once *"less a man"*.[26]

He seems to have been zealous in routing out wrongdoers. He had four girls excommunicated for having illegitimate children, all of whom left the village rather face doing penance in church. In one of these cases James Miles, in whose house the child had been born had to do penance for letting the girl go away.[27] Two of the Fathers are named - Richard Bannister, who went away with the girl and Mr. Maye, the ex-schoolmaster, who had a child with Margaret Tydnam.[28]

Breakers of the Sabbath also appear - Richard Smythe for carting corn and meal to St Albans on New Years Day; Henry Strayte for mending hedges on St James day and John Beech for allowing his son to cart corn from St Albans during the time of Sunday service.[29]

At the turn of the century things started to go wrong for Bradley, first an ugly little incident when John Miles had threatened to give him *"a dash on the mouth"* saying in *"a scoffing and mocking manner" that* he lied in his throat and was - *"a knave Sir Domice & Priest"* and that he, Myles *"was as honest a man as he"*.[30]

In 1601 one of the Bacon's remarked - *"I heard that Mr. Bradley did not preach today as he is excommunicated, or too careless of his charge"* [31] However, he illegally took a marriage in 1601, and the following year resigned.

RICHARD GAWTON, Vicar 1602-16

Of all the Puritan inclined Vicars sent to Redbourn, Richard Gawton must have been the 'hottest', Urwick describes him as *"one of the foremost among Puritan leaders of the day"*.[32] His most exciting period was spent in Norfolk where he was well known for his sermons in Norwich for which he was cited before the Bishop, well known as a persecutor of Puritans. They had a long and heated theological discussion, which turned into a trial, chiefly centred on preaching without a licence and not wearing a surplice. The Bishop proceeded to suspend him from all ministerial functions in the Diocese.

Gawton later published a detailed account of the interview, calling it *"The Troubles of Richard Gawton"*. Like William Dyke, he sought refuge in Hemel Hempstead, becoming Vicar in 1580. His appointment to Redbourn was the last made by Lady Anne Bacon.

His Churchwarden's reports indicate that, at over 50 years of age, he had lost little of his preaching zeal but settled into the life of a country parson - *"ever since he came unto us* [he has] *diligently preached every Sabbath day twice, and against the administration of the Holy Communion he hath also preached once in the week before to prepare the communicants to the worthy receiving thereof.*[33]

In 1615 he was unable to provide the full set of armour required, but said he would provide what he could. He claimed to be over-rated, but the authorities said he should be charged with more, i.e. one Calyver, but did not press for this [34]

Gawton died at Redbourn, leaving a widow, Ann, who died 10 years later.[35]

HENRY BOWMAN, Vicar 1616-27

Sometimes spelt "Bourman", he was the first appointment of a Redbourn Vicar by Sir Francis Bacon, after the death of his mother, Lady Anne.[36]

Thomas Cromwell ordered the keeping of parish Register books in 1538, but none have survived for Redbourn. The earliest date from 1617, signed by Bowman. The fragments that remain appear to be the last few pages of an earlier volume, perhaps dating from 1538.

His eleven years at Redbourn were unremarkable, there were the usual cases of fornication, incontinancy and illegitimate children. There were also the demands for the Vicar to provide a 'Corslet furnished'. A new demand resulted in the Vicar and the Churchwardens being charged (for money) to support the *"plantation of Virginia"*.[37] Presumably this was an early sign of its well-known failure some 16 years later.

When Bowman was cited to appear at the Convocation of Canterbury, it would be nice to know what business they had with him, as such courts were mainly concerned with matters of State, Faith and the Litany.[38]

Bowman's wife died in 1625 and he followed 18 months later.

EDMUND BRASY, 'Parson' 1617

It is puzzling to find a single reference to Edmund Brasy as *"parson of Redbourn"* only 7 months after Bowman became Vicar.[39] Yet he was clearly named in Archdeaconry records; being presented by the Churchwardens as being responsible for repairs to the roof and windows of the Chancel. This is a good example of the legal responsibility of a Vicar for the repair of his Chancel.[40]

PHILLIP LEIGH, Vicar 1630-43

The date 1630 is given by Urwick; he also records his marriage at Totteridge to Sarah Smith in 1634.[41] A year later their first son was baptised at Redbourn.

The Vicar's responsibility for repairs to the Chancel did not extend to work in the Nave, which might explain why he appeared to have no part in some high handed work by Gabriel Whitley, in 1631.[42] George Simmons and Martha Beamond (of Beaumont Hall) complained to the Archdeacon that Whitley had erected a pew for his own use, and that they could not sit upright in their seats due to his seat pressing on their knees.-

> *"betwixt the body of the church and the chancell, in which alley labouring men, yeomen, men servants...usually sit, and through which the Churchwardens cannot passe through to collect any Briefe or do any other duty but are forced to goe about either through the Chancell or the other side of the church. The men's servants and others which did usually sit in the alley are forced to seek themselves new seats or else absent themselves from their parish church".*

Whitley answered by saying that the pew had been erected in a vacant place and in accordance with a Faculty granted to him. He knew of no grievance against it but would submit to the judgement of the Bishop.

A more permanent 'fix' may have come with replacement the old pews with the current fashion for 'box pews', as shown in *Fig: 12.4*. However, it must be pointed out that there is no evidence that the box pews dated from this time, but many such pews date from early 17th century.

An Inventory of five years later, signed by *"Phil Leighe"*, does not solve any of these problems as it does not mention pews of any type [43]:-

<u>Inventory dated May 1638</u> (Not quoted in full)

A Great Bible, two Prayer books, a book of Martyrs (2 volumes), a Register book and a book of Canons for the Churchwardens

Two chests, one with 3 locks and keys (i.e. one each for the Minister and Churchwardens)

A Communion table and frame *"encompassed round about with a rale lately made"* (Known as 'Laudian Rails', to protect the Altar from dogs etc.)

"One fayre carpet of Broade Cloathe with a silk fringe" for the table and a runner of damask, also a napkin

A silver chalice with cover (from 1577)

A pewter flagon and pewter collection dish

A *" fayre pillow & needleworke lyned with silke damaske"* for the pulpit

A surplice for the Minster

A table at the west end for receiving & distributing moneys for the poor

"A very [hole] *and a cover for baptising"* - obviously referring to the Font, of an
    earlier date than today's Queen Anne type

In the Vestry, 2 great spits, 1 mattock, 1 shovel

One bier to carry corpses

Five tuneable (Turnable ?) bells in the steeple , one rope, a table and form

Rents (on Glebe property ?) amount to 25s.5d.

The Archdeacon was told that the church is *"wanting* [in need of] *a decent and sufficient surplisse"*, obviously connected with another report that - *"Phillip Leigh, the Vicar, had his weakness for drinking the King's health in a very poor surplice cut short"* [44] Leigh's weakness as – *"a common drunkard and haunter of ale-houses, usually drinking healths and pressing others thereto, a common swearer and quarreller and hath expressed much malignity against Parliament"* eventually resulted in the loss of his living at Redbourn.[45]

His behaviour obviously set a bad example. John Finch got into trouble for drinking, quarrelling and fighting in the "Holly Bush" at the time of Evening Prayer. Finch would come into church late, if at all, sit with his hat on, not kneel for the confession or Lord's Prayer and not stand for the Gospel or the Creed.[46]

The sudden sequestration of Leigh's living caused hardship to his wife and family, who 2 years later was able to get an Order, ratified by Parliament, for payment of 1/5th of the *"tithes, rents, profits and the Easter Book of the Vicarage"* [47] They continued to live in Redbourn after this, at least until his death in 1656. He was described in the Burial Register as - *"late Vicar of this parish"*.

RALPH ROTHERAM, MA. Minister 1643-49

He could not have been too happy with the burden of finding one fifth of his living to pay to the Leigh family. He served Redbourn through the troubled Civil War period, the execution of King Charles and the setting up of the Commonwealth under Cromwell. The only thing we know about him is that Urwick describes him as *"a Godly, learned and orthodox minister"*.

SAMUEL MACHARNIS, MA. Minister 1650-54

Urwick describes Macharnis as *"a Godly and able preacher, by sequestration from Mr Leigh"*, indicating that he still had to pay Sarah Leigh 1/5th of his tithes.

A change under the orders of Cromwell was that the keeping of the Registers and the solemnisation of marriages was to be transferred to the Justices of the Peace. This change is marked in the Redbourn Register by this note, in 1653:-

"Memoranda that Edmund Grover was made choice of to be this parish Register and to have the keepinge of this booke, and was sworne and approved by William Beamont Esq., one of the Justices of the Peace".

From this point the registers record 'births' instead of 'baptisms', though it is not long before these start to reappear. Marriages records cease after 1649 only reappearing in 1685 long after the Restoration.

THOMAS QUINCY, BA. Minister 1654-57

A new system for the appointment of clergy now appeared involving approval by Cromwell's Commissioners. Quincy was first proposed by three lay people, (none from Redbourn), then the Patron, Sir Harbottle Grimston, gave testimony, of his *"holy and good conversation"*, finally he was adjudged suitable *"as fully and effectually as if he had been instituted and inducted according to any such laws and customs as have in this case formerly been made or used"*.[48]

An instance of the generosity of Redbourn people is seen in a collection made for the *"distressed Protestants of Piedmont"* in 1655; in spite of being so far from home the quite respectable sum of £2.10.3d. was raised.[49]

JAMES BARKER, Vicar 1657-62

Barker came from St Paul's Walden. He wrote a book in 1661, dedicated to Lady Grimston, with the long title of *"The Royal Robe; or a treatise on meekness, wholly tending to Peaceableness"*.[50]

By the 1662 Act of Uniformity Clergy were compelled to follow the Book of Common Prayer and to declare their assent to conform to it and the principles of the Church of England - or resign. James Barker was one of about 2000 ministers (1/5th of English clergy) who resigned or were ejected as a result.

THOMAS DRAPER, Vicar 1663-85

Referred to by Urwick as *"Conformist"*, meaning that he conformed to the 'new' 1662 Prayer Book, Thomas, was instituted in 1663. His father was probably Joseph Draper, Vicar of Sandridge up to 1661.

Non-Conformity to the Prayer book was punishable with imprisonment after the third offence, Roman Catholics also came under surveillance, churchwardens being required to report any such 'Recusants'.

One such Recusant was John Wogan, who in spite of being a confessed Papist still had a licence to teach.[51] With the uncovering of the 'Popish Plot', he changed his views and agreed to be guided in all things by the Vicar, who certified that he had indeed attended church and taken the Sacrament. His conversion was short lived as within only two weeks he stopped coming to church and later the same year (1680) he reappeared on the list of Recusants. In 1706 occurs a report of *"one Wogan, a beggar"*, perhaps indicating that he had been deprived of his livelihood because of his religion, and fallen on hard times.

I suspect that the following tale of Michael Beynon, is largely fictional, but must have been a popular story at this time.[52] He was the brother of Eignon Beynon of Beaumont Hall, not himself a Roman Catholic.

Michael was a Popish Novice engaged to be tutor to a prominent Roman Catholic family. On his journey he was awakened one night by *"a very bright light, darting up and down on the wall"* this he took to be the visitation of an Angel. After a day of prayer and fasting, another visitation took place, this time by a beautiful child. The third night it was by *"a great lion with a chain about him and appearances like dogs surrounding him"*. This time he thought it to be the Devil and prayed for deliverance so loudly that the whole household was awakened, but were unable to see the apparition. This was the last straw and Michael renounced *"the communion of the Whore of Babylon"*, i.e. Popery.

In 1671 the Vicar was reported to the Archdeacon because the Chancel was needing repairs. This part of the church was a Vicar's responsibility while the Churchwardens looked after the rest, which they reported The date *1678* carved on a stone forming the apex of the Chancel gable seems to indicate that Thomas had done his duty by that time - unfortunately this stone was to be *"omnia bene"*.[53] dropped during repairs in 1984 and could not be salvaged.

This seems to have been a time of caring for the church and its equipment. Archdeaconry records tell us of what Silver, books and other 'goods' existed and of a new 'great Bible that was purchased. A 1684 Terrier of Church Glebe lands also contained a complete description of the Vicarage of Draper's time.[54]

Water-colour by Thomas Baskerfield, dated 1789   *Poor water-colour of 1802*

Fig: 12.4 – Drawings of the Vicarage about 100 years after description below

The Vicarage 1684

It was built in the north east of the Churchyard mostly built - *"Studde by Studde broade of good oaken Timber, having a porch over the dore and a study over it "*

A Hall, (perhaps indicating this was quite an early, hall type, house), a Kitchen with an oven, Milk house, Brew house and two Butteries

Five small chambers (on the first floor) and one Garret (in the roof)

An old Barn, House Office, Hogg Sty and an Orchard of fi acre

The house described compares with drawings made later - see *Fig: 12.4*

The Registers record the burial of *"Mr Draper"* in December 1685.

JOHN COLE, Vicar 1686-88

Urwick tells us that John Cole came after Draper, who died in December 1685, so we can only assume that he came in the following year. Urwick also says that he was probably the son of William Cole Rector of St Albans Abbey and Archdeacon in the 1680's. He was Vicar of both St Michael's and Redbourn, probably employing Curates in each parish.[55] John Cole gave up both parishes to become Archdeacon of St Albans in 1688 and moving to Great Munden.

JOHN BIVVY, Vicar 1688-1703

Sometimes spelt Bivy or Bibby, he is only remembered by the gift of silver in his memory, after his death at Caddington in 1729. This consisted of a Flagon, Paten and Alms dish. If there was also a Chalice, it is now missing.

WILLIAM MARSTON, Vicar 1704-26

Like the previous Incumbent, William Marston was Vicar of both St Michael's and Redbourn. He appears to have lived here while employing a Curate at St Michael's. His son, William, was baptised at Redbourn in 1706 and as will be seen, twenty four years later this son followed his father as Vicar of the parish.

William must have brought no small degree of national prestige to Redbourn as Chaplain to John Churchill, Duke of Marlborough. He was not slow in acquainting his parishioners with details of the Duke's campaigns such as a sermon preached in 1709 during a thanksgiving for the *"protection of Her majesty from the attempt of her enemies, and for the many and great successes throughout the campaign"*.[56]

Maybe the Duke had something to do with getting the Queen Anne Font, which we still have. Less likely is his involvement in the new peel of 6 bells in 1716, replacing 5 on a timber frame itself bearing the date 1704 and initials I.C.[57]

The inscription on one of these bells mentions the name of H. Knight, who was the Curate that William put in charge of the parish when he moved to St Michael's in 1713. An incident on a Sunday morning in August 1716 leaves us intriguingly in suspense as to what happened - George Carpenter, senior, was reported for - *"disturbing ye Rev. Henry Knight and ye whole congregation"*.[58]

Another addition to the church *"built at the charge of several young men of the village in 1705"* was a gallery.[59] There are two possibilities where this might have been. The first was above the Rood Screen, in the traditional medieval position, the second more likely position was at the west end of the Nave, where seating for 50 people was known to exist up to 1850.[60]

William's burial place, is marked by a, stone in the floor of St Michael's church, he died in 1726 aged 51 years, his son, William, lies next to him.

JOHN RAMSEY, BA Vicar 1726-30

Unlike Marston, Ramsey did not also hold the living at St Michael's

It was during his time that the silver in memory of John Bivvy was bought. Also major work on the Nave roof is indicated by the date '1727' and the initials 'TB' carved on one of the timbers 251 years after the Clerestory was built.

Ramsey resigned in 1730, and his name disappears until seen again as Vicar of Abbots Langley 18 years later. He died there, aged 61, one of three John Ramseys who died as Vicar of that parish.

WILLIAM MARSTON, MA Vicar 1730-46

William took the living four years after his father's death, at the very youthful age of 24. Like Ramsey he was only Vicar of Redbourn.

Nothing really notable seems to have happened while he was at Redbourn. However, several monuments appeared in the Chancel. One in particular is notable, bearing the bust of Mary Beynon widow of Eignon Beynon of Beaumont Hall, who died in 1732 and 1717 respectively.

Mary's mother, Mary Eccleston was also interred here, the inscription explaining that she was the daughter of John Crosse, who was – *"fined for High Sheriff of London"*. This is rather intriguing, but I have been told that this refers to the practice at one time of preferring only Church of England men as Sheriff, others being subject to a fine. Thus by appointing Non-Conformists to the post, £9000 was raised towards the building of the Mansion House.[61]

William Marston died in 1746 at the age of only 40.

JOHN BOYS, Vicar 1746-87

John Boys has the distinction of being our longest serving **Vicar**, only surpassed by a later clergyman who spent more time here as both Curate and then Vicar.

John Boys was perhaps one of the best Vicars at keeping the Registers, he was particularly meticulous about his family details. These began with a note announcing that he was married at Flamstead in 1751 to Ann Seabrook. There then followed careful records of the birth of 15 children, five of whom died in infancy. Eleven of these were not only dated but the times of birth were included.

It is only during his time that burials in wool, as required by the famous 'Woollens Act', are seen in the Registers. The Act was designed to support the flagging wool trade from 1678, and required that.[62]:-

"no corpse of any person.....shall be buried in any shirt, shift, sheet, or shroud or anything whatsoever made or mingled with flax, hemp, silk, hair, gold or silver or any stuff or thing, other than what is made of sheep's wool only"

To ensure that these terms were complied with, an affidavit had to be made to the Churchwardens, non-compliance incurred a £5 fine. Some of the richer families treated it as a tax, which could be halved by a member of the family reporting the shortcoming and claiming half the fine back.

A typical case recorded that John Ogilvie - *"was buried in linnen and the Churchwardens received the money for the same"* There are 36 such cases out of 1221 'Woollen' burials during the recorded period. Some parishes kept separate records of affidavits; no such records survive for Redbourn. A typical entry he made was - *"Affidavit of his* (or her) *being buried in woollen according to the direction of and within the time prescribed in the Act of Parliament"*. The Act remained in force until 1814, but no records exist for the last 26 years.

The four Register books that were used in Boys time are a mine of additional information. Several other clergy appear, Henry Osman for 8 years from 1765, he was Curate at Flamstead but took many services at Redbourn. Rice Hughes, Vicar of Hemel Hempstead, Frederick Delafont and Richard Griffith who took many services in Boys' declining years.

Mention has been made elsewhere of 'Briefs', designed to collect money to help with repairs, mostly to churches, but also to communities, like that following a major fire in Redbourn village.(see page 126). The registers detail 140 such collections between 1755 and 1781, ranging all over this country and abroad. 105 collections were for churches, including 7 "steeples" which had either fallen down or needed urgent repair. The rest were for Fires in other places (17), Hail damage (80), 1 for *"building fortifications at Brightheimston (?)"* and 1 for the colleges of Philadelphia and New York.

The total collected, all during Boy's time, was £15.8.5d. After they were abolished in 1828, the Church Building Society came into being, their role now taken over by English Heritage.

The recording of 'Stamp Duty' payments from 1783 was another piece of book keeping.[63] Three pence was charged on every Baptism, Burial and Marriage, 10% being allowed to the clergy who collected it. All people unable to pay were excused and marked as 'poor' or 'pauper'. The payments to Mr. Mason of St Albans were all dutifully recorded. In one case Mr. Dolling, the Churchwarden, made the payment but was censured for not getting a receipt.

Another Act of Parliament concerned the tightening up of illegal marriages by requiring the calling and recording of Banns.[64] These were entered with the marriage records in special tabulated registers; the first such register starting in 1754 when the Hardwicke Act was passed.

An interesting list of *"Surplice Fees"*, dating from 1777, was found loose in one of the Register books, see *Fig: 12.5*. This gives the fees payable on everything from a marriage with banns (8 shillings), to a burial - 4s.6d. in the churchyard, to £20 in a new vault in the Chancel. Monuments cost from one guinea for a head or foot stone in the churchyard, to £10 for a stone monument in the Chancel. Needless to say these cannot be compared to current figures.

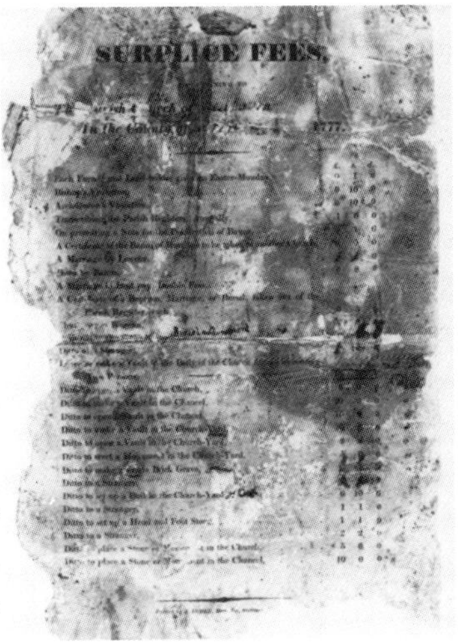

The demands of his growing family and all the new paperwork must have taken much of his time, so it is not too surprising to see that he received several reminders from the Archdeacon, not to neglect these duties.

Fig: 12.5 - Table of surplice Fees - 1777

An 'Injunction' received after a five-hour visit by the Archdeacon in 1757, showed that the Chancel still needed repairs to its roof, floor and the windows *"made good."*.[65] The Nave was in a much worse condition, particularly the north side, needing *"substantial repair"*. A new Belfry floor and new doors on the south and west were also required while the whole inside wanted whitewashing. The font, pulpit and desk (i.e. the three-Decker pulpit) needed repair. Furnishings for the Communion table were to be provided, also a new surplice, which was *"to be kept whole clean and decent"*.

Certification that these jobs had been done was *"very deficient"*; so it is not surprising that eight years later, at the next Visitation, things were just as bad. In fact the roof was now in such a state that - *"...for want of a plastered ceiling, in the winter season* (the rain) *drops down through the leads very fast upon the ministers and peoples heads and greatly damages the church books in the desk"*. As a result - *"The Incumbent and Church wardens...and all others concerned are hereby admonished to repair forthwith the above defects..."*.

The posts of Parish Clerk and Sexton were often held by the same man for quite long periods; one such was Jos. Brown, who served for 37 years, in 1764 he waxed lyrical by writing instructions to the Bell Ringers in verse.[66]:-

"All who intend to take these ropes in hand
To ring, mark well these lines and understand
Which, if with care you read, will plainly see
What fines and forfeits are the Sexton's fee.

He that doth break a stay or turn a bell,
For the forfeit is a groat, it's known full well.
And carelessly to ring with spur or hat
The forfeit is a groat, beware of that.
And they that fight or quarell, swear or curse,
Must pay two pots, turn out, or else do worse.
And for unlocking the steeple door,
And for sweeping of the belfry floor,
And to buy oil, you know it's very dear,
And for my attendance here
If you will observe such rules as these
You're welcome for to ring here when you please
Pray remember the Sexton,   Jos. Brown May 1764"

John's wife, Ann, to whom he had been married 25 years, died in 1776, aged 42, he lived a further 12 years, dying at the age of 72. Both he and Ann were buried in St Peters in St Albans.[67] He had rooms in the Inner Temple, London, where he died, and also owned the "Peacock" inn at St Albans.[68]

JAMES CARPENTER GAPE MA., Vicar 1788—1826

James Carpenter Gape was another Vicar not wanting for money. He came from a prominent St Albans family involved in local politics, having been Mayor of the city in 1809 and 1822, one of his sons later filling the same post.[69]

He was also Chaplain to King George III in 1794, perhaps it was in honour of this position that the Arms of the King were put up over the Rood Screen (now over the south door). He may also have used his influence to obtain one of a batch of Cedars of Lebanon, which appeared around St Albans in about 1803.[70]

His portrait, *Fig: 12.6,* is the earliest known of any Redbourn Vicar. Major D. Gape, who let me have a copy of the original, said he was one of the most colourful of his ancestors.

Fig: 12.6 -
James Carpenter Gape

He lived in St Michael's Manor (now a hotel), while curates looked after his two livings at St Michael's (from 1778) and Redbourn. He was married at St Michael's in 1786 and had 7 sons and 4 daughters. His Redbourn curates can be deduced from the dates of their signatures in the Registers as follows:-

Caleb Lomax   1788-91
James Preedy   1791-95
Jeremiah Lowe   1795-1811
Barnaby Rudge   1810-14
Thomas Pugh   1813-24
Charles Gape   1824-27

A prominent member of the congregation during much of Mr Gape's time was Thomas Baskerfield, who lived at "The Priory" in the High Street (see chapter 8). He was a well known antiquarian responsible for several significant alterations to the church, he boxed in the Lady Chapel to make a meeting room for the Parish Vestry meetings in 1783, and took down the Hertfordshire Spike from the tower in 1802.[71]

He was also responsible for making the earliest drawing of the Church and Vicarage, in 1789 – see *Fig: 12.7*

Fig:12.7 - The church & Vicarage in 1789 - notice the 'Hertfordshire Spike' on the tower

While making a family vault in the Chancel in 1801, he improved its appearance as described by a note in one of the Registers:-

"Let all things be done with decency and order (made)- *a new vault in the Chancell; under the Holy Table. That this house of prayer might strike with greater reverential awe on the minds of the congregation, raised and floored within the rails of the altar and wainscoted round the walls".*

Gape's third Curate at Redbourn, Jeremiah Lowe, took part in a bit of national history by taking the first Census of Population, recorded in the Register as shown overleaf.

Gape resigned both Redbourn and St Michael's in 1826, and appointed himself to his own living at Croydon-cum-Clapton in Cambridgeshire. He died in St Albans in the following year, aged 72, and was interred in the spacious family vault behind the High Altar screen in the Abbey.

A copy of the statement of the Population of the
Parish of Redbourn delivered in to the Magistrates
(As the Act for that purpose directed) at Saint Albans
April 10 [th] 1801

    No. of houses of every description   239
    Families inhabiting do.   237
        Males.....595   Females.....553   =   1153
                  Occupations
      Agriculture   Trades
        318   358   =   676

Persons too old or too young to be included in either of these
    classes 411

    Total Number of persons   **1153**

        Jeremiah Lowe....Curate
        John Lord............Overseer

LORD FREDERICK BEAUCLERK, Vicar 1827-50

"Lord Fred", as he was known, was the last of the absentee Vicars who we shared with St Michael's. Before being instituted into both parishes he had been Vicar of Kimpton. He was the great, great, grandson of Nell Gwynn and King Charles II, the 4th son of the fifth Duke of St Albans.[72.]

He lived mostly in London, letting his curates run his two parishes on their own, only 10 of his signatures appear in the registers in his 23 years. Cussans suggests that one reason for the rise of Non-Conformity in the village can be attributed to there being no resident Vicar here for so long. Noting that though the church could accommodate 600 people, the chapels, combined, could seat more than a thousand. Certainly all the village chapels were built during the 'absentee' incumbencies of Gape and Beauclerk.

His main interest in life was cricket, though said to be shy and retiring, he became another man on the cricket pitch, being a good all round player and captain. He was chosen to play for England 46 times between 1796 and 1823, not because of his position or money, but for his sheer ability. He was somewhat of a showman, even accentuating a slight limp to gain crowd support and sympathy.

Fig: 12.8 - Rev. Lord Frederick Beauclerk   *Fig: 12.9 - Beauclerk in cricket silks*

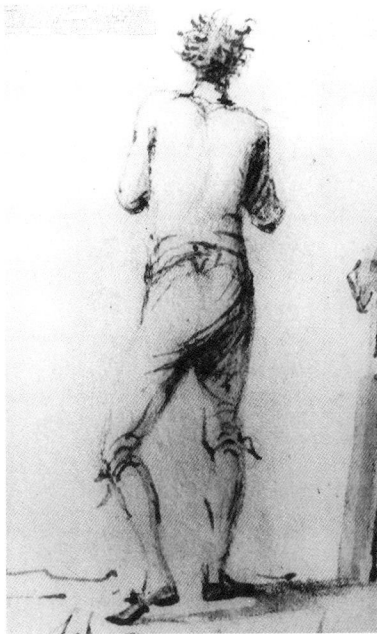

Beauclerk started playing in 1791 and continued into his fifties. He was a founder member of Lord's Cricket Ground and President of the MCC. in 1826; it was mainly through his influence that cricket was saved from extinction, and became the National game. There is no evidence that he ever played at Redbourn, but perhaps his example helped our club to flourish, as will be seen in chapter 15.

He incurred disapproval in many quarters (even for playing cricket!); one critic remarking - *"A clergyman! - why so he is; but he ne'er preachers once in a twelve month.*[73] However, it was for his playing for large sums of money that the most criticism came, some of the matches were advertised as paying £1000 to the winners. Letters were even sent to the Archbishop of Canterbury pointing out his gambling as unseemly conduct for a clergyman, but they had no effect on position.

He was a little more discrete about another sporting activity - he owned a race horse called "The Poet" (see chapter 15).[74]

WILLIAM SEROCOLD WADE, MA Vicar 1850-84

When Beauclerk died, his curate Mr Wade, became Vicar and remained here until his death in 1884; thus becoming Redbourn's longest serving clergyman, 56¹/₂ years first as Curate, then as Vicar. Like Beauclerk, he was also a 'sporting gent' who occasionally let these interests take precedence over his clerical duties. On at least one occasion getting his clerk to give out the following notice.[75]:-

> *"The Vicar is goin' on Friday to the throwin' off of the Leicester 'ounds, consequently he will not be back till Monday next week. Therefore, next Sunday there will be no sarvice in this church on that day".*

This Parish Clerk was most probably Moses Moody, clerk for many years and possibly the subject of a sketch that I found in one of the registers (*Fig: 12.10.*) He was born in 1756. His name started to appear as witness to weddings from the age of 20. By trade he was a tailor and a redoubtable village character of that time - see chapter 8.

Fig: 12.10 - Sketch in Registers, perhaps of Moses Moody?

The registers give us a glimpse of his family life. His first wife was Mary Coultman, by whom he had three children. After her death, and before his next marriage, he fathered an illegitimate child who died in infancy. His second wife Susannah Scrivener, bore him another eight children. They died within a year of each other, she was 70 and he was 91.

Mr Wade's name can still be found in many things around St Marys. A book of - *"Psalms and Hymns, adapted for use in Redbourn Church"*, was given by him in 1839 also a 1734 Prayer Book, in 1851. The Tenor bell bears his name, amongst others who collected for its recasting in 1875. A set of handbells, in the care of the Sexton in 1859, are unfortunately neither dated or named.[76]

The reminiscences of Mr Harry Miller, a Churchwarden, describes the church of 1850/60 in detail (slightly abridged) as follows.[77]:-

> *"The walls inside were quite green with damp, and in the winter-time the roof used to glisten with the frost. Sometimes during service the frost would melt, owing to the warmth which came form the one stove, and water would drop from the roof to the great discomfort of the congregation - especially the ladies if they happened to have on a new bonnet! The church had no lamps, but the clerk would come round with tallow candles, deposit a few drops of melted wax upon the edge of the pews to affix the candles.*

> *"The Vicar's family, together with a few parishioners who lived in the larger houses, were allowed to sit in the Chancel; the central aisle was occupied by the farmers and trades people; the south side by labouring men; the north by women. The singing was accompanied by an old barrel organ, which stood where the font now stands. Very often, after the congregation*

had started singing, the clerk discovered he was playing the wrong tune – the congregation, therefore had to stop singing and wait until the big rollers had been changed.

"An old inhabitant, still living, distinctly remembers his Grandfather playing a clarinet in the men's gallery over the Rood Screen – the women's gallery was at the west end over the entrance o the vestry.

"The churchyard used to be in a sadly neglected state, it being treated more like a place for recreation than a sacred spot".

Some of the defects noted in Miller's description were addressed in Wade's time, others not until much later, and the most serious, the leaking roofs, had to wait 40 years. Perhaps, in an attempt to keep up with the Non-Conformist chapels, the most major job in Wade's time was to replace the old Box pews with more comfortable 'chapel type' pews, about half of which remain today. This was started while Beauclerk was still alive and was completed the year he died.

Fig: 12.11 – The Box Pews in 1839

The architect's application to the Diocese described the need for an increase in accommodation, noting *"The dilapidated state* (of the church), *owing to ye bad arrangement and decayed state of the pews and seats."* [78]

The schedules from which the following details are taken give us information about the seating in the church before 1850, as well as the proposed new seating. Unfortunately no plan of the arrangement of the box pews was included, but the schedule gives their capacity as 323 seats, with a marginal note - *"Very irregularly pewed"* This irregularity is obvious from *Fig: 12.11.*

The new arrangement is scheduled and shown in a plan, (reproduced as *Fig: 12.12)* the seating accommodation adds up as follows:-

NAVE - Front, 9 lines of pews, some divided	150
Back 4 lines of pews with 3 lines in the gallery above	53
SIDE AISLES, north, 15 lines with family pew at east	85
south, 12 lines, with gallery at west	77
TOWER - 6 lines, with organ between	50
Total –	415

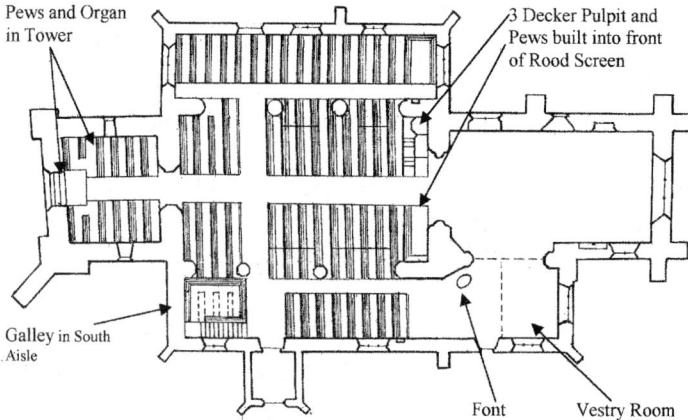

Fig: 12.12 - Reproduced from 1850 plan of new seating arrangement

The new seating gave an increase of 28% on the old haphazard Box Pews. Another improvement was in the number of 'free' seats; as against 'appropriated' seats (i.e. those set apart for certain families who probably paid for the privilege). Now 84% of the seating was free, previously there had been only 18%.

The plan also gave other information showing that the old Three Decker pulpit had been moved up against the screen and had its sounding board removed. A family pew was built into the screen opposite the pulpit. The position of the organ (barrel?) in the tower is unusual, and must have been very ineffective acoustically. Notice also the Font in the Lady Chapel with the boxing in of Baskerfield's vestry reduced in area.

The cost was estimated at £525, but escalated to £600. A mortgage was raised and a grant obtained from "The incorporated Society for promoting the Enlargement, Building and Repairing of Churches and Chapels". The rest came from a Church Rate and public subscriptions.

No further major work was considered until 1872; by which time the external structure was giving cause for concern. So a Luton architect, Henry J. Pearson made a report estimating the cost at £215.[79]

The Tower he said was *"in a dilapidated condition"* and advised fitting an iron band above the Belfry windows and ties on the inside; there is no evidence that this drastic action was taken or indeed necessary. As a cure for damp penetrating the walls, he advised building a drain channel around the outside, made of brick, and draining off to "dumb wells". This channel still functions, having only to be cleared of weeds occasionally. He advised reconstruction and re-leading of the South Aisle roof, a Herts Advertiser article of confirming that this had been done by 1879.[80]

In the same year the Vestry minutes recorded work on the inside - *"A vote of thanks was unanimously recorded to Mr J Hawes for his great kindness of renovating the interior of the church at his own expense".*

In mid-century there was a sudden crop of Ecclesiastical surveys. The first was made for the Baptist Union between 1847 and 1850 by William Upton, Pastor at Dagnall St Church. [81] He based his findings on first hand, personal knowledge making it of particular interest. He commented on St Mary's clergy -

> *Revd. Lord Frederick Beauclerk, 80 - the Vicar is quite laid aside"*
> *Revd. W S Wade, Curate, 45 -is a sporting gentleman, cricketer etc.,*
> *reading tolerably Evangelical sermons"*

In his general remarks he is quite damning -*"Redbourn is as dead and dull a place religiously as can be imagined. Few pious people to be found and among them few care for their neighbour's souls".*

The 'Ecclesiastical Census' made in 1851 in conjunction with the Census of population, and was chiefly interested in the number of people attending all the churches.[82] The figures for St Mary's were more optimistic than Upton's, and exceed the figures planned for the new pews. The average attendance, including Sunday School children, being 350 in the morning and 500 in the afternoon. Several events of note took place in the village in which Wade was prominently involved. All three National schools were built on the Common during his time, and he was a frequent visitor to them all. He also saw the opening of the railway, no doubt being one of the guests on the first train, and afterwards at Hemel Hempstead Town Hall for the celebration lunch. He was one the patrons of the first Horticultural Show, but due to ill health was unable to attend, his place being taken by Rev. Pope, who was to succeed him as Vicar.[82]

Serocold Wade had three children by his first wife, Elizabeth. After she died, he moved out of the old Vicarage and took lodgings at "Dairy Farm" on the Common.[83] In 1863 he married Isabella Pugh who lived at her Father's home, "The Elms". Rev. Thomas Pugh was Rector of Lilley, and was earlier Curate of Flamstead; his name also appeared frequently in St Mary's registers he appears to have helped Wade, probably when he was away at the hunt.- Wade and his new wife moved to "The Poplars" (now "Greyfriars"), an ugly scene which took place here, involving a blocked right of way, is described in chapter 8.

The marriage of his daughter, Mary Alice Margaret to Sir Charles Lawrence Young in 1871, was a much grander affair than his own. The local press described it as a morning of*"surpassing brilliancy"*, going on to relate how the villagers had erected three triumphal arches on the Common, the shops were closed and the. schools on holiday. Everyone turned out to see the bride, with her seven Bridesmaids - their dresses were, of course, fully described.

Details followed of the reception in a Marquee at "The Poplars", tea and plum Cake for the children, gratuities for the widows and sick, cricket bats and balls to be played for by the cricket club, and a *"substantial dinner"* for the tradesmen of the village at "The Bull" in the evening.

Wade suffered poor health from at least 1879, when *"condolences on his late affliction"* were sent by the Vestry meeting. He was able to get assistance from various clergy in his latter years, as evidenced by a variety of signatures in the registers. He died in 1884 aged 84 years, after 23 years as Curate followed by 34 years as Vicar, making him our

Longest Serving Clergyman

Fig: 12.13 - William Serocold Wade

His grave still exists, but there is a more prominent memorial in the church, given by his family. This is the east window in the Chancel, showing the Ascension of Our Lord. The names of all his children and his first wife are recorded on it, but nowhere is his second marriage acknowledged. Whether this omission troubled Isabella, his second wife, is not known, however, she had the window in the South Aisle, showing St Alban, Amphibalus and the Virgin Mary added in 1896 (see *Fig: 5.3*). This is a much better window, made by Messrs Heaton, Butler & Bayne.[84]

PHILLIP DEEDES, Vicar 1884-6

Phillip Deedes came in the same year that Wade died but stayed less than two years, perhaps finding it difficult to follow a Vicar who the parish had known for over half a century.

The only significant addition during his short time may in fact have happened at the instigation of; his predecessor, this was the acquisition of a pipe organ. It was not a new instrument, having been bought from a church in Luton, but coming originally from the Temple Church in London.[85]

Fig: 12.14 - Phillip Deedes

WILLIAM ALEXANDER POPE, Vicar 1887-97

William Alexander Pope came to us from Flamstead, where he had been Vicar from 1884. He had come several times to take services for Mr Wade and the deputised for him at the first Cottage Garden Show in the village, *Fig: 12.15.* He is seen sitting beside the Earl of Verulam (4th from left, centre row) one of three wearing straw boaters - perhaps made in the village Straw hat factory.

Fig: 12.15 – Group at the first Cottage Garden show in 1883

Another occasion for wearing straw boaters may have been that August day in 1887 when members of the St Albans Archaeological and Architectural Society visited the Redbourn area.[86] They started at Redbournbury at 10.30am, and visited "The Priory", and the church at noon. At each place being treated to a lecture by an expert. At the church Canon Davys told them its history and Rev. Fowler talked about the brasses. After the AGM in the Church Vestry, lunch was provided by Mrs White at "Cumberland House". After lunch they continued to "The Aubreys" and a talk by Dr. Griffith before leaving the parish for Flamstead church and Beechwood mansion and their homeward journey about seven o'clock. Perhaps it was as a result of this visit that the church was given some pews for the choir and two large reading desks, formerly in the Abbey.

(I managed to arrange a centenary celebration of the event with a lecture in the Church about Redbourn Priory by Dr. Eileen Roberts, members were encouraged to visit some of the 1887 sites before the lecture.)

Fig: 12.16 - The church 1887, drawn by Canon Davys to illustrate his lecture

The most major work, probably since medieval times, was carried out in Pope's time, so major that it required closure of the church. The reason for the work was dramatically presented to the village in 1890 -

> *"For some considerable period the state of the Nave Roof has been such as to cause grave anxiety, and during the past winter it was found to be absolutely necessary to take steps for its restoration".*[87]

The work and the finances are well documented in account books kept in the Parish Chest, but the best description can be found in one of the Registers.[88]

> *"...with the exception of two tie beams and a few other pieces, the Nave roof of the church was renewed, as was also the roof of the east end of the South Aisle (i.e. The Lady Chapel). The roof of the North Aisle was also re-leaded and sundry work made good".*

The *"two tie beams"* can be recognised because of their charred appearance. The reason for the charring has been put down to a fire in the church, but no record can be found of such a major event; I suggest that they were being burnt with the rest of the timbers, until it was decided to salvage and reuse these two.

Mr S. Redhouse of Stotfield was contracted to do the work, supervised by Mr E. J. K. Cutts, the architect. A pencilled note was spotted on one of the boards in 1993, recording this work - *"Church restored 1890 - S. Redhouse"*.

The Church was opened by the Bishop of St Albans, December 3rd 1890

After spending £433 on the roofs, it was hoped to - *"to place the Church in a similar position with those of equal importance in the neighbourhood"* The cost was estimated at between £1500 and £2000, but by 1893 the work had cost £711.12.0d and as no more money was forthcoming in spite of wide ranging appeals. The subscription list had been headed by the Earl of Verulam with £100 and ranged down through Lord Salisbury, Lord Grimthorpe, Sir John Bennett Lawes of Rothamsted, the Bowes Lyon family to *"Master Head 2 shillings"*. There was still a deficit of £4.17s.2d. but the Vicar undertook to 'liquidate' this.

Some of the work completed included widening the centre aisle between the pews, installing the oak screen in the Tower arch, to the memory of Mr W. T. White of Cumberland House, and reopening the west door. The latter being possible because the organ that stood there had been replaced by a pipe organ.

Like Serocold Wade before him, Mr Pope moved out of the old Vicarage; he rented the "Red House" in the High Street. This large mansion seemed far too large for him, with its spacious living rooms, 10 bedrooms and coach-house for 5 or 6 carriages. When a new Vicarage was completed at Church End in 1894; he moved. In modern times this has been converted into flats - see *Fig: 12.17.*

Fig: 12.17 – Side of the 'New' Vicarage

In 1894 there was a major change in local government, nationally, with the separation of parish affairs from the Vestry meetings. The new, publically elected, Parish Council having to find meeting places away from the church; initially in the schools, until purchase of the old hat factory in the 1920's. (see page 182).

Meanwhile the Vestry meetings had to confine themselves solely to church matters. The minutes of the second such meeting hinted at a change in Churchmanship, reading :- *"Easter Day 1898 - Candles lighted and used at 8 am Celebration of first time probably since the Reformation"*.

Later in the same year another note informs us -*"Harvest Festival - Bells rung for the first time after restoration by Mr S. B. Goslin of London at a cost of £100 raised by the Vicar by private subscriptions"*. This was for re-hanging the bells and quarter turning the Clappers.

Mr Goslin queried the security of the carriages as the vibration from the bells was causing cracks in the walls of the tower. The Society for the Protection of Ancient Buildings made a report and suggested repairs and checks for movement, but no action was taken for a further 13 years.[89]

Mr Pope died in 1897 when he was only 56.

GEORGE AUGUSTUS LEWIS BROWNE, Vicar 1897-1908

The new century was heralded by a low-key collection by Mr Harry Miller for an avenue of trees from Church End to the Church, later altered to run from gate to gate. A century later it is a fine shady avenue. A note in the Register, dated 13th Nov. 1899, gives us the facts - *"First tree of the new avenue, extending from Church End gate to Hemel Hempstead Road, and paid for out of a fund of about £20 planted by me on this date G. A. Lewis Browne, Vicar"* (Note: this was for 28 Lime trees). In some of the older photographs of the inside of theChurch hanging oil lamps can be seen - *Fig: 12.21.* With such inadequate

Fig: 12.18 - Rev. Browne

lighting it is not surprising that the PCC.jumped at the chance to have gas lighting installed with lights on all the pillars - *Fig: 12.22.* The offer did not come from the 42 year old Gas Works in Fish Street, but from Mr Laxton who was to install it, together with an acetylene gas generator in a hut near the Hemel Hempstead Road gate.

Fig: 12.19 - Oil lamp hanging in the Nave　　*Fig: 12.20 - Gas lamps on the pillars*

This system was far from trouble free, an amusing incident, related to me by the late Anne Peake, told how the lighting failed during one Evensong and Mr Laxton went off to see what was wrong. When he came back the congregation thought they were seeing a ghost - he had lit a match to see what was wrong and the gas had blown up and covered him in white ash!

The Vicar was absent from Vestry meetings in 1905 and 1906 and spent some time on sick leave. Although reported to be greatly restored to health, part of taking life easy may have been to sit in church and write about its history and architecture. He expressed a degree of uncertainty by adding the note - *"This is written in Church, and so all mistakes must be overlooked"* [90] It is quite a comprehensive account, with not too many errors, and a few interesting comments, such as saying that the east window, to the memory of Serocold Wade, is a *"reproduction of a very handsome window, with dreadful glass"*.

When the 500th edition of the Parish Magazine was published, the Editor calculated that issue one must have been during Browne's time, in about January 1907. It has continued in unbroken sequence to the present-day, but now called - "Common Round".

LEONARD BUXTON, BA Vicar 1909-14

Two new books were opened by Leonard Buxton, first for Vestry minutes in 1909, the old 'Orderly Book' had been in use since 1800 and was a jumble of Vestry minutes and Workhouse accounts all mixed together. The new book eventually had only 79 of its 295 pages used, that is until 1959 when an economical secretary decide to utilise the unused pages for current PPC. Minutes. The other new book started with PCC. minutes from 1913, but with a note to say that no minutes had been kept since 1911. The item of chief concern was with Mr W. J. Oldred Scott's report on the exterior condition of the church.

Fig: 12.21 – Leonard Buxton and wife (left), family (right)

Oldrid Scott, was the second son of Sir Gilbert Scott who was responsible for much of the early restoration work on the Abbey. Oldrid took over his father's work there, amongst other things, being responsible for the design of the Bishop's throne.[92] At Redbourn he reported on the condition of the church in 1913.[93]

He spoke well of the repairs already done saying that, apart from re-pointing the external flintwork, little needed attention, apart from the Tower. As repairs had been delayed since 1890, the Tower was found to be now in quite serious condition. Some stones had deteriorated, and there were cracks that needed attention: but it was generally the external plastering that was extremely patchy and needed removing and re-facing properly. He said the Tower *"..though sadly disfigured externally, has much dignity and picturesqueness"* commenting - *"It is quite hopeless to make the tower other than a rugged old monument of antiquity and on the whole less done to it to alter it's present appearance the better".*

One other thing we have to thank Scott for is his discovery of the small Norman window in the North Aisle described on page 50.

Work on the Tower had finished by the end of 1913, but other work continued into the wartime years, until stopped in 1916. The cost had reached £1163.6s.1d when Mr Peake, the Treasurer and General Superintendent of the Work, offered to pay the final deficit of about £28.[94] He also produced a very good set of photographs showing the work in progress - see *Fig: 12.22.*

Workmen (left) and timber scaffolding on the east   *Work on the north*

Fig: 12.22 – RESTORATION WORK ON THE TOWER IN 1913

Late in 1913 the Vicar announced a new scheme for Diocesan finance, later known as 'The Quota', now 'The Parish Share'. The PCC. were shocked at our share being £30, and because of the current commitments on the tower repairs, they voted to pay only £5; but later, by taking a special collection, they were able to raise the full amount. The same pessimism still persists over this ever-increasing payment, which is now in excess of 1000 times the 1913 figure.

Also in 1913 Mr H.G.Spary made a useful contribution to the church history by drawing plans of its architectural and monumental features.[91] These detailed drawings (scale of 1 inch to 1 foot) show the principal features and tombs. A third drawing gives a section through the Tower, showing the old oak bell frame.

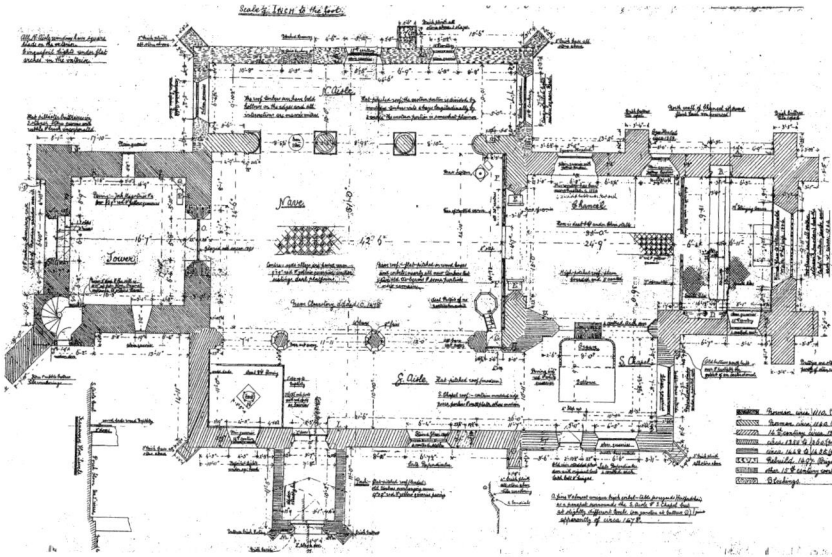

Fig: 12.23 - One of Mr Spary's plans, reduced about twenty times
Notice the position of the organ in the Lady Chapel

Before Leonard Buxton left in 1914, the threat of possible Suffragette raids on the church had to be considered. It was suggested that volunteers should be sought to walk round the church between 10 and 11pm. And 4 to 6am. but after lengthy discussion, it was decided to engage a night watchman.

HENRY WALTER BIRKHEAD BERRY, BA Vicar 1914-42

Mr Berry came just as repairs were nearing completion. Instead of concern about suffragettes, discussions turned to much increased Insurance Premiums due to the threat of damage from zeppelin raids, so much so that a 'deficit balance' had to be declared. This threat is probably what prompted a valuation of the church silver and a suggestion to have the registers copied.

In September 1915 a Zeppelin brought the war to our doorstep, leading to a Thanksgiving Service being held to celebrate *"the marvellous escape of Redbourn from bombs dropped on Saturday 2nd September"*

Fig: 12.24 - 'Mr Berry'

The untimely death of Harry Miller, the Vicar's Warden, of a heart attack resulted from a Zeppelin raid on Hertford. The raid took place on 13th of October 1915, when 44 bombs were dropped by a single Zeppelin killing 19 people. Harry's widow made the handsome gift of a new Pulpit to his memory, this was made by Harry Hems & Sons of Exeter, in 1916. *(Fig: 12.25).*

Fig: 12.25 – The new Pulpit
(Makers photograph)

Quite a bit of extra work had to be done to accommodate this on the north side. A pew, built into the screen for the occupants of "The Priory", was removed, other pews moved and a new oak-block floor laid. The vestry meeting recorded their appreciation for Harry Miller's work and *"his intense love of the church"*.

Meanwhile the old pulpit, Described by Spary as *"a deal Pulpit of no particular merit"*, was sold by the PCC. to Mrs Pope for £2. Perhaps she passed it on to the Baptist Minister living in Church End? See next chapter.

The late Anne Peake told me how the congregation could be greatly amused watching a visiting preacher trying to find his way up into this pulpit. It could only be reached by going into the Lady Chapel and finding a red beige covered door which led through a small arch beside the screen and up to the pulpit steps.

The removal of 'The Priory Pew' from the front of the screen and a similar one on the south side, left two unsightly holes through which the rough wall behind was visible, see *Fig: 12.29*. The screen was in a poor state generally, having earlier had the panelling on the top removed when seating there was not required. Recognising that the screen was a *"valuable relic"* a report was commissioned and a repair fund started.

The report, with the approval of Aldrid Scott, was made by Mr T. M. Robinson. This recommended that some work could be done by a local builder, but a skilled man was required for the bulk of the work. For the former Mr. Edward Peck was used, while the skilled craftsman chosen was Mr Eustice Salisbury, brother of the well-known artist Frank Salisbury.

In 1917 the Vicar announced that he had bought the inside of an organ from Watford on *"very reasonable terms"* and had engaged a man to do work on it for *"a small remuneration"*. Three months later he had to regretfully report that the man had failed to do the job satisfactorily and had *"absconded"* before finishing the work.

Fig: 12.26 – The Screen awaiting repairs, about 1920, notice the holes in the screen where pews had been, also the 'Harry miller' Pulpit (left)

At this stage the opinion of the Abbey organist, Mr Luttman, was obtained and a London firm of organ builders contacted. The outcome was that the organ was repaired - *"as a good instrument, worthy of a church"*. The final cost was three times as much as originally estimated and included a small remuneration to the man who had 'failed'.

The ongoing 'Organ saga' will be continued a little later in proper date sequence. Meanwhile the PCC. expressed their appreciation to Mr William Woodstock, who had been organist for 30 years

The 1920's were marked by a series of gifts to the church:-

1920	A small silver flagon in memory of Charles Lee, who had been ChoirMaster, Sunday School teacher, Sacristan and Bellringer.
1920	Mr Frederick Hall, of Cumberland Cottage, gave the carved oak Altar rails in memory of his wife and of two sons killed in the war.
1924	Mrs Sanson (see Watercress in chapter 10) and Miss Cooke gave two Persian carpets, two carved oak chairs and a stool.
1927	The South Aisle screen in memory of Colonel de Falbe - see Chapter 8
1928	A silver Pyx, given by ladies of the congregation and a processional cross by the choir
1929	The present oak 'Eagle Lectern' given in memory of Sarah Bucksey, Lady Trevanion's maid, replacing a brass lectern which can be seen in *Figs: 12.29*

The 1927 Faculty for the South Aisle screen also included reordering of the Baptistery with panelling round the wall to form a War Memorial.[95] The Queen Anne Font, was to be replaced a new one to the memory of Mr. H. T. Moore, see *Fig: 12.27.*

Since the pipe organ was bought (1884) it had stood in the Lady Chapel, initially with the organist backing the South Aisle, then being rotated to fit under the Lady Chapel arch so that the organist was now with his choir in the Chancel.

Fig: 12.27 – Proposed Font

In 1931 Mrs Moore offered to have the organ rebuilt, still unsatisfactory after the 1917 repairs, the work this time being completed without a hitch. However, on his annual visitation the Archdeacon uncovered the fact that this work had been done without a Faculty being applied for from the Diocese. Unfortunately the retrospective application for this and two other items was not good enough and a Consistory Court was convened in the Abbey, to which the Vicar and Churchwardens were commanded to attend.

Representing the Church were Dr. Totton and Mr Laxton the Churchwardens, Miss Gertrude Peake the Secretary with Mr Ottaway their Solicitor. Vicar had just undergone a serious operation in Hospital and could not attend. The following notes are from the Herts Advertiser account.

Fig: 12.28 - The Organ and Choir stalls in the Chancel

Besides the organ restoration work, the faculty asked for retrospective approval for the installation of Electric lighting and for the oak Lectern in memory of Sarah Bucksey. Knowing of the impending court case, the Bishop had been advised not to accept an invitation to dedicate these new items.

The Chancellor's complaints against the organ were entirely to do with its appearance, he said it had *"completely spoilt a very interesting old arch"* it had a *"hideous front and stupid little doors.* The defence stated that there had been no complaints about its position in the arch, that the renovated organ was more compact and allowed 20 more people to be seated in the Lady Chapel. The verdict was that the organ could remain, but that something must be done to improve it.

As mains electricity was not available, a system using a generator had been installed by Messrs Henry Smith of St Albans. Though there was a possible a fire hazard, it was the light shades that offended the Chancellor. He would not even have them in his kitchen he said and described them as like *"great biscuit tins"* which caused *"the greatest disfigurement"*. He was not even satisfied when told that a similar system had been approved for St Peters. He ruled that the electricity could not be used without alterations to the architect's instructions and the shades changed.

The Diocesan Advisory Committee had condemned the Eagle Lectern outright, but Lady Waller said it was a good design, very suitable for the church. Fortunately the Chancellor had seen both the old and the new Lecterns and while not seeing much in favour of either, allowed the new one to stay.

Mr Laxton appealed to the court, that to do the extra work, the church might have to be closed. To this the Chancellor replied that it was none of his business-it was up to the Bishop. The church did not close, but the PCC. insisted that the Quota should not be met until the Consistory Court expenses had been paid.

The Churchwardens gave their unreserved apologies for not applying for a Faculty. After the court they were admonished by their own solicitor, who said that *"they should not return to the 19th century, when we suffered in all parts of the country from **Churchwardens restorations"***.

Subsequently the Churchwardens were very careful to apply for faculties for all work done - re-flooring the Chancel in 1935, new stained glass in the Lady Chapel (to the Peake family) in 1936, additional grave space in 1937 and a blower for the organ in 1939 But no Faculty was later sought for re-hanging the Porch door in 1940, this was done as thank offering for Jack Dexter who had been reported missing, but later found to be a prisoner of war.[96]

Mr Berry died in 1942 at the age of 71, and was buried at Redbourn. Dr. Totton summed up his contribution to life in Redbourn, saying that he had been a guide and friend in time of need to everyone and that due to his efforts there had been much co-operation between the churches of all denominations.

In expressing gratitude for his efforts to beautify the church, he said he would not forget the treatment received from the *"Authorities and Busybodies"* over these matters (referring to the Consistory Court case) at a time when he was grievously ill; he thought the memory of this had remained with him to the end.

DAVID BICKERTON, Vicar 1942-52

David Bickerton came from a Curacy at Thaxted, taking over in the difficult years at the end of the war. During Mr Berry's time 94 bombs of various types had fallen on the parish, Mr Bickerton got off lightly with just one Flying Bomb.[97] He did have to contend with blackout restrictions But here the friendly relations built up by Mr Berry with the Non-Conformist churches helped a willing acceptance of his request to hold winter evening services in Fish Street chapel, St Mary's paying for the blackout materials and the Electricity.[98]

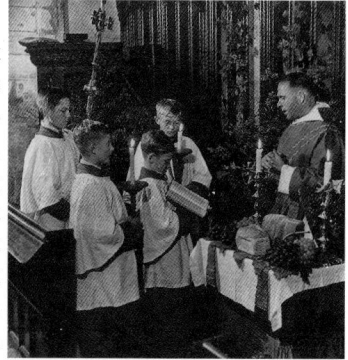

Fig: 12.29 - Rev. David Bickerton reading the Gospel

Another result of wartime concerns was that the Registers were Microfilmed and a transcript made.[99] The transcript has been very useful (my copy is well thumbed), but the microfilm was of such poor quality that it had to be re-photographed in 1973, both are kept in the Hertfordshire Record Office.

In 1944 Mr Bickerton was keen to uncover evidence of where the stairs to the Rood Loft had been.[100] On the north side he found a square headed opening but no evidence of stairs, perhaps a ladder had to be used from the North Aisle. On the south a round-headed arch was revealed with spiral steps leading up to it. However, the lower third of the flight had been removed to make a short passage leading to the pulpit, the original medieval entrance making the opening.

The following year the walls of the church were closely examined for traces of mural painting by Monica Bardswell, an assistant to Professor Tristrum.[101] Due to earlier scraping of the walls and re-plastering she found only scattered fragmentary traces, but came to the conclusion that in Medieval times the wall behind the Holy Rood had been painted a dark red.

Up to this time there is no mention of there being a Church Hall until in 1944 Mr Bickerton attempted to fill this need by buying a wooden hut measuring 46 feet x 16 feet, costing £300, from Kimpton.[102] The problem was where to put it, there were two options – in the Churchyard near Church End Gate or on a plot in Library Lane. However, the project had to go on hold as there was a wartime ban on the erection of buildings - so it was put into store at Fish Street Farm.

With the end of the war, discussions began again but now with the better alternative of the conversion of the old stables in the Vicarage drive suggested. These were purchased from the Earl of Verulam for £315, and the wooden hut was brought out of storage and sold for £20 less than it was bought for.

The PCC held its first meeting in the new Hall in 1946, and agreed that to pay for the costs incurred, bookings would be advertised as *"widely as possible"*.

Another 'saga' started to develop about this time concerning ways of heating the church. The Medieval congregations had to be content with any heat given off by the candles and torches burning in the church. The first heating stove was that installed by Thomas Baskerfield when he converted the Lady Chapel into a Vestry room in 1793 - see earlier in this chapter. It is well known that people using box pews in churches brought hot water bottle with them, or perhaps had some kind of stove; probably this happened also at Redbourn. Mr Spary's plan of 1913 shows only one stove in the church - under the western arch of the north arcade, perhaps this was the one which had earlier been used by Baskerfield.

A *"proper system of heating"* was considered in 1921 at a cost of £375, but the alternative of buying new stoves at £20 each looked more attractive. Five years later there were two stoves, probably Baskerfield's and one at £20; these were moved around so that there was a big one in the North Aisle, and the smaller one elsewhere, probably in the Lady Chapel. Then in 1937 two stoves were given to the church by the Abbey.

David Bickerton was not satisfied with this form of heating, so he called in an Architect to advise. Consultations continued over the next three years, with many different systems being looked at. Hot air was the preferred choice, but at £980, this was too costly. North Met were asked to quote for heating by electricity, their estimate is unknown. Next we hear that Mr Kell, of Messrs Oscar Faber, talked to the PCC about a hot water system.

This system looked promising, so thoughts turned to applying for a Faculty, but suddenly the price was increased from £950 to £1200. Later they revisedtheir estimate to a much more reasonable £800. A plan of the system held by the PCC. shows radiators in similar positions to those we now have, except that there was one in each of the Clerestory windows.[103] It was possibly the deletion of these six positions (which could only have heated the roof) which gave the above price reduction.

By 1949 the new system had been installed and was reported to be working well. The fund for the work closed at £1171, which was enough to also re-decorate the church after completion of the work. However, as will be seen later the saga of St Mary's heating systems was not over yet !

Fig: 12.30 – Charlie Stevens, & one of the pre 1949 boilers

An earlier, undated, system was found when a 'dry moat' was dug along the North Aisle wall in 1971. This revealed an under-floor horizontal chimney, which could only have functioned by down draught from a boiler in the aisle. The extreme inefficiency of such a system was indicated by the complete blockage of the chimney with soot. The high chimney shown in *Fig: 12.30* must have been a great improvement.

In 1948 the Vicar's work in Redbourn was put on film, called *"Men at work - The Vicar".*[104] This Filmstrip consisted of 34 frames, with commentary, showing just about every aspect of a Vicar's life. Unfortunately the parish does not have a copy, but a few of the scenes were reproduced in the 500th edition of the parish Magazine.

Also shown in the same Parish Magazine is a photograph of Mr Bickerton taking the prestigious part of Orator in the 1948 St Albans Millenary Pageant. He was given this part because of his - *"rich, strong and clear voice"*. A rehearsal of his prologue oration was filmed by Mr John Heather, but as this was a silent film we could not sample his voice.

After the end of the war various necessary work could now be tackled. In 1948 all the pews in both aisles were removed and the floors tiled. In 1951, thanks to the work of a French Polisher evacuated from London during the war, the thick, dark Victorian varnish on the front of the screen was carefully 'pickled' off.[105] The effect of this typical Victorian 'improvement' can still be visualised by looking at the back of the screen, which he did not complete.

The robbery of the lead from the Porch roof in 1951, necessitated its replacement with copper. Serious Death Watch Beetle attack was noticed the following year in the South Aisle roof timbers. This resulted in three having to be replaced and the weight on the roof lightened by replacing the lead with felt.

Miss Anne Peake noted that about this time there was an interesting gift of a table for the North Aisle Altar. She tells how this table had been in the Vestry for many years before being sold to a local farmer by the Vicar, Mr Wade. It was later bought from him by Dr. Bovill and after his death was given back to the church by his daughter. There is some doubt about the age of this item which appears to be of about 1600, but could be 200 years younger.[106]

When Mr. Bickerton decided it was time to leave the parish, the massive job of recasting the bells the replacing the old oak bell frame with steel joists was well advanced. He left the village for Sandon, in North Herts., and later Sampford Courtney in Devon. Though he died more than 40 years after leaving Redbourn, he was always fondly remembered by many people, even the Earl of Verulam remarked to Miss Peake that he had *"fallen under the spell of your Vicar"* He died in 1994, aged nearly 85, and is commemorated at St Mary's with a Chalice bought by friends who knew him.

HAROLD GEORGE FORES, Vicar 1953-58

Mr Fores came to Redbourn after 7 years at Hatfield Hyde. During the first World War he had served in the R.N.V.R. and during the second as Chaplain in the R.A.F.V.R.[107]

Two months after his arrival at Redbourn the newly recast bells were ready to be re-hung on the new steel bell frame. The fund collected around the village stood at the magnificent total of £1666, grateful acknowledgement was given by the PCC. to the former Vicar, David Bickerton. The Bishop of St Albans came to Dedicate the bells on 28th March 1953. All the details were recorded in an illuminated book, housed in a glass covered cabinet made by boys of Redbourn school, still on display in church.

Fig: 12.31 - Harold Fores

The Bellfounders, Messrs John Taylor cast inscriptions on the bells giving details of who paid for recasting and also historical details taken from the old bells). The inscriptions on the peal of six bells are as follows, note that the historical facts are given in italics bracketed:-

Treble - Recast 1953 with the help of the Children of Redbourn
(Praise the Lord 1716 H. Knight)

Second - Recast 1953 by the gift of the people of Redbourn
(John Waylett made me 1716)

Third - Recast 1953 by funds raised by the bellringers of Redbourn Church, Joe Hobbs, Leader *(John Waylett made me 1716)*

Fourth - The work of recasting and rehanging the peal of Six was begun in 1951, David Bickerton being Vicar and Anna Vowe Peake and James Gordon Imrey being Churchwardens, and was completed in 1953, Harold G. Fores being Vicar, and Anna Vowe Peake and Kenneth Gilham Betts being Churchwardens. John Taylor and Company, Bellfounders and Bellhangers *(Pack and Chapman of London Fecit 1770)*

Fifth - Recast to celebrate the Coronation of HER GRACIOUS MAJESTY QUEEN ELIZABETH II, 2nd June 1953 *(Taylor and Symondson, Bellfounders, Oxford, London and Loughboro' 1839)*

Tenor - Recast 1953 by gifts in memory of dear ones departed *(Recast by John Warner and Sons, London. Revd. W. S. Wade, Vicar. Joseph Beaumont, James Hawes, Churchwardens, 1875)*

Two gifts associated with the Peake family were given in 1956. First was a Garden of Rest, as a memorial to Dorothy Lilian Peake. The second was the Tower clock, given by the Redbourn Women's Institute *"as a memorial to their beloved founder & first President, Gertrude Vowe Peake JP."*

The history of the church written by the Vicar G. A. L. Browne in 1907 was never published, it was not until 1956 that such a history and guide appeared. It had been prepared by a large group of people studying various aspects of the village. The Vicar and his wife were members of the section studying the church. It was so popular that reprints were made in 1958 and 1961. This stood until the present book was published by the Redbourn Research Group in 1973.

Mr Fores had to resign because of ill health in 1957, he and his wife moved to a house on the Gorhambury Estate, where he died in 1958. A silver wafer box was given to his memory.

EDWARD JOHN MOTLEY, Vicar 1958-67

St Marys was now in urgent need of rejuvenation, Mr Edward Motley was just the man for this job; he came from a Modern church at Mill Hill, with a wide experience, combined with an inspired vision and enthusiasm, he soon started making changes. He put new life into the services by building up the Sunday School and Choir. He formed groups to involve all ages - the men's group, named "The Commoners", a new group for young wives called "The Fly-by-Nights" and for the youth, a branch of the 'Anglican Young Peoples Association'

In the church building itself he saw a great need and opportunity to improve and beautify the interior, while making it more suitable for modern worship. He was able to visualise the effect of removing the organ from the arch between the Chancel and the Lady Chapel thereby widening the vista in that part of the church, an effect which is still much appreciated. He finished off this area by rearranging the steps and Altar Rails and re-paving the area.[108]

Fig: 12.32 – Chancel & Lady Chapel decorated for the 1966 Flower Festival   *Fig: 12.33 – Rev. Edward Motley*

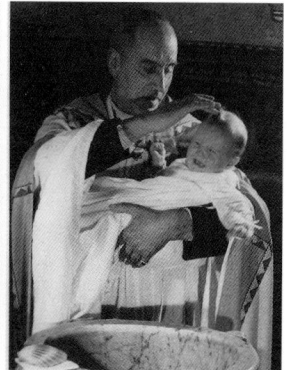

The major part of this undertaking was taking the old organ apart and moving it to a new loft built at the back of the Nave. This was carried out by Messrs Cedric Arnold, Williamson and Hyatt of Thaxted, who improved the instrument and provided it with a separate console. The latter was thoughtfully given a very long lead so it could be moved around the church to find the best position; the ideal spot not actually being found until long after Mr Motley had retired.

All this meant that the church had no organ for best part of a year, a problem he solved by the loan of his own grand piano. When the organ was put back into use, the congregation was not prepared for the improved acoustics - the organist gently being required *"to play a little softer"*.

Part of the 'opening up process' was the removal of the choir from the Chancel, the old choir stalls being moved to the back of the church where they still remain. Mr Motley thought that the Poppy heads on them looked out of place in their new position - so he cut them off such drastic action got people coming to church – if only to see what he was going to do next!

When the Bishop came a few years later, to take a Confirmation, he found the vestry a most uncomfortable place - having to don his robes while jostling elbows with the choir and the servers. However, he suggested adding another floor in the tower so as to make a new 'Upper Vestry' just for the clergy; Mr Motley needed no further prompting, and by 1966 this job was put in hand.

Other important jobs undertaken were the repair of decayed stonework on two of the Norman pillars and the exterior of some windows where the stonework had seriously deteriorated; the insertion of stained glass in the North Aisle east window to the memory Dr. Totton, who had served the village for 40 years. A major difference to the interior was the installation of new lighting in 1967.

After the new heating system was installed in 1949 all went well until 1963 when the boiler burst during a wedding service. This gave Mr Motley one of his favourite stories. He Jokingly summed up the service by saying that the bride arrived in white and departed in grey. On the recommendation of he Diocesan Advisor an electric type was fitted. However, this proved unreliable and new parts impossible to obtain.

The major works that were carried out in Mr Motleys time have been mentioned, however, there was plenty of other things going on in the Parish, rather too many to do justice to in this account, some of themost interesting of these were as continued overleaf.

Fig: 12.34 – Mr Motley's 'Grey Bride'

(Painting by Ruth Peirson)

The 'Christian Stewardship' system of using offers of time, talents and money was started in 1962, this organisation still flourishes today.

Conversations with the Methodist Church, nation wide were aimed at unifying the two churches. Redbourn was not backward in this, and lively meetings took place. The project failed, but other initiatives followed - 'The People Next Door' and eventually the 'Redbourn Council of Churches' (now the 'Redbourn Churches together') to oversee and encourage co-operation between all the village denominations.

For over a hundred years the Redbourn schools had been managed by the Church of England, but in 1965 control passed to the County Council, however, useful contacts with the schools have continued, clergy still visiting by invitation of the head teachers.

'St Mary's Drama Group' was formed in 1965 by the Mother Union and Young Wives groups; this is still going strong as the 'Redbourn Players'.

1965 The long process of designing a new Vicarage, to be built in the old Kitchen Garden, was started. It was not completed until after the Motleys had left Redbourn, chiefly because of the time spent over the sale of the old Vicarage and some of its land to the developer building Ben Austins and Sabeton Close.

1966 A most successful Flower Festival, master minded by Mrs Motley, set a very high standard for the many held since.

1967 Television came to Redbourn - the 9.30 service being broadcast live by ATV. on St George's day. The Rt. Rev. John Trillo, Bishop of Bedford, who lived in the village, being the preacher. Glowing letters were received from viewers as far away as Devon and Cumberland.[109]

1967 Saw the establishment of the first Redbourn Mission House by Mr Gordon Hoskins, St Mary's taking a significant part in preparations, as they have ever since - see the next chapter.

Mention must be made of the clerical assistance that Mr Motley had while at Redbourn. First there was Deaconess Thelma Barton from 1959 for two years. With the licensing of Mr Cyril Harling as a Lay Reader 1961, he gained some valuable assistance which was, supplemented by Curate Bill Berry from 1963 to 1965. Finally Fred Conisbee came as Curate from 1966, being already known to the Motleys. He became a much-loved member of both the church and the community and continued to live in a cottage at Church End, and serve St Mary's for many years after his retirement.

Mr Motley retired to Pentlow in Suffolk at the end of 1967, before moving to his wife's ancestral home at Standen House in Sussex.. His widow, Elizabeth Motley, came back to live in Redbourn for several years after his death.

IAN LEONARD ROBSON, Vicar 1968-72

Ian Robson was appointed Vicar before Mr Motley had left, he came from All Saints Batford, having been spotted there by the Churchwardens and offered the living - a procedure not at all approved by the Bishop. This appeared to have been the first time that the parish had much say in the choice of a new Vicar.

Fig: 12.35 - The 'New Vicarage' – 1969

Fig: 12.36 – Rev. Ian Robson

Almost immediately Ian Robson benefited from his predecessor's planning of the new Vicarage, enabling he and his family to move out of the old, 'expensive to run', Victorian Vicarage to the modern building shown in *Fig: 12.35*

In the services the most radical change I remember was for the Celebrant to move from the front of the Altar, with his back to the congregation, to the other side where he faced the people over the table. The earlier repositioning of the steps in the Chancel gave space for this change - perhaps one already foreseen by Mr Motley?

Other changes were being considered, so seriously that a PCC sub-committee was formed to look at ideas. The most radical idea was to remove all the remaining pews and pave the whole area so that flexible seating arrangements could be tried. However, the idea of an eastward-facing Altar in the North Aisle alarmed many people.

Meanwhile more important jobs were tackled, one of which was necessitated because, after 167 years of telling Redbourn the wind direction, the old weathercock was not only in a dilapidated state but was also lose on its rotting post. Thanks to an offer by John Nowill, an exact replacement was made, clothed in gold leaf. This culminated in topping it out one evening, made memorable when in was dropped into place too fast and wood preservative in the hole squirted out and drenched Churchwarden Terry Biggs – I'm afraid we all laughed! (*Fig: 12.37*).

Fig: 12.37 –The new Weathercock   *Fig: 12.38 – Smoke bombing the church*

A year earlier the cleaners reported finding red coloured beetles, particularly in the North Aisle area - these were identified as Death Watch Beetles, dreaded for their devastating effect on old timbers. Pending expensive replacement of roof timbers, it was decided to try a new idea which only involved setting off smoke bombs in the church annually for at least ten years. The smoke left a sticky, toxic, deposit on the timbers, fatal to emerging beetles. Thus after Evensong one Sunday, the congregation stayed behind to watch as the smoke drifted upwards from the smoke canisters, towards the roof timbers. Later in the spring over 200 dead beetles were found on the floor, some of which had even laid their eggs.

(NB. We no longer use these bombs, as their effectiveness is limited and they can be fatal to other wild life living in church, principally bats)

A long overdue job was to replace the temporary felt roof on the South Aisle. The material chosen was aluminium, but unfortunately the flashing along the nave wall was inadequate and led to leakage when the wind and rain were in a certain quarter. Another damp area was along the North Aisle wall, where the whitewash was always green. The architect suggested digging a dry moat on that side as the outside ground was some 30 inches higher than inside floor level.

In 1970 the village was given a rare honour by being chosen to feature in the Church of England display at "Expo 70". A photographer was commissioned to produce illustrations of all church activities, including the Mission Fair, a staged Wedding and Confirmation featuring the Rt. Rev John Trillo Bishop of Hertford.

Ian Robson left the parish in 1972 for Ashford in Middlesex, followed by the huge and prestigious church of St Mary Abbots at Kensington.

ALAN JOHN COLE, Vicar 1972-80

Changes in Liturgy were taking place as Alan Cole came to St Mary's; a musical setting being composed by Anthony Jennings, known as the "Redbourn Mass". Never before or since were there so many new people taking their first steps to ministerial training. We already had a Curate and Lay Reader; then Richard Leslie became a Deacon, while Alex Osborne was studying to be a Priest, Christine Farrington to be a Deaconess and Terry Clements to be a Lay Reader. Christine was our first Lady Deacon, later being Priested and becoming a Canon of Ely Cathedral and an Honorary Chaplain to the Queen.

Good relationships continued to develop with the other Redbourn churches, an example being that Alan Sharpe, a Methodist Local Preacher, became our Organist. His arrival coincided with the Organ Console at last finding a permanent home under the North Arcade, with the front three pews being rotated 90° and adopted by the choir.

Fig: 12.39 – Rev. Alan Cole

The great saga of the heating system was brought up to date in 1973 by the installation of a gas type boiler, with full protection systems; conversion to natural gas followed a year later.

Fig: 12.40 - Detail of damage & repairs to stones of the Tower quoins

A long programme of church restoration work started in Alan Cole's time. Some repairs had been carried in past years where the original Tottenhoe stone, (sometimes called "Clunch"), had become porous with age and exfoliated. The architect Mr Sean Lander had been watching the condition for some time and now advised that restoration should not be further delayed. The most urgent area was the Norman Tower, but the plan included costing of work on the whole building.

The cost for the Tower was estimated at over £5000, eventually reaching £9205. The PCC were not able to raise such a sum from their own funds, so an appeal was made by letter to every household in Redbourn.

The response was better than expected. The work was able to proceed with additional funds from the newly founded "Friends of St Marys". All four faces were treated, *Fig: 12.41* shows repairs on the north side.

Repairs had barely finished when disaster struck the North Aisle – lead thieves started to strip the lead but were stopped by heavy rain *(Fig: 12.42)*

Fig: 12.41 – Work on the Tower in 1978
From an exhibition print where all the
stones replaced were indicated with lines
from beyond the edge

Their visitation was evident to the Vicar when he came into church next morning and found an inch of water in the North Aisle

This was not the only theft the Vicar experienced, a few years earlier he had been alerted to a suspicious man leaving the church with a heavy sack. When Alan

Fig: 12.42 – After the theft of lead
from the North Aisle roof

offered to help him with the bag, the man ran off leaving his sack, whichwas full of brass items from the church worth about £80. The Police soon caught the thief. A headline in a local newspaper read -

"HAVE-A-GO VICAR"

When it was decided to decorate the interior of the church using only volunteer labour, it brought an unexpected bonus. It was hoped the work would be finished by Easter, but the architect wanted the scaffolding left until some reinforcing of the roof tie beams was completed. The bonus was that this provided an unusual stage for a production of dramatic play in the church.

One highlight of Alan Cole's time at Redbourn was the celebration of the 400th anniversary of the 1577 Chalice. This took the form of an *"Elizabethan Fayre"* at Church End and a *'Sol et Lumiere'* in church. Another centenary celebration was of our only (as far as I know) centenarian, Mrs Ecuyer, whose recipe for longevity was to be *"content with life"*.

In 1980, Alan left for Thorley, later moving to Cambridge, then Gamlingay, where he became an honorary Canon of Ely Cathedral.

JOHN GLANVILLE PEDLAR, BA Vicar 1981-98

With his cathedral training at Exeter and later as Precentor at St Albans Abbey, combined with his musical experience and talents, it is not surprising that St Marys gained enviable reputations for its Liturgy and music under John Pedlar. Thus was the church used for a great variety of musical events, many of which were enriched by John's fine tenor voice, all of which brought audiences from far and wide and greatly helped with raising fund for a number of charities.

There was also varied events, such as the Flower Festival in 1983, an exhibition celebrating the centenary of the separation of the Parish Council from the Vestry Meetings in 1984. A broadcast of the Parish Eucharist, also in 1984, produced many appreciative comments from far and wide. The Wedding Festival of 1991 was another unique event attended by the Earl and Countess of Verulam - the Earl being Patron of the Living. Many couples, married in years past at St Marys, also attended and together with all couples in the congregation renewed their vows.

Fig: 12.43– Rev. John Pedlar

Undoubtedly the most ambitious project, still talked about with emotion by those who took part, was the staging of the Passion of Our Lord called "The Way of the Cross", in1985. The parish was inspired by the Rev. Jeremy Davies from Exeter, whose idea was to show the scenes culminating in the Crucifixion using as his stage venues around the village, and recruiting members of all the Redbourn churches for the cast. The Last Supper took place at St Marys, other scenes took place at the Cricketers, Cumberland house, the Methodist Church, Down Edge and Junior School. It was dark and wet when the Crucifixion took place at St Luke's School, finally the Entombment and Resurrection were movingly re-enacted at St John Fisher, Roman Catholic church. One complaint from someone Down Edge was nicely countered by a duty police sergeant, who pointed out that the church had waited 2000 years to do this and had the full support of the law.

After John Pedlar arrived at Redbourn the restoration work, which started with repairs to the Tower, continued to an ongoing programme agreed with the architect. The badly deteriorated stonework of the Lady Chapel east window was repaired in 1983 and the following year the chequer-work on the Chancel gable end was tackled. Various types of stone, not so prone to water damage as the original Tottenhoe stone, had previously been used, but English Heritage (from whom a grant was obtained) insisted that the original type of stone must be used on the chequer-work. Also the timbers showing in the gable, though entirely decorative, had to be replaced in oak - a good decision.

The attention was now turned to the roofs, starting with the Chancel, where tiles had been slipping for years. This was completely stripped on both sides, repairs to the timbers carried out and an accumulation of birds nests removed.

BUILDING IN FAITH +

Church Development Appeal

Fig: 12.44 – "Building in Faith" brochure drawing

As long ago as Mr Bickerton's abortive wooden hut, (page 227) attempts to provide a much-needed hall for social activities had come to nothing. John Pedlar was determined that now was the time to bring this into being. A brilliant design by David Lelay caught everyone's imagination, it nicely echoed the chequer-work of the Chancel and harmonised with the rest of the church, while providing all the desired facilities. It was going to cost a lot of money, much more than the parish could see itself finding, but the title of the campaign summed up the determination to succeed - ***"BUILDING IN FAITH"***

Lt. Com. Harold Harvey, the appeal chairman, (holder of an RNLI. medal for gallantry) borrowed a typically nautical phrase and 'launched' the fund raising campaign. The final cost was to be nearly a quarter of a million pounds, however, thanks to much concentrated fund raising and the amazing bequest of his house by the Rev. Walter Simmons, a retired clergyman living in the village, the money was raised with only a small bank loan at the end.

The new Transept Hall as it was called, was Dedicated by the Rt. Rev. John Taylor, Bishop of St Albans, in 1989. It has proved a great asset to the church, not only for Sunday use and in-house events but it is also widely used by many church and secular groups. The weekly venue as a Day Centre for old and infirm village people, is surely its happiest use.

Had it not been for the opportune bequest by Walter Simmons it would have been impossible to consider more restoration work for many years, but by 1990 ladders and scaffolding were again to be seen at St Mary's. By this time Mr Lander had resigned as Church Architect and been replaced by Mr Bruno Hooker. His priorities were for work to concentrate on the roofs.

The first to be tackled was the Nave roof in 1993, which had some disconcerting leaks in uncomfortable positions in church. A nice reminder of previous work was a pencilled note found on one of the timbers reading – *"The Church was restored 1890 –SR"*. This referred to the work carried out by Mr Samuel Redhouse (see page 218)

The South Aisle roof was also still leaking, when the wind was in the wrong direction, but before this could be tackled more money had to be raised. Even with the Friends of St Mary's help funds were not available for all the work, so the Vicar decided the time was ripe for another appeal to the village under the title *"Save our Roofs"*. He sat in church to receive donations; which proved so successful that twice the amount aimed for was actually received. This covered the Nave work and enabled work to start the following year on the Aisle roofs.

The South Aisle, Lady Chapel and the North Aisle roofs were restored in 1994 using stainless steel. The first two did not cause too much trouble, but the west end of the North Aisle the roof, dating from 1497, was found to be in a dangerous condition due to wood rot and Death-Watch Beetle attack', its main timbers had to have new pieces of oak spliced on to replace the rotted ends (*Fig: 12.45*). Keith and Garry, did most of the work for Messrs KKS, used their many skills, from joinery to metal working, they could hardly have done a better job.

The total sum of all these repairs came to over £122,000. It says much for the devotion of our small congregation and the high regard that so many friends in the village and elsewhere hold for St Marys that this money was raised. No grants were sought for any of the roof repairs, so all the money came from church funds, the Friends of St Marys or from individual donations.

Chancel roof repair, north side,
before re-tiling, 1990

Damage to the Nave roof being repaired
(notice double skinning),1993

South Aisle and Lady Chapel roofs
completely re-clad, 1994

North Aisle new ends being scarf jointed
onto rafter, 1994.

Fig: 12.45 – REPAIRS TO THE CHURCH ROOFS, 1990 TO 1994

Simon Chiwanga from Mpwapwa in Tanzania became well know and liked at St Marys when he stayed in one of the Mission Houses and joined our congregation. On returning to Africa he was made Bishop of the Diocese of Mpwapwa. From there he wrote to John Pedlar with the suggestion that he ran some seminars to train his African clergy run their parishes more effectively. John decided to do this as part of a Sabbatical and asked David Walker to accompany him to give lay depth to the training.

David took this work seriously, feeling the call to work there using his artistic and acting talents. He went to Theological College and has since returned to work there, currently for a second three-year term.

In 1998 'JP', as he is called by many, had his own call to the church of St Pauls, Bedford. Thus after 17 exciting and productive years at Redbourn he moved to a city church with very different and challenging problems to the friendly country parish of Redbourn.

DUNCAN JAMES SWAN, MA BSc. Vicar 1999

Duncan has been with us for two years and he is starting to bring in changes both to the services and to the building itself. So far the new lighting (started before John Pedlar left), has been switched on, the inside of the church has been whitewashed and a hearing loop installed. Now a new appeal is collecting some £80,000 for repairs to the remaining roofs – the Tower (lead) and the Porch and stonework generally

VICARIAL TITHES

Nowadays our Vicars receive their salary from the Diocese sponsored mainly through the PCC's payment of the Parish Share. However, in earlier times there was a much different method of payment based on an allocation of land, known as "Glebe", from which he obtained income. A small amount came from fees for services memorials etc., (see page 206) but the major part was from 'Tithes'.

Tithes were a tenth part of certain crops and animals - a Rector was entitled to the **Great Tithes** from the crops of corn, hay or wood, while his Vicar could only have the **Small Tithes**, like milk, eggs, honey etc.[110] In Medieval times the Abbot of St Albans reaped the Great Tithes, which were allocated towards the maintenance of writers in the Abbey Scriptorum.[111] After the Dissolution they went to the Lord of the Manor of Redbourn.

Valuations given for the Vicarage in Medieval times actually represent the Tithes available to a Vicar - in 1291 being £17.6.8d. (see page 54) Tithes were commuted to a money payment by Act of Parliament in 1836. To assess their value, surveys had to be made of land, property and owners in each parish. Redbourn was surveyed in 1841, from the schedule of which the chief amounts due were as overleaf.[113]:-

Lord of the Manor (the Earl of Verulam)	£757.17.0d
Other land holders	£295.16.6d
The Vicar (then the Rev Lord Frederick Beauclerk)	£313. 0.0d

(Out of this he paid his Curate, Rev W. S. Wade, his salary)

Subsequent redemption of tithes into a cash payment was allowed by Act of Parliament, certificates for some of these exist between 1906 and 1935.[112] This money had to be paid into Queen Anne's Bounty, out of which clergy salaries were supplemented.[114]

DIOCESAN CHANGES

The division of this country into ecclesiastical districts known as Dioces date form the 7th century.[115] In Medieval times St Albans came under the huge Diocese of Lincoln, but with the Abbey claiming freedom of jurisdiction under its Archdeaconry from at least 1190.[116] With the Dissolution, Henry VIII proposed to found new Sees including St Albans, this did not happen, instead Edward VI annexed the Archdeaconry to the Diocese of London. In 1845 the small diocese of Rochester was reconstituted to include St Albans. Finally St Albans became a Diocese in its own right in 1877.

ST MARYS CHOIRS

Historically Redbourn enjoyed quite a reputation for its music and singing. In the Priory, Masses were sung every Sunday and at major festivals. Abbot Thomas de la Mare, when at Redbourn, *"took great pleasure in the tunefulness of his monks, which he considered to be beyond comparison with the best of singers"*.[117]

Fig: 12.46 – St Mary's Church Choir c.1907, The Vicar, George Browne in front row

The use of the gallery above the Rood Screen has been mentioned earlier, (page 175), also the barrel organ in the South Aisle and later in the Tower. This instrument was replaced in 1884 when a pipe organ was bought from a church in Luton and sited in the Lady Chapel. It may have been at this time that a choir was formed, as three years later St Albans Abbey gave St Marys some second-hand choir stalls [117] Reports given annually, by the Vicar, often expressed appreciation for the choir and money was also forthcoming for new books etc.[118]

During Mr Berry's time the choir was said to be of such a high standard that they were able to pack the church when "Messiah" or similar works were performed. Mr Woodstock, probably our longest serving organist, for 30 years up to 1920, has also been noted. These music traditions have been carried on particularly when a Vicar was also musically talented, such as John Pedlar.

SUNDAY SCHOOLS

The national Sunday School movement dates from c1790.[119] Traditionally the clergy were associated with teaching, in Medieval times, often using the porch of the church as a schoolroom. At Redbourn, although a 19th century plan indicates bench seats here, there were no windows, so this use is rather unlikely.[120]

The earliest mention for Redbourn was in an Education Return of 1833, which stated there were 70 boys and 45 girls in the Church Sunday School.[121] Ladies of means sometimes gave money towards Sunday education, one such was Sophia Baskerfield, who bequeathed £4 per annum in 1846 *"towards the maintenance and support of the Sunday School"*.[122] The Ecclesiastical Census of 1851 gave the following figures for all the village Sunday Schools.[123]:-

St Marys Sunday School -	130 – 150 children
Fish Street Congregational Chapel -	76
Wesleyan Methodist -	60
Mt Zion Baptist -	137 - 143

Pupils were encouraged with a "Sunday School Treat", often on the Vicarage lawn.[124] In 1922 the Vicar, Mr Berry, had the idea of organising a train outing to Southend-on-Sea, this became an annual event for many of the children providing their first ever glimpse of the sea.[125] One of them, Mabel Olive Luck, was inspired to write about it in the Parish Magazine, ending with these two verses:-
There was a great cry,

About going to Southend,	That "Sunday School Treat"
A band of people gaily met	It was a united one
Happily that day to spend.	At Southend again we had to meet,
We shall never forget	And now we're at "Home Sweet Home

This annual event was filmed by Mr John Heather in 1948 and 1949.[126] The latter, although it only shows the departure and return of the party to Redbourn, is always demanded at any public showings of his films.

REFERENCES

NOTE - Much of the information for the later parts of this chapter are taken from PCC. Minutes - no separate references are given for these

1   Prerogative Court of Canterbury, Register of wills, ref. Welles 6
2   PRO. Ref. – Augment. Off. Miscell., Vol.497 as quoted by John Cussans, ref. 6, p.238
3   Rev. Edward L. Cutts - "A Dictionary of the Church of England" pp.138-9
4   William Urwick -"Nonconformity in Hertfordshire" 1884, pp. 290-1
5   The Bishop's Transcripts for the Archdeaconry of St Albans are kept in the HRO.
6   John E. Cussans - "History of Hertfordshire" 1879, pp.240-1
7   As 4, p.292
8   As 4, p.193
9   HRO., Wilton Hall - A Calendar of Papers – Answers to Articles, 23.3.1579
10   As 9 - Answers to Articles 13.3.1583
11   As 10 - Miscellaneous Papers, Book 2, 21.11.1584
12   As 10 - Miscellaneous Papers Book 3, Letter from Edward Spendlove, 26.7.1585
13   As 4, p.107, note 2
14   As 10, dated 13.3.1583
15   "Oculus Episcopi"   Administrations in the Arch deaconry of St Albans 1580-1625
16   As 11, book 2, 29.4.1585
17   As 4, p.294
18   "The Herts Genealogist & Antiquary" (Ed.) W. Brigg, Vol. 1 p.115 also As 9, 1588
19   As 10, Letters dated 18 & 19.7.1588
20   Robert Peters - "Administration of the Archdeaconry of St Albans, 1580-1625", p.167
21   As 4, p.294
22   All the facts about Mr. Dyke are taken from - Urwick (4 above), pp.106-15 & 291-2
23   As 4, p.294
24   As 9, 1590-2
25   As 9, 31.1.1592
26   As 9, Answers to Articles 19.11.1595
27   As 11, Book 4, 21.12.1600
28   As 9, 31.1.00
29   As 11, Book 3, 1597
30   As 11, Book 4, 7.7.1600
31   As 4, p.295
32   The account of Gawton's early life come for Urwick (Ref. 4),pp.69-71
33   As 9, 5.6.1603
34   As 9, 22.8.1615
35   As 15, Will - HRO. ref. 68AW37
36   As 6, p.241
37   As 9, 29.7.1616
38   As 9, 16.1.1623
39   As 9, 8.1.1616
40   As 3, p.140
41   AS 4, p. 297

42   As 11, Miscellaneous Papers, book 4, 1631
43   Inventory in HRO. ref. No. 13
44   As 4, pp. 297
45   As 4, pp.297-8
46   As 4, Miscellaneous Papers, 24.9.1638
47   British Library Add. MS. 15669 fol.67
48   As 4, pp298-9
49   As 4, p.838
50   As 4, p.299
51   Taken from P. R. Knell, "A Papist Schoolmaster in Hertfordshire" pp.19-20, from -
         "The Essex Recusant", vol. 2, No.1, 1969
52   From a printed account in the Parish Chest, Historical box, source unknown
53   As 11, Miscellaneous Papers, Book 7, 1671 & 1672
54   Gerish Collection in HRO. Box 62, Folder 5
55   John Everett, "A Fair Field" pp.70-73
56   Parish Chest ref.HB/6
57   Records of the 'Redbourn Historical Group' (no longer in existence)
58   As 11,Miscellaneous Papers, book 7, 1716
59   Victoria County History - Hertfordshire, Vol. 1, p.369, note 111
60   "Application - Increase in Accommodation", Lambeth Palace ref. ICBS.4042
61   Letter to the author from Mrs Gwenoline Page, Markyate
62   W. E. Tate - "The Parish Chest", 1983, pp.67-69
63   As 62, p.50
64   As 62, p.49
65   Records of the Archdeaconry of St Albans, HRO. ref. ASA.18, 1757
66   As 2, p.237
67   As 2, p. 241, note †
68   "Hertfordshire 1731-1800 as recorded in the Gentleman's magazine", p.214
69   Duncan Warrand (Editor) "Hertfordshire Families" p. 163
70   Hertfordshire Countryside, Vol. 4, No.15, p.102
71   British Museum ADD.MS.9063.fol.248b
72   Unless otherwise referenced, the information in this section comes from an article in
         The Listener, by Harold Hobson - "The Cricketer without a Rival" 9.4.1942
73   Article from MCC. Archives Titled "Jus Eccesiasticum Angulicanum" p.52
74   As 59, Vol. I, p.365
75   As 54, folder 4
76   Note in Register book, HRO. ref. 1/4
77   Parish Magazine August 1910, article by Mr. H. Miller
78   Documents held in Lambeth Palace, ref. I.C.B.S. 4042
79   Parish Chest, ref. LB/10
80   Herts Advertiser dated 3 May 1879
81   Judith Burg "Religion in Hertfordshire 1847-51" transcript of William Upton's survey
82   Herts Advertiser and St Albans Times, September 1883
83   May Walker, "Redbourn", 1960, p.56
84   The author was given this information by Mrs Joyce Wallis, of NADFAS.

85   As 59, p. 369
86   St Albans Architectural and Archaeological Society Transactions, 1887, pp.8-90
87   Report on the work and the subscribers, held by Mr C. Harling
88   Account and subscription lists etc., Parish Chest LB/15
89   Report in the Parish Chest, ref. LB/10
91   HRO. ref. Miscellaneous 37425-9
90   Copy in the Parish Chest ref. HB/1
92   Dr. Eileen Roberts - "The Hill of the Martyr", chapter 17
93   Copy of Oldrid Scott's report kept in the Parish Chest, ref. HB/1
94   Vestry Minutes, 1916, page 55
95   Faculty, HRO. refs. DSA2/1/231/66 & 67, Plan ref. DSA2/1/8/53 & 54
96   In notes given me by the late Anne Peake
97   HRO. - HCC, & DC. Records – 'Air Raid Damage'
98   Fish Street Chapel records held by Redbourn Village Museum, ref. 97.050
99   PCC. Minute Book 1937-51
100 Parish Chest, ref. LB/16
101 Parish Chest, ref. LB/10
102 Faculty 1948, HRO. ref. DSA2/1/78/68
103 Parish Chest, ref. LB/20
104 Made by J. Mc.Farlan for Common Ground Ltd. ref. CGB.383 - copy held by the
       late Beryl Draper, viewed by the author before her death, present location unknown
105 PCC. minutes and notes on the church given the author by the late Anne Peake
106 Report requested by the Redbourn Research Group from "Questor" Antiques
107 Un-dated cutting from the Herts Advertiser, c.1953
108 Faculty 1961, HRO. ref. DSA2/1/130/138
109 "Common Round" June 1967
110 John Richardson – "The Local Historian's Encyclopaedia" ref. C.134
111 Thomas Walsingham - "Gesta Abbatum", Rolls Series Vol. 1, p.57
112 Tithe Map, HRO. ref. DSA 4/79/2
113 Parish Chest, ref. LB/5
114 As 110, ref. C129
115 As 3, p.229
116 As 59, Vol.4. p.363
117 As ref. 111, Vol. 2, page 401
118 Copies of Annual reports held by Mr C. Harling
119 Rev M.W.Patterson – "A History of the Church of England" 1914, page
120 Plan of the church by J. C. Buckler, c.1840, HRO. collection of drawings
121 Education Returns, from copy held in "Kyngston House", by the St Albans
       & Hertfordshire Architectural & Archaeological Society
122 Redbourn Parish Chest, Charities box, ref. RC2.846
123 Ecclesiastical Census, 1851, from copy in HRO.
124 Herts Advertiser ,.8th Dec 1894
125 Parish Magazine, August 1922
126 Filmed by Mr John Heather in 1949, held by Redbourn Village Museum

CHAPTER 13

THE OTHER REDBOURN CHURCHES

In the reigns prior to Queen Elizabeth, dissenting from the established doctrines and practices of the Church of the time could be an offence punishable by death on the block or at the stake. However, other views supporting the ideas put forward by John Calvin, were gradually surfacing. Such Puritan minded clergy called themselves "Ministers". They would not wear a surplice, would not sign the cross when baptising and would not kneel at Communion. They also challenged Royal Supremacy over the Church and sought to introduce a system of church government, which was above the state.[1]

Clergy were required to conform to the Prayer Book requirements, or to resign their livings. The holding of public religious meetings, or using a building for such a purpose except if specially authorised, was punishable by imprisonment or a heavy fine. However, the movement became so strong and widespread that eventually the state had to give way, but still sought to control such groups by requiring registration with their Archdeaconry. Thus a separate 'Non-Conforming' community was accepted and grew in Redbourn. By the end of the 19th century there were five such separate groups, each with their own chapel.

Meanwhile Roman Catholics, or 'Recusants' as they were called, had also to be recorded and if possible converted back to the Church of England. A few Recusants were reported by the Churchwardens, but it was not until a century after the emancipation of Roman Catholics in this country, in the mid 19th century, that they built their own small church in Redbourn.

As will be seen later, reconciliation and friendly relationships between all the denominations have taken place in Redbourn and nationally, more and more sharing worship in each other's churches.

ACT OF UNIFORMITY

The 1662 Act of Uniformity demanded a public demonstration by all clergy of conformity to the principles of the Church of England, as laid down in the Prayer Book. Amongst two thousand clergy who found this unacceptable and resigned, was James Barker of Redbourn, who resigned, but afterwards changed his mind and conformed.

This Act had the effect of driving ministers and congregations underground and forcing them to hold illegal meetings in each other's homes, often in remote places to avoid detection. When such 'Dissenters' were discovered, fines or imprisonment could be imposed. Cases known at Redbourn are as overleaf: -

1665 - A long list of *"Persons exercising Religion otherwise than allowed by the Liturgy"* included Thomas Eggleton of Revellend, a labourer, all were given a 3 month sentence or a £5 fine.[2]

Meeting Place	Situation	For whom	Date	By whom certified	Notes
Barn of Elizabeth Leighton	Redbourn	Independants	6th May 1796	Henry Atley, Minister, Samuel Hill, John Wood, George Gill	
House of William Chapman	Redbourn	Independants	9th June 1796	Henry Atley, George Gill, J. N. Bacon, Samuel Hill	
House of Sarah Law	Redbourn	Methodists	10th August 1798	Sarah Law, Samuel Copleston, John Humphrey, John Wood	
Building of Tomas Rogers	Fish Street	Independants	20th Sept. 1802	Samuel Burder, Minister, Henry Geary, Jos. Ellis, Thomas Rogers	Possibly a barn later made into a chapel
Tenement of Mr Walter Kent	Fish Street	Independants	20th August 1806	John Smith, Minister, Edmund Friday, Thomas Southam	**Present chapel**
House of Edward Smith	Redbourn	Independent Calvinists	29th Sept. 1817	Edward Smith, George Homan, James Horond, William Piggott, Edmund Friday, Richard Wells, Thomas Southam	
Barn of John Abbott	Tassel Hall	Protestant Dissenters	6th June 1822	George Homan, Thomas Southam, John Abbot, James Horond, Richard Wells, Edward Smith	
House of William Piggott	Back Lane	Protestant Dissenters	1st Oct. 1822	George Homan, Thomas Southam, John Abbott, James Horond, Richard Wells, Edward Smith	
House of William Whitehouse	Redbourn	Protestants	13th April 1825	John Wilson Pipe, William Whitehouse, John & Thomas Wood, W. Irons, Edward Herbert	
House of Williams Eams, Miller	Redbourn	Protestants	10th Nov. 1825	Richard Cooper of St Albans, Minister	
Mount Zion, belonging to Edward Pratt	Lybury Lane, near Tassel Hall	Protestant Dissenters	12th July 1835	George Gristwood, E. Pratt, Edward Smith, J. Pratt, Matt. Grace, Thomas Lawrence, George Wheeler	**Mount Zion chapel**
Building	Redbourn	Wesleyan Methodist	31st March 1837	Josiah Wingrave, Jacob Harrison (Trustees)	**First chapel**
	E. Common	Primitive Methodist	c.1869		
	Crown St.	Baptists	1869		**Crown St.**
	N. Common	Wesleyan Methodist	1876		**Second chapel**

Fig: 13.1 – Meeting places of Redbourn Dissenters 1796-1876 (Based on Urwick)

1669 - A list of "Conventicles" compiled for Archbishop Sheldon included [3]: -   *"At the house of William Barber, gent, and Thomas Bigg, yeoman, a meeting of Quakers every Tuesday, number and quality forty ordinarily, sometimes two or three hundred"*
"At the house of Richard Stringer, joyner, a meeting of Anabaptists, number sixty or eighty"

1683 - Friends meeting at Caddington were arrested and convicted, including John and Richard Jackes of Redbourn.[4]

ACT OF TOLERATION

This Act of Parliament introduced toleration of Dissenting ministers and congregations, (excluding Roman Catholics) but required registration of their meeting places. Records of the St Albans Archdeaconry only survive from 1760, but a return made by the Vicar, William Marston, in 1724 said there were ten Dissenting families, out of two hundred and ten in the parish. Urwick lists those for Redbourn, the first in 1796, see *Fig: 13.1* [5]

INDEPENDENTS – FISH STREET

From the first registration of the Independent cause in 1796 it is obvious they were well established and organised, sharing a minister, Henry Atley, with St Albans. By 1802 Samuel Burder was given as Minister and in 1806 John Smith. The first trust deed indicates that a barn in Fish Street was *"converted into and used as a meeting house"*. Some cottages were also part of the property, all of which were Copyhold to the Manor of St Amphibals.[6] It was John Smith who enlarged this small chapel to nearly twice its size in 1807, work which must have provided the frontage of the pleasant building which remains, little changed, to this day - see *Fig: 13.2*

Fig: 13.2 – Fish Street Chapel Sunday School Anniversary c.1920's

Even with Smith's enlargement it was only just big enough - attendance being described as – *"quite full on the Lord's evenings and all seats nearly occupied in the afternoon"*. By 1807 all bills, except for one guinea, had been paid, but the following year Smith was again planning further enlargement. Not only did he raise £200, but also remitted a third part of his stipend to help the fund.

The signs were of a healthy church, catering for the future with a Sunday School of forty children. John Smith was also taking his mission beyond Redbourn by starting a 'lecture' in Flamstead. But there were also unhealthy signs, starting in 1817 with some members leaving Fish Street to set up a chapel elsewhere – (next section) Sadly, with the infirmities of old age, Smith's capability seems to have left him. Membership dropped to three, though Upton's survey of 1847 gave reasonable attendances as fifty to two hundred. The chapel was in a *"dilapidated state"*, and Smith described as a *"Good man, but inefficient"*.[7]

A plaque in the chapel commemorates John Smith's ministry thus: -

"Sacred to the memory of John Smith, for 43 years a faithful minister of Jesus Christ in this place. By his indefatigable exertions funds were raised for the purchase of this estate and the erection of the chapel for the use of the people of this village as an Independent place of worship for ever. After he had served his own generation, by the will of God, he fell asleep on the 12th of June 1848 and in the 74th year of his age and at the 51st of his ministry".

He is said to have been buried under the pulpit.

The Herts. Union, who had been asked by the Trustees to manage the Chapel, introduced William Robinson for a probationary period. In 1850 he was accepted as Pastor. Things immediately began to improve, repairs were carried out, a gallery and a schoolroom being added.

During his busy time here the national Ecclesiastical Census was made, recording 120 free sittings and 100 other, with congregations of 95 morning and 100 in the evenings. He also bought the first Record Book for the chapel, most entries beginning in 1855, including marriages for which the building had just been registered. Robinson's burial (in 1854) is the third recorded in this book. He also left notes detailing the history of the church, which his successor thoughtfully entered in the front of the book..

The next two pastors stayed for four years each; they were John Cooke Westbrook and Edmund Russ. The latter minister invited a frail, but very talented young lady of 26 to stay with them called Emma Tatham.[8] Her talent was for writing and poetry – her book "The Dream of Pythagoras" went to five editions. While staying with them she became ill and died, her dying wish to be buried in the chapel graveyard was honoured and marked with a stone.

David Richardson was the next Pastor, he stayed 10 years and a further 15 after retirement. It was he who transcribed William Robinson's historical notes into the Record book.

The highlight of Richardson's time was a programme of modernisation between 1863 and 1865. The chapel was lit by gas, piped from the newly built Gas Works across the road. The frontage was improved by adding railings and a weathervane on the front gable, summed up by a plaque reading – *"Congregational Chapel, Built 1806, Enlarged 1865" The weathercock cost £1.1s.6d. Both the receipt and the weathercock can be seen in the Redbourn Village Museum – Fig: 13.3*

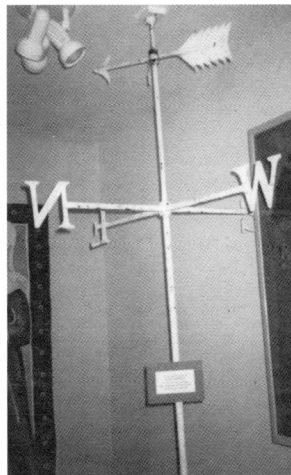

Fig: 13.3 - Weathervane

The most distressing part of his ministry must have been when a second splinter group' broke away and built a new chapel in Crown Street. However, one member made up for this by long faithful service. This was Michael Harborough. After acting as Deacon for several years he accepted the office for one year, but served until his death 27 years later. His son, Russell, (who started the Jam Factory - see chapter 11) followed him in this office.

Following Richardson's retirement, the spiritual needs of the members were supplied by students from New College, London, working also with the chapel in Harpenden. In 1892 Michael Holland became Pastor, but four years later the members could not afford to pay their part of his salary (£50). He solved their difficulty by resigning.

An offer of help came from the group who had broken away from Fish Street very acrimoniously only 23 years before and gone to Crown Street. Perhaps they too were in financial difficulties, however, there is no indication that their offer to share a pastor was taken up. Instead, they went to St Albans for help, thereafter sharing a succession of pastors. First William Carson, up to 1908, then with Mr A. T. Hallowes sharing the work from 1904. Frank Wheeler served from 1909 to 1914. From then until at least 1926 students from New College returned.

On page 190 a nice piece of co-operation with St Mary's has been recorded during the Second War. After the war the chapel went out of use, and in 1948 it was leased to the County Council for use as a Library, Welfare centre and for further education and other meetings. However, services were still held there, latterly being taken by Mr Harry Harborough, until his death in 1960.[9]

However, the chapel has since returned to its former use, (see next section). This well loved building will soon celebrate its Bi-Centenary as a place of worship - the first Non-Conformist chapel to be built in Redbourn.

MOUNT ZION BAPTIST CHAPEL (1817-1979)

In about 1817 a group, with differing views from other members of Fish Street chapel, broke away and started holding meetings in each others houses, (see table - *Fig: 13.1*). This was the beginning of the Strict Baptist cause in Redbourn, although as early as 1669 an illegal meeting of Anabaptists was recorded (see page 214). They initially called themselves – "Independent Calvinists", but later appeared as "Protestant Dissenters". Yet another name – "Hyper-Calvinists" was used by Upton in his survey.

Their chapel, called "Mount Zion", *(Fig: 13.4)* was built in 1835 on land given by one of their members, Edward Pratt, cost £330 to build, but after raising half the amount they complained that more would have been raised *"but for the Birmingham railroad having spoilt Redbourn's coaching trade"*.[10]

Fig: 13.4 – Mount Zion in the 1920's

Fig:13.5 – Richard Figg, aged 98

Upton gives the pastor in 1847 as Rev. J. Figg, but the Ecclesiastical Census of 1851 corrects this to Richard Figg, who is also seen as a grocer in the High Street up to 1899.[11] *Fig: 13.5* shows him in 1903 at the age of 98. He wrote a long poem entitled "The Backslider's Confession", probably written before he became a pastor, as near the end he gives his commission from God to *"Go forth and preach my works and blood"*.[12] At the celebrations for Queen Victoria's Diamond Jubilee he made a speech as the oldest man in the village.[13]

The next pastor was William Cartledge between 1857 to 1871. On the 34th chapel anniversary the debt was finally cleared. The following year (1870) gas lighting was installed. William Cartledge resigned over disapproval at his intended marriage. He stayed in the village for a further 10 years.

During the 1870's the graveyard was getting full and had to be restricted to church members only. During this period there was no pastor until 1880 when Mr Newman came, at first on a temporary basis. We do not know how long Newman stayed, but by the First World War there was no resident pastor.

The system of using pastors from neighbouring chapels to supply their needs continued, but other more weighty matters were under discussion. One was the need to constitute the church on Strict Baptist lines; this being necessary before an application for financial aid to cover essential repairs could be made. The worst happened when the chapel was declared unsafe for use because of cracking of the walls in 1969. Fortunately they were able to move back to the old Fish Street Chapel, at first sharing it with the Library. Thus the Baptist congregation had come back full circle 155 years after breaking away from Fish Street.

They have much improved the old chapel and renamed it Mount Zion. For a time they again had their own pastor, Alan Gilliam, but later found that they could not afford to keep him on. The cause continues in very good shape, taking an active part with the other village churches in "Redbourn Churches Together".

As a postscript to this history it must be stated that the Lybury Lane chapel was saved from demolition by Mr Saxon Aldred, who for many years has effectively used this as his workshop to make and renovate pipe organs.

CROWN STREET TABERNACLE (1869-1950's)
In 1869 a far from friendly separation of some of the Fish Street congregation began. It started as a peaceful withdrawal by some members who wanted to hear the preaching of one of C. H. Spurgeon's students, Mr Dunnington.[14] The latter politely requested Pastor Richardson of Fish Street, to release these members of his flock from their membership. He got a sharp reply, to the effect that they had already dismissed themselves.

After addressing open-air meetings on the Common, Mr Dunnington used the Assembly Room at the "Bull". These meetings were attracting 150 to 300 people, indicating that there was a real need for quite a substantial chapel. After obtaining a site in Crown Street, a fine looking chapel was built there. They named it "The Tabernacle" after Spurgeon's Metropolitan Tabernacle in London, because he had made a £200 interest free loan for the new building – *Fig: 13.6*

The chapel cost £555 and from its inception was lit by gas from the Fish Street works. It opened in 1870 and was completed the following year, with Mr Dunnington as the pastor. Its members were described as "Particular Baptists but of open Communion principles". Meaning that membership was by baptism by full immersion, but that communion was open to other baptised Christians.

Fig: 13.6 – "The Tabernacle" c.1900

There was a strong Sunday School of 90 to 100 children, in 1880 hosting a united teachers' tea meeting with the Congregational and both Methodist churches. A better relationship also seems to have developed with the Fish Street congregation by this time, as is evidenced by their offer to share a pastor in 1896.

The cause survived the Second World War but closure came because of falling membership in the 1950's. The quite imposing chapel was then demolished and a house called "Old Walls" built in its place.

METHODISM IN REDBOURN

The first registration of Methodists in Redbourn came 7 years after the death of John Wesley. This was in the house of Sarah Lowe in 1798, but there is no mention of a chapel building until 1836, by which time they were known as 'Wesleyans'. This reflects the slow start that was typical of the St Albans area.[15]

Things had been starting to happen from about 1835, when there were said to have been 120 "hearers". This indicated an obvious need for a chapel building.

THE FIRST WESLEYAN CHAPEL

The first chapel was opened in 1836 on land on North Common purchased for £20. The building itself cost a further £180 and can still be seen, now part house, part store and part shop. In *Fig: 13.7* it can be seen on the right next to the "Greyhound" inn (with a lean-to in front); the later chapel is on the left. Many stories are told about this first chapel and

Fig: 13.7 – The first Wesleyan Chapel – RHS

hardships suffered by its people. One man used to be pelted by his wife with pots and pans when he returned from a service. While a Luton girl had to sneak out to avoid being stopped by her parents from attending.

The services were often powerful and dramatic, the many candles in the chandelier being snuffed out, leaving one on the pulpit for dramatic effect. There were many conversions, including an old lady of 82.

By 1845 membership had grown to 70, equalling that of Watford and Hemel Hempstead put together, but two years later was described by Upton only as *"useful"*. By the 1851 Ecclesiastical Census seating was given as 200, with average congregations of between 90 and 150.

Fig:13.8 – Two views of the Primitive Methodist Chapel on East Common

PRIMITIVE METHODISM

The other Methodist cause may have grown from the same beginnings as the Wesleyans or broken away from them or some other group. They favoured more outgoing, revivalist services such as provided by 'Camp-Meetings'.[16] The Herts Advertiser recorded that they had been holding such meetings at least twenty years before building their chapel. The stone-laying took place in 1869, after a procession through the village.[17] Their chapel, though small, could hold 200 people, some in a gallery – *Fig: 13.8*. It was a flourishing cause in the late 19th and early 20th centuries with a Sunday School of 60, a choir and both Sunday and weekday services.

George Draper was one of the preachers and the Anstee family also played a leading part in chapel affairs.

"Methodist Union" with the Wesleyans on North Common was not greeted with enthusiasm at first, but had to be accepted in 1939. To soften the blow it was decided to keep both chapels open, using that on East Common for the Sunday School and Women's meetings. Eventually the chapel was sold, briefly to the 'Open Brethren' for £400, but later turned into a store for used car parts. It has since been demolished and replaced by a house.

THE LATER WESLEYAN CHAPEL

Meanwhile the Wesleyans were flourishing on North Common, so much so that only 35 years after their chapel was built, they needed a larger one.[18] Extension was out of the question. Instead they were able to purchase a nearby plot of land on which two cottages and a barn stood. On this site they built a fine new chapel for £947, offset by £100 from the sale of the old chapel. – *Fig: 13.9*

Fig: 13.9 – The 1876, North Common, Chapel in c.1900

That was in 1876. By 1882 they had not only cleared their debt but were ready to consider further extension. There were two proposals, either to build a gallery or to extend to the rear. The latter was accepted and this was put in hand for £302 and included a Vestry tacked on the end.

A report made on Methodism in St Albans by Rev. George Geaves in 1907, stated that the Redbourn society, except for the City itself, was the largest cause in the circuit.[19] Even so, and in spite of playing a major part the development of Methodism in the area, Redbourn never had a resident minister. The nearest it came to this was the brief appearance of Sister Elsie in 1898 for one year. Initially it came under Marlborough Road chapel, later being linked with Hatfield Road chapel.

Many well known local names appear in the records as preachers, leaders or workers. The local dentist, Mr F. G. Boucher, became too popular by his free treatment of sufferers, on Sundays, so he had to charge them, but put the money in the collection. Tom Pratt was Chapel Steward for 47 years, *Fig: 13.10* Harold Anstee was also active here after the closure of the Primitive Chapel on East Common.

*Fig: 13.10 – Tom Pratt, Chapel Steward for 47 years from 1892. (*Drawing by Derek Mather)

Between the two World Wars, though money was tight, more progress was made. There was still enough to spend on some renovations and on the installation of electric light. The congregation was thriving and during the period there was an abortive suggestion from Fish Street for amalgamation.

In modern times the chapel has continued to flourish, though now the emphasis is not so much on housing large congregations as to providing other accommodation. In 1957 the seating was reduced to a more realistic number, with a partition to bring the pulpit forward so as to increase the size of the primary room at the rear. New kitchen and toilet facilities have been added, making this a popular venue for some village activities, including a Playgroup. The basement room, thoughtfully provided in the original layout, is a great asset, though the necessity for high entry steps make disabled access a little difficult.

CHURCH AND CHAPEL IN THE 19TH CENTURY

The Ecclesiastical Census of 1851 was too early for either the Primitive Methodist chapel or the Tabernacle in Crown Street. After these had been built the total count of chapels reached its maximum – five. A picture can be drawn of the village situation at about this time. William Serocold Wade was Vicar, St Marys having seats for 550 people 90% of which were used on most Sundays. The five Nonconformist chapels could seat about 1270, thus, including the church, there was a potential to seat 1820 people (about 87% of the village population). The chapels thus outnumbered the church by more than two to one.

To bring the picture up to date, the five chapels are now reduced to two - the Methodists on North Common and the Baptists from Library Lane now in Fish Street. Arising initially from a study campaign called "The People Next Door" all the churches in the village have got together, and while retaining their own churches and organisations, frequently share services and fellowship, under the umbrella of "Redbourn Churches Together".

THE PENTECOSTAL CHAPEL

A further chapel remains to be recorded, this is the small Pentecostal chapel which sprang up some time after the last war. A small chapel was built on the site of a cottage at the corner of Lamb Lane and Crouch Hall Lane, see *Fig: 13.11*. Mr George Berry, a draughtsman at de Havillands, was the only pastor I recall. Their building is now the home of the "Redbourn Players".

Fig:13.11 – The Powell's cottage before being replaced by the Pentecostal Chapel

ROMAN CATHOLIC CHURCHES

After the Reformation, until the mid 19th century, Roman Catholics in this country suffered much persecution. Some were burned at the stake, others driven into hiding or exile, fearing for their lives, at the least others were excluded from public office or teaching. An example of the latter has been seen in the case of John Wogan (see page 198).

Churchwardens were required to report any such 'Recusants' but few were made, reflecting a similar lack of cases in the county as a whole.

Full emancipation in this country did not begin until the Roman Catholic Relief Bill of 1829 and the abolition of religious tests for university in 1871.[20]

It was not until about 1936 that a Roman Catholic Church appeared in Redbourn. This was a small hut, its site described by Father Durkin in 1977 [21]:-

"The only evidence of a church was a notice board, peeping over the hedge. The entrance through the hedge led to an avenue of cypresses, which had been planted in the late 1930's, the seclusion added to the charm of the small, well cared for, friendly, little church".

Father Durkin went on to describe how his predecessor, Father A. M. Putts, had planned a new church to cater for an ever increasing congregation taken not only from Redbourn but also neighbouring villages. Thus was the present church built and dedicated to St John Fisher –*Fig:13.12*. It was consecrated in 1967 by Cardinal Heenan, Bishop of Bedford, with local clergy and civic leaders present.

Fig: 13.12 – St. John Fisher, Roman Catholic Church

Nikolaus Pevsner describes the church thus [22]:-

"An arresting west front with uneven gable above a plain red brick wall and a lower projecting porch with side entrance. The asymmetrical elevation continues inside, with different spaces ingeniously grouped within the basic rectangle, yet avoiding a sense of clutter through carefully worked out effects"

THE REDBOURN MISSION HOUSES

This remarkable project was undertaken with enthusiasm and dedication by Mr Gordon Hosking and his wife Elaine, who lived in "Cumberland Cottage". The property included an acre of land with a coach house at the end of an avenue of Horse Chestnuts, formerly part of the Bowes-Lyon estate.

Recognising the need for a house where Missionaries, home on furlough, could be united with their families they had left behind in England, the old coach house seemed to be ideal for this purpose, except that it needed much work done on it. He took out a mortgage to provide funds, which were put in the hands of Trustees. The other churches in the village recognised Gordon's need for their practical help and pitched in to clean and decorate the house. When it was ready, Norman Nunn and his wife, from the Sudan Interior Mission, were the first to move in.

The requests for lettings from other missionaries soon indicated the urgent need for further accommodation. Overcoming a multitude of financial and practical problems, Gordon succeeded in building five new houses and four flats adjacent to the coach house. A Common Room was also provided, but sadly the avenue of Horse Chestnuts had to be sacrificed. The whole complex was named "Harding Close" after the Rev. F. Harding of Spicer Street Church in St. Albans - a founder member of the Trust.

Fig: 13.13 – "Harding Close" Mission houses
Notice the Old Coach House in background

The foundation stone was laid by the Rt. Rev. Maurice Wood, Bishop of Norwich, the 69th successor of Bishop Herbert Losinga who consecrated St Mary's Church eight and a half centuries before. The Hoskings had a new house built nearby for themselves. They also offered this new house to the Trust when they retired and moved from Redbourn. It became a home for retired missionaries in their declining years. Sadly this had eventually to be closed when it failed to meet new requirements for nursing homes. The site is now a small housing estate (not for missionaries) known as "Flint Copse".

REFERENCES

1   Rev. E. L. Cutts – "Dictionary of the Church of England" page 489-90, also other books, such as – John Richard Green – "A Short History of the English People", page 468

2   Session Rolls of the Liberty of St Albans, Vol. 1, page 176

3   William Urwick – "Nonconformity in Hertfordshire", page 300

4   As 2, Vol. 1,page 335, also - Joyce Godber – "Friends in Beds & West Hertfordshire" 1975, page 29

5   As 3, page 302, the earliest for Redbourn being 1796

6   From a Newspaper cutting in the Church Record book, pages 78-9. Most of the subsequent information in this section is also taken from this book which is kept in the Redbourn Village Museum, ref. RDBVM.97.050-060

7   Judith Burg – "Religion in Hertfordshire 1847-51" The survey made by William Upton for The Herts Union

8   W. B. Gerish Collection in the HRO.- Biographical notes

9   "The Story of Redbourn", by members of Mr Munby's WEA., class, 1962, page 70

10 As 9, page 65

11 Trade directories between 1862 and 1899, given "Henry Figg" in 1850, probably his father

12 From a printed copy given to me Ann Skillman

13 Herts Mercury 26 June 1897, via Kyngston House archives

14 Most of the subsequent information about this chapel is taken from – "The Story of Redbourn", (ref. 9) pp.66-8

15 Most of the information about Methodism in Redbourn is based on – Roy Craske, "Redbourn Methodist Church" 1876-1976"

16 As 1, page 398

17 Cutting found in the Treasurer's Book, 1894-1939, Redbourn Village Museum ref. 00.007

18 As 15. Also – Rev. George Geaves, "Wesleyan Methodism in the City of the Proto-Martyr & The St Albans Circuit", 1907, pages 114 to 119

19 As 18, Geaves, page 119

20 John Richardson, "The Local Historian's Encyclopaedia" section P92

21 "Redbourn Village Souvenir Brochure – Silver Jubilee of Queen Elizabeth the , Second article by Rev. B. Durkin, page 9

22 Nikolaus Pevsner, "The Buildings of England – Hertfordshire" 1977, page 277

CHAPTER 14

REDBOURN SCHOOLS

In Medieval times the chief source of learning came from within the Monastic Houses, such as St Albans Abbey. It is doubtful if any village boys could read or write except by joining that community as novice monks.

Educated clergy were not necessarily always the norm for country parishes, but some of these are known to have attempted some teaching of their younger parishioners. The Church Porch was often used as such a classroom, and some churches can be found with seats and large windows. Redbourn church has a dark porch and no seats, however, the earliest known plan shows what appear to be benches along each side, such as could have served such a purpose.[1]

The interest of the Church of England and its clergy in education continued through the centuries, including the mainly church run National Schools of the 19th century. Today less participation is allowed in our multi-national and multi-faith schools, but most clergy try to retain a foothold in their local schools - this is still the case at Redbourn.

EARLY REDBOURN SCHOOLS

At least one Vicar was also a teacher, this was Humphrey Wyldblood. He was deprived of the living in 1592, but was allowed to continue teaching.[2] Other teachers can also be named as follows:-

1595	**Michael Anne**, a schoolmaster [3]
1600	**Mr Maye**, described as *"Late Schoolmaster"* after having an illegitimate child and being dismissed [4]
1675	**John Wogan**, a Papist but with a licence to teach, ended up a Beggar (see page 214)
1731	**Thomas Carpenter** left £10 per annum to Mr Collett, master of a school at Redbourn.[5] This was a Charity School, rent from a piece of land paying for *"poor scholars there"*. His nephew, who ran the charity, eventually fell out with the schoolmaster and stopped payments; leading to closure of the school.
1762	**Adam Redpath**, the only schoolmaster seen in the Militia Lists.

REDBOURN BOARDING SCHOOL

The first definite location of a Redbourn school was at "Beamont Hall" in 1771. This is known from an advertisement in the "Public Advertiser" which read [6]:-

> *"Youths from five to sixteen years of age are boarded and taught English, Latin and French; Writing, in all hands; Arithmetic, in all its parts; Mensuration, Surveying, Gauging, Dialling etc., with several branches of the Mathematics, and Book-keeping".*

The advertisement stated there were 43 boarders and went on to detail the terms. Basic schooling and boarding cost £14 per annum, with mending and *"School Articles"* £16, with clothing £20. A guinea entrance fee was charged, with dancing at an extra half guinea per quarter. This was obviously a very up-market school, with an emphasis on subjects involving mathematics, totally at the opposite end of the scale provided by Mr Collett at about the same time. The Headmaster or Mistress, are not named, but the Gould family were known to be occupying Beaumont Hall at that time.

OTHER EARLY SCHOOLS

During the 19th century Redbourn was increasingly well catered for with schools, even children in the Workhouse had some degree of education. This seems to have started when Mr Potter was appointed Master in 1818. He was ordered [7] – *"to teach...the children in reading, spelling and the Church Catechism..."* The Poor Law Commissioners did not lay down such a requirement until 1844, so Redbourn was ahead in this respect.

The number and variety of schools operating in the village during the 19th century perhaps reflects the prosperity of villagers during the Stage Coaching period. I have found the following from Trade Directories and Census Returns:-

1830's	**John Ball** ran a day and boarding school in the barns behind the 'Doctor's House' in the High Street, he was a noted maker of quill pens – page 127
1832	**Susannah Bassil**, Charity School (Robert Smith Bassil is listed under 'Gentry')
	Sarah Lawrence, to at least 1839
	Robert Sibley, Day school
	Sarah Slythe, Boarding school, also in 1839 as a day school, in 1861 on the Common, and retired in 1871
	Daniel Wilder, Boarding school
1839	**John Whithouse**, School in the High Street. A former pupil described how the children sat on two forms with the master sitting in the middle – *"with a rule in one hand and the spelling book in the other. He would ask a boy to spell a word, and if it was spelt incorrectly, the boy would receive a sharp blow over the head with the rule"*
	Thomas and Ann Bull had a night school at North Place, also described by the same ex-pupil saying they paid a penny per night, or three pennies per week. He noted that – *"many a Redbourn boy had to rely for his education on this evening school, having to go to work during the day on a farm. The boys would often present the master with half an ounce of snuff to keep him in good humour so that he would let them out early"*
	Sarah Slythe, see above
1841	**William Whitlock**, Harpenden Lane
	Mary Hickman, Lamb Lane
	Mary Balls, The Common

1850	**Miss Kitty Dixon**, a Seminary, The Dixons were millers at Do Little Mill
1851	**Mrs (James) Arnold**, The Common
	Miss Ashby, Fish Street
	Sarah Stephens, Infants, The Common
	Mary Trowth, Snatchup
	Mr & Mrs William Whitehouse, High Street
1861	**William Ottway,** North Place
	Sarah Slythe, The Common
	Jane Whitehouse,
	Two others in Fish Street
1878 & 82	**The Misses Matilda and Ann Strong**
1890's	**Miss Slythe**, a former governess to Lady Glamis' two daughters, a school near Redbourn House, possibly the daughter of Sarah Slythe (see above)

It will be noticed that many of the teachers were single women, this giving rise to the title of 'Dames Schools'. Most of these disappeared in the late 19th century, but Redbourn is reputed to have had the last such school in the country, it was run by Miss Laura Quick, who died in quite recent years.

Yet another type of school existed in the village during the century, this was the 'Straw Plait School'. These existed when this local cottage industry was at its height in the county. In Redbourn there were at least three –

> **Ann Grover**, in the High Street (1861)
> **Mary Smith**, in Mount Pleasant (1861-71)
> Plait school at the "Jolly Gardener" (date unknown).[8]

Plait Schools existed to teach children to plait straw so that they could earn useful money for the family. About 2d to 3d per week was charged, for which they were supposed to be given some rudimentary education, but the teachers were sometimes uneducated and perhaps even non-plaiters themselves. Children as young as 2fi years attended these very overcrowded establishments.

REDBOURN'S NATIONAL SCHOOLS

Moves to build a church run school in Redbourn began in 1847, with the Vestry proposing the sale of the Market House to build a – *"school room or rooms for the education of the poor of the parish"*. It was another nine years before the auction took place, providing enough money for two schools. Plans show the original school with a central fireplace, and a bell on the chimney stack.[9] (see *Fig: 14.1*) A site on the Common was given by the Earl of Verulam .

A foundation stone, still in place, records the date, 1857, and the names of the Vicar, Rev. W. Serocold Wade and the Churchwardens. The Conveyance of the site to the Vestry gave its purpose as – *"a school for the education of children and adults, or children only, of the labouring, manufacturing and other poorer classes"* [10] It was to be conducted according to the principles of the National Society for promoting the education of the poor, hence its title of "National".

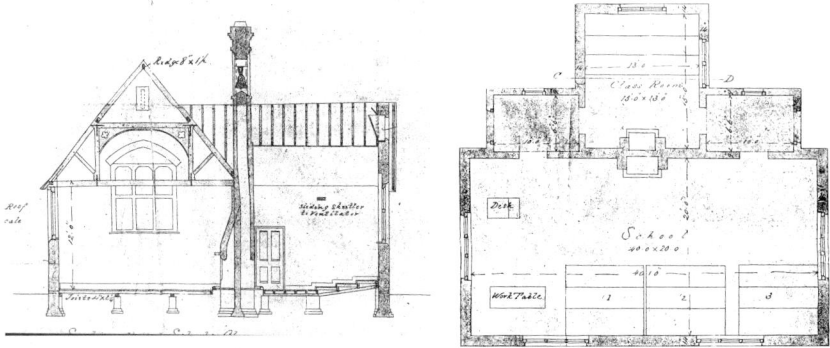

Fig: 14.1 – Elevation and Plan of first school, 1857 (From original drawing in HRO.)
Notice the bell in the chimney stack

It was to be under the control of the Vicar and a management committee headed by the Hon. Claude Bowes Lyon. The committee were expected to contribute £1 annually to the funds and the heads were to be practising members of the Church of England.

The name of first headmistress is not recorded, but by 1863 a logbook was started by Sarah Elizabeth Parker declaring herself as *"Mistress in charge"* [11] She was to remain for the next 30 years during which time her school, for all ages and sexes, was split into Boys, Girls and Infants. In 1884 she married Charles Harvey, Headmaster of the Boys School.

Fig: 14.2 - The first National school seen from the Common

Conditions in the new school were at times very difficult, at first they had to manage without desks and in winter the two back-to-back fires were far from adequate. In the very cold weather *"the children could scarce hold their pens and pencils"*. The remedy was to spend half an hour rubbing their hands together, or if that failed they had to march up and down to get warm.

Fig: 14.3 – Infants School (right centre) 1950's

Fig: 14.4 –Boys School, now Ravenscroft, (modern photograph)

During Miss Parker's time as headmistress the number of pupils nearly trebled, thus new premises had to be built, first a school for infants on the same site in 1872, followed by a separate Boys school on a site near the present War Memorial in 1879. The land for this was again given by the Earl of Verulam; the management committee consisted of four ladies, headed by the Vicar's wife, Isabella Wade.

SCHOOL LOG BOOKS

The school logbooks from 1863 are kept by the present schools and form a very useful resource both for village historians and pupils. They have been used by the children to recreate conditions in their schools from Victorian times, being particularly fascinated by the 'Punishments Book', dating from 1902. The use of the cane from earlier times is given by a note made by Sarah Parker *"broke my cane, therefore, determined that the next one should be stronger and more costly, the broken cane costing only fid"*.

The logbooks shed interesting light on the reasons given for absence from school, usually governed by youth employment, illness or weather conditions. Sunday school treats, village fetes, cricket matches, Sangers Circus etc., appear until the school 'legalised' many of these by giving half-day holidays. Such official days included the Harpenden Races, the Cottage Garden show and the Queen's Silver Jubilee. Also noted were times to attend church to mark the relief of Mafeking (1887) and to pray for relief from the "Cattle Plague" (1866).

Illness was, of course, a major reason for absence. Some illnesses were fatal – Whooping Cough – one child died in 1872, two deaths from Measles in 1892 and several dangerously ill. Other illnesses such as Mumps, Blister-pox, Chicken pox, Bronchitis, Pneumonia, Influenza, Scarlet Fever also St Vitus Dance and water-on-the-brain were recorded. Vaccinations were given by the doctor in 1880. Sometimes children were sent home with Ringworm, one boy being off school for ten weeks. Others would be sent home *"to be washed and made tidy"*.

The weather was another reason for absence, especially as many children had to walk across fields to school. Snow could make this impossible. 1874 was a particularly bad year, the schools having to close because the snow was so deep. If the weather was bad the school sometimes closed at lunchtime to enable the children to get home. 1893 seemed to make up for all the bad winters, the school log recording – *"Extraordinary fine weather for the past three months"*.

Absence by children working at the Silk Mill caused conflict between parents and teachers until a system of half time working was arranged (page 183)

1895 Boys class,
"Best in Drawing"

Girls class early
1900's

Fig: 14.5 – EARLY CLASS PHOTOGRAPHS

SCHOOL INSPECTIONS AND VISITS

Annual visits by HM. School Inspectors produced a variety of comments, mostly favourable such as – *"The school was only opened in May, but appears to be progressing satisfactorily"* (Boys) *"Very bright and happy school"* (Infants), *"One of the best schools in the area"* (Girls). Another spoilt the good name – *"Prevailing disorder and inattention, discipline is absolutely disgraceful, every kind of dirty, disorderly habit going on without the slightest check"* (Infants).

Getting a good report was of great importance as the size of the 'Grant' awarded depended on getting a good overall report.

The Factory Inspector was another visitor - on the lookout for under-age children who also attended the Silk Mill. Other, more welcome visits, were from the Vicar or his Curate, who took some of the weight off the teachers, at least for Religious education. Another regular visitor was Mrs How from "the Heath", who referred to the Infants School as *"my flower garden"*.

SCHOOL DAYS

The logbooks depict the schools as seen by the Head, but the scholars, sometimes told of their earlier school days. A girl described the 1880's when the infants had to sit on back-less wooden forms and copy letters and figures written on the blackboard onto their slates.[12] The Common was their playground on which there was no supervision or organised games. Another ex-infant remembered entering school aged three years and later on being *"Breeched"* in knickerbockers for the first time, feeling like *"the King of Persia"*.[13] The prospect of transferring to the Boys School filled the same boy with horror and nightmares, the headmaster, Jobby Laxton, having the reputation as a tyrant. His arrival was a dramatic event started by a quick rap on the barometer and then a *"Good morning boys"*, greeted with an answer in unison.......

Fig: 14.6 – Mr Jobby Laxton

"GOOD MORNING SIR"

PRESENT-DAY SCHOOLS

The three schools on the Common continued in their separate buildings until after the Second World War, but meanwhile an extension was required for the infants who were given a pre-fabricated building near the War Memorial. This has remained in use as a Youth Club and retaining its name of "the Annex".

Modernisation came with new buildings sited in Long Cutt. The Junior School, for both girls and boys being opened in 1966, while the adjacent Infants a year later. Preceding these, a new Secondary Modern School had been built in Crouch Hall Lane in 1962 to serve not only Redbourn but the surrounding villages also. However, closure came in 1981, after which it has been used as a school for children with learning difficulties, called "St Luke's".

Meanwhile of the old schools on the Common have been put to other uses. The Girls and Infants School has been taken over by firm of accountants, while the Boys, after a period of use as an pipe organ workshop, has become a school for children of pre-school age, called - "Ravenscroft".

REFERENCES

1   HRO. collection of drawings by J. C. & J. Buckler, vol. 3
2   "Oculus Episcopi"   2 WH. Misc2,
3   H. R. Wilton Hall, "A Calendar of papers 1575-1637", Miscellaneous papers book 2
4   As 3, Answers to Articles
5   "Report of the Commissioners of Charities and Education in Hertfordshire, 1815-39", page 291
6   May Walker, "Redbourn", pages 68-9
7   Vestry Minutes, kept in the Parish Chest
8   As 6, page 75
9   HRO. ref. DES.1/63
10 Vestry Minutes, kept in the Parish Chest, Historical box
11 The School logbooks are kept by the Redbourn Junior and Infants Schools. Most of the information in this section is taken from these or from – Roy Craske, "Redbourn Girls School 1863-1951"
12 Hertfordshire Countryside, Vol. 22, No.106, Feb. 1968
13 "Common Round" January 1965

CHAPTER 15

THIS AND THAT ABOUT REDBOURN

In this final chapter I am including miscellaneous items which do not fit comfortably into any of the preceding chapters, but which never-the-less demand inclusion in any history of the village.

EARTHQUAKE 1896

About 5.30am on Thursday 17th December 1896 Mr E. W. Arnold at Redbournbury farm woke up to feel his bed rise up at one end and then at the other.[1] He realised he was experiencing an earthquake. His sister in the next room had a similar sensation, and also heard the rattling of crockery. At Redbourn Little Mill a rumbling sound was heard, while many other villagers had similar tales to tell. The heavy sleepers heard nothing and were very sceptical of their neighbours. The article giving these details showed a map marking all the places in Hertfordshire from which reports had been received.

One aged inhabitant recollected experiencing another earthquake 34 years earlier, again in the early hours of the morning.

REDBOURN'S POPULATION

Estimates of the possible population of the village have been made for 1086 and 1344 (chapters 2 and 3) based on the number of tenants multiplied by five (an average family size). The same factor can be applied to the Rental of 1455 which gives a figure of about 410. Further estimates can be made but it is uncertain how accurate these are. It is only when we get to the National Census Returns, starting in 1801 (see page 209), that fairly reliable figures become available.

There are various ways of attempting to fill in the years between 1455 and 1801. One makes use of the Register figures and applies factors to them as follows [2]:-

$$\begin{array}{ll} \text{Baptisms} & \text{x } 30 \\ \text{Burials} & \text{x } 31 \\ \text{Marriages} & \text{x } 125 \end{array}$$

Alternatively the population figures can be progressively updated by the difference between Births and Burials (increase or decrease in population). I have looked at all these methods and double-checked them for the periods when figures are available; the results are very inconsistent and disappointing.

Another method is to use the x5 factor on the number of occupied buildings listed in Surveys taken in the 17th and 18th centuries. This must also be unreliable, as the surveys were for the Manor of Redbourn only and thus did not include tenants outside the manor. Therefore, the only accurate part of the graph, shown as *Fig: 15.1,*is after 1801.

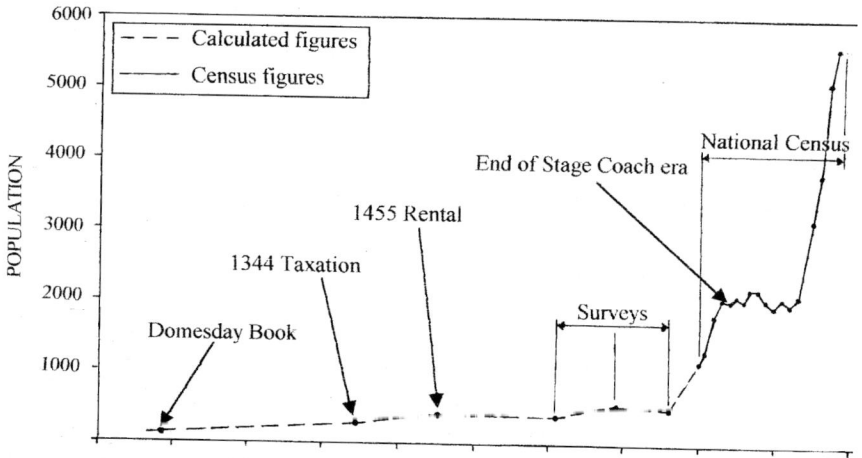

Fig: 15.1 – Graph of Population figures from 1086 to1991

The things to notice from this graph are:-

> The very gradual growth from early times to the mid 18th century.
> A jump in population caused by the prosperity of the stage coach era.
> The static population from the end of stage coaching to the 1930's.
> The steady increase, with the expansion of housing, chiefly after the last war.

After the first (1801) Census, the next three decenial Returns only gave the number of people, trades and houses, it was not until 1841 that names of each resident were recorded. The latter were entered on printed sheets with columns for the place, name, age/sex, employment and place of birth of each resident. Subsequent Returns gave additional information as to, relationships, marital condition, employment, etc.

Census returns dating back less than 100 years are unavailable to the public; except as overall data figures, thus as we wait with anticipation for publication of the 1901 figures. As can be imagined the material available to historians and analysts is vast; they have been used to compile information for some of this book, particularly relative to the houses and occupations of villagers.

THE PARISH BOUNDARY

The boundary of Redbourn parish was established in Saxon times, as is proved by a charter of 1060 which delineated the bordering parish of Wheathampstead and Harpenden. (see pages 16-17 and *Fig. 1.12*) There is no evidence to suggest that the parish boundary has changed much, if at all, from then until the mid 20th century. Only one boundary dispute is recorded, this was when the Prior of Ashridge persuaded the Abbot of St Albans to let him have half the road width on the west side of the parish. (see page 38).

Only with a review started in 1935 did the Herts County Council sanction the changes indicated in *Fig. 15.2* [3]

The first perambulation of the entire parish was not laid out until 1609.[4] This was a long and detailed description following a survey of the manor. It can be easily followed in some stretches, but where field names and tenants holdings are used as landmarks it is difficult to be certain of the position.

Modern descriptions of 'Beating the Bounds' at Rogationtide help to bring the boundary to life. Such walks were intended to confirm and establish the exact boundary and to impress its importance on the rising generation by 'bumping' them at strategic points. This old tradition is still kept alive though is now irrelevant with the accurate delineation given by modern large-scale maps.

Such events were very enjoyable and memorable, especially to the youngsters and were popular as shown by the large turnout for the 1927 'Beat', *(Fig. 15.3)*. Not only parishioners, (often including the Vicar) but sometimes visiting celebrities attended. 1948 was one such occasion. Mr Wood, First Assistant to the St Albans Rural District Council, walked the whole 17 miles and afterwards wrote a detailed description of the event.[5] This was published in abbreviated form in "Common Round" in 1960, but failed to mention the final surprise 'bumping' of Mr Wood himself – on the Start/Finish point!

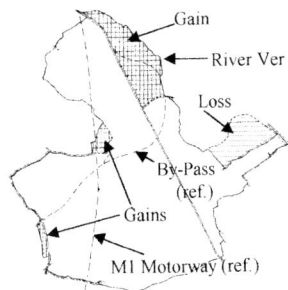

Fig: 15.2- Losses and Gains, 1935-7

Fig: 15.3 – Beating the Bounds,c.1927

THE REDBOURN CINEMA

A cinema was set up in the Village Hall some time before 1946, a projection room being made at the back of the hall: which still exists as a storeroom. From here that the son of a local dentist showed films, as a hobby [6.] After the war Mr John Heather, then living in Harpenden, revived the film shows, again as a hobby.

Poster in place for the next show　　　*Mr Heather with admirers (at Harpenden?)*
Fig: 15.4 – Mr Heather's Cinema shows

His first show was on Friday 21st Feb. 1946 and included, as the feature film, Jack Hulbert in "Bulldog Jack". He put on two showings each Friday, but later had to cut them to one because of the pressure of his work. He charged 6d. for children and 1/- for adults, but if he knew a family to be very poor, he would let them all in for price of one.

In spite of increasing rents, he held his prices to a maximum of 2/-, often being out of pocket by as much as £155 in a year. Threat of a further rent increase and the increasing popularity of Television brought final closure in December 1958. The films shown were "The Atomic Kid" and "When Gang Land Strikes", which in spite of their titles, were non-violent films suitable for family viewing. His audiences were mostly children, whose bad behaviour worried Mr Heather, and caused to him sometimes to stop the programme and sort them out.

Mr Heather, a quiet and unassuming man, moved to Redbourn in about 1951. He was a Civil Engineer of some standing,, founding and running the British Railways training school in London, until his retirement in 1965. He continued in engineering by writing articles to journals in both English and German.

He was known in London playhouses as an avid 'first nighter' often invited 'back stage' to meet the actors, such - Dame Edith Evans and Dame Flora Robson.

The work he himself would probably wish to be remembered for, is as a friend and constant visitor to the children at Bretby Hall, Orthopaedic Hospital, near Burton-upon-Trent. He made fortnightly visits to the hospital from Redbourn for at least 50 years, clocking up over 200,000 miles. At the hospital he entertained the children by doing conjuring tricks, ventriloquism and of course by giving film shows. At Christmas time he dressed up as Santa Claus, and satisfied every child's desires which they had expressed to him previously. On Sundays he took services in the chapel as a Lay Reader - he had considered going into full time ministry but engineering and his hospital work took precedence.

It is not surprising that a ward was named after him at Bretby Hall. He was also asked if he would let his name be put forward for an MBE. - presumably the answer was no.

The memory of John Heather will not be easily forgotten in Redbourn and unwittingly he has left his own memorial. This is the series of 16mm. Black and White Cine films which he made of village scenes, people and of course of children. Making them between 1947 and 1953, he used to slip them in during performances in the hall, they were always a great hit with his audiences - who thrilled to see themselves as stars of the big screen.

These films are still very popular, not only with the people appearing in them, but also with their families and even with people new to the village. By popular demand they have been shown for several years in their original venue, the Village Hall, but unfortunately not by using the old projection room. They have been combined on three reels and cover the following subjects, the 1949 Southend outing being the most popular of all [7]:-

1947 -	Children arriving for the first film show; High Street scenes
1948 -	Southend outing; St Albans Pageant prologue by the Vicar; Children playing on the Common; Dancing at the Vicarage
1949 -	Remembrance Day parade; Scenes on "Snow Sunday"; Southend outing
1950 -	Opening of the Children's playground; Cycle racing at Hilltop; Remembrance Day parade
1951 -	Remembrance Day parade; Horse racing at Friar's Wash; Bonfire night
1952 -	Planting Lime trees in the Common avenue
1953 -	Coronation Day and races on the Common; Harpenden Carnival; The Queen's Birthday as seen by Mr Heather from the Pall Mall.

SPORTING ACTIVITIES

Activities which would be considered as 'sport' in later centuries were often of vital importance for survival in Medieval or earlier times; horse riding, archery and fishing are good examples. Hunting, vital for early man, became the sport of kings in Medieval times, but severe penalties could be incurred if a peasant tried poach 'game' this on his Lord's park lands.

Court cases show how this was enforced by the Abbot and later Lords of the Manor, but it was not just the peasants, desperate for food, who ran into trouble. In 1240 Gadfrid of Childwike, his sons and others were called to answer why they hunted and caught hares in the Abbot's free warren at St Albans without his permission.[8] This was not just a once off trespass, but had taken place over many of the Abbot's lands, not only at St Albans, but also at Kingsbury, Park, Langley, Cashio, Rickmansworth, Codicote, Walden, Sandridge, Tyttenhanger, Barnet and Redbourn.

The charges were contested by Gadfrid, who stated that he and his forebears had *"enjoyed hunting peacefully and lawfully from the time of Henry II"* and that they had paid the present King (Henry III) 5 marks for such rights. The case was tried on neutral ground at Cambridge, but as the Abbot was one of only three in the country who had been granted rights of warren by William the Conqueror, he won the case and 40 marks (£26.13.4d) for the damage caused. It is interesting to find later records of grants made by the Abbots, to Geoffrey de Childwic (1249) and to John de Bassingburn (1300) for free warren in some of the same lands.[9]

The people of Redbourn resented not being allowed to hunt in the manor, especially on land they themselves farmed in the Common fields. Their resentment came to a head when they joined with St Albans and the surrounding villages in the Peasants Revolt (Chapter 3). The new Charter which they tried to extract from the Abbot demanded - *"the free exercise of hunting, fowling and fishing rights..."*.[10]

Later Lords of the Manor kept an equally sharp eye on the poaching activities of their tenants – one case recording a £2 fine for a man caught poaching an eel from the river near Fish Street Farm.[11]

It was not until about 1700 that fox hunting with hounds became popular, Hertfordshire must have been one of the early counties to have a pack kept for this purpose, with kennels at Chesham and Redbourn, in 1725 [12]. Twenty years later, the Duke of Cumberland built his hunting lodge at Redbourn for his guests, but kept his hounds at Dunstable (see Chapter 8).

A map of Hertfordshire, made in 1880, shows the places in the county where hunting took place.[13] Another indication of its popularity in this area is seen in a sale document of 1823 for "The Elms"; which tried to encourage prospective buyers by noting - *"the neighbourhood is justly celebrated for field sports"*.[14]

In more recent times the Aldenham Harriers held hunts in this part of the county, Mr G. H. Hartop of Beaumont Hall being one of its early masters.[15] They continued to use Redbourn Common for their popular Boxing Day Meets until Animal Rights protesters, with Media attention, forced them to give up

Geoff. Hartop, besides his hunting interests, was a frequent rider in the annual point-to-point races held at Friars Wash where attendances at its peak reached 20,000.[16] Such meetings were held from as early as 1890 and the same course continued to be used up to 1964, except for gaps between 1906-26 and during the Second World War.

The Vicar, Rev. Lord Frederick Beauclerk, owned a racehorse called "Poet". This came third in the St Ledger and also won a Steeple Chase between Tyttenhanger House and Beaumont Farm in 1834.[17] Beauclerk, to avoid any trouble with his Bishop, he ran this horse under "Mr Brand's" name. The celebrated jockey, Jem Mason rode for him.

Archery was one of the very necessary Medieval activities and space was set aside for practice on most village greens. No location for archery butts can be suggested other than somewhere on the Common. Butts existed at least up to 1621, when a court order was issued to - *".. the inhabitants of Redborne for that they have suffered their butts to be in decay by the space of three months last past"*, the fine was 20 shillings.[18]

Several fields in the parish, such as - Butt Field, Long Field Butts, Clay Butts and St Mary's Butts were not archery butts. They were actually lands at the end of a field, which because of their size and shape were difficult to plough.[19]

The Common was the scene for many other sports which probably coincided with the two annual fairs; Cock fighting and Pugilistic combats are two that have been suggested.[20] When winter days were much colder than now, skating took place when the Moor, along the south side of the Common, became frozen over.[21]

A more recent sport was golf, with a 9-hole course which ranged over the entire Common, starting at Cumberland House and ending on the cricket pitch. A map of the course can be seen in the Museum, dated 1906. *(Fig: 15.5)* One of the golfers can be seen in action near the Moor in *Fig: 15.3* [22] More seriously, a rifle range was provided for troops billeted locally during the First World War.[23]

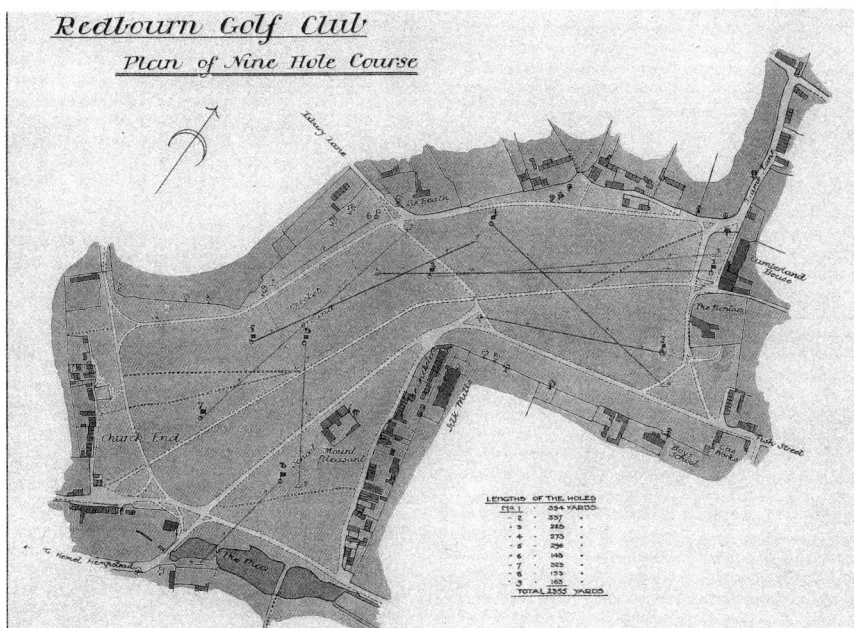

Fig: 15.5 – Plan of Golf Course across the Common, 1906

Another scene of combat was just beyond the parish boundary past St Agnells Farm, known as "Jacks Dell". This was the traditional arena for battles on Good Friday afternoons between the youngsters of Redbourn and Flamstead.[24] They fought there with their caps tied on pieces of string which, when whirled around their heads and aimed at an opponent, made a very effective weapon. This continued until one village routed the other, thus taking possession of the Dell. Here too, more serious fights took place between grown men in earlier times; these sometimes lasted all day, only stopping when darkness fell.

The start of cricket in Redbourn is somewhat shrouded in mystery. Authors of County histories are divided, some saying that it was first played in the County at Redbourn in 1666, while others say that it was the St Albans Cricket Club that was formed in that year. Branch-Johnson's version is that Redbourn Common saw some of the earliest cricket matches in England; while the first cricket club in the history of the game was formed at St Albans in 1666.[25]

Although Lord Frederick Beauclerk was a founder member of Lords Cricket Ground and also absentee Vicar of Redbourn, it is doubtful if he ever played here (see page 231). However, during his declining years while still, Vicar of Redbourn and St Michaels, the M.C.C. did play at Redbourn, winning by 7 wickets.[26]

The Redbourn team showed its worth towards the end of the century, when they competed for the Hertfordshire County Cricket Club, Challenge Cup. In the first three years of the competition the cup went to Potters Bar, Watford and Hemel Hempstead, but then Redbourn won the next three years in succession, becoming the permanent holders in 1890. The cup is still in the proud possession of the club - see *Figs: 15.4*

The Challenge Cup (above)
The winning team 1890 (left)

Fig: 156 - Hertfordshire County Cricket Club, Challenge Cup

In the early years facilities for the players were very basic, a marquee being hired for important games, until a tent was bought for £9 in 1898.[27] But, probably because of its age, the club was allowed to put a hut on the north side of the pitch in c.1932.[28] When they outgrew this old green pavilion and sought a new site nearer the pitch, opposition came from non cricket playing Commoners. Everyone has since got used to today's modern, low profile, building which has served since 1966.[29]

Football has also been played on the Common, the sport having roots in Redbourn back to at least 1888, but it was never allowed a permanent pitch or changing facilities there.[30] Like the Cricket Club, it had success in the county, winning both the Bingham Cox Cup in 1907 and 1931, and the Mid-Herts league in the same year.[31]

Though they have been allowed to play football on the Common, They have only fairly recently been able to find a permanent site in the village. Only temporary and far from satisfactory solutions were available for serious

Fig: 15.7 – Redbourn football team who won the Bingham Cup in 1906/7

play, Helen Keeley described how they had been *"pushed from pillar to goal post over the years"*, and listed the fields used.[32] These included Silk Mill meadow, the Park, Dunkley's Meadow at Scout Farm, Long Cutt Meadow, and at the back of the Secondary School.

The idea of having a Sports Centre with playing fields attached, goes back at least to 1938. With the start of war plans were shelved, but in 1946 the "Playing Fields Management" took charge [33] It was not until 1969 ,when the Redbourn Playing Fields Trust was formed, that things really started to move.

Eventually after getting some stony ground in Long Cutt Meadow they were able to provide a pavilion after years of frustration. In the same year, 1985, seeds of the final solution appeared with a land deal offered by Peter Frost of Hillbury Farm. The plan was to exchange the Long Cutt meadowland for housing development while the old farmland was earmarked for a Leisure Centre site. The final scheme came to fruition when the centre was opened in 1996. This comprises a large Sports Hall with adjoining, Fitness, meeting and social facilities, and the outside pitches including, of course, football.

In spite of all these problems over pitches, Redbourn produced some outstanding footballers. There was Albert Day who played in two international matches in the mid 1930's; Fred Lawrence whose many football medals between 1929 and 1949 are kept in the Museum and in more recent times Ron Henry, who was captain of Tottenham Hotspur.

In this section I have only been able to touch on some of the success stories in which Redbourn people and teams have been involved; likewise only a few of the sporting activities have been able to be mentioned - perhaps some day someone will write a whole book on the subject.

"REDBOURN'S GREATEST OCCASION"

From Ancient times the Common, formerly referred to as the Heath, had been owned by the Lord of the Manor, but with the villagers enjoying Common Rights of pasture, turbary etc. In chapter 3 we saw how these Common Rights were threatened by the people of Flamstead and protected by the Abbot of St Albans.

After the Dissolution, the ownership of the Manor and it's Common passed through several hands before coming to the owners of Gorhambury in 1629.[34] After the sale of most of the Manor to the Crown Commissioners in 1930, the Common remained in the hands of the Earls of Verulam.[35] Since 1937 the Parish Council had been made responsible for the maintenance and upkeep of the Common. This involved them in the expense of repairs of damage to seats, railing etc., caused by vandals; sadly this is a problem which has not gone away.

The Herts Advertiser put the above heading to an article describing the handing over of Redbourn Common by the Earl of Verulam to the Parish Council in 1947. James Walter Grimston, the 4th Earl of Verulam, came to Redbourn to officially hand the Common over to the Council [36] The old cricket pavilion was chosen as the scene for this great occasion.

Mr Harry Harborough, as Chairman of the Parish Council, supported by the Vicar, Rev. David Bickerton and other leading parishioners received the gift on behalf of the village. Mr Harborough referred to the "wilful and wanton damage" which had been experienced and appealed to everyone to *"try to preserve this great gift"*. The Earl described what the people of Redbourn were receiving was *"a really valuable asset"* and he hoped that the Common would always remain the beautiful thing that it had been in the past.

Other speakers included Mr Fred Bradley, who, speaking for the cricket club, said they would endeavour to maintain the amenities of the Common because *"cricket and the Common were inseparable"*. For the youth of the village and for future generations, a Boy Scout, George Reading, hoped that the youth would remember their promise to look after the Common and hand it over to their children well cared for.

Thanks on behalf of the villagers was summed up by Miss Gertrude Peake who expressed the opinion that - *"the village had always possessed one of the most lovely commons in the country"* and she hoped that the Council would *"take the greatest care of its privileges and always be jealous of the rights of the common, and not let it be spoilt in any way"*

The Avenue near Church End, c.1890

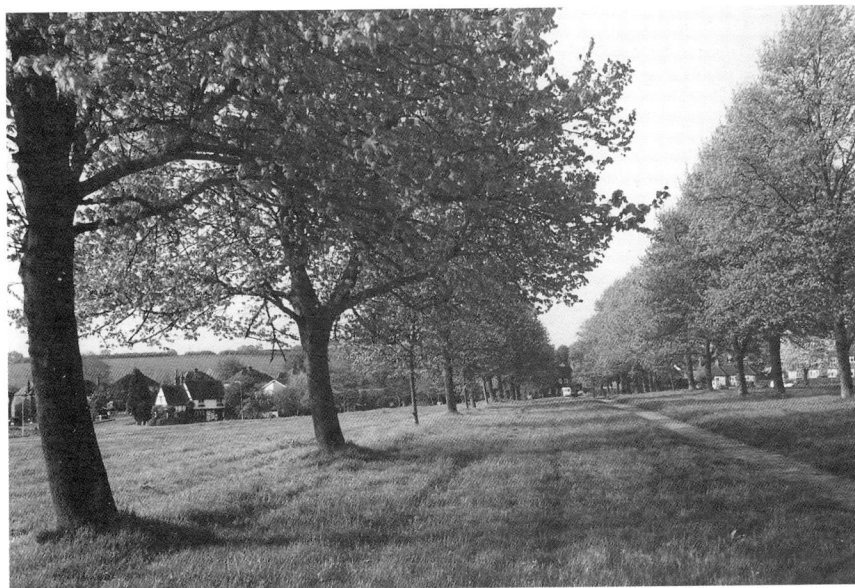

Similar viewpoint to the above, but taken in 1994
Fig: 15.8 – Two views on Redbourn Common about a century apart

REFERENCES

1   Transactions of the Hertfordshire Natural History Society, Vol. IX
2   W. E. Tate's "The Parish Chest", page 81 and J. C. Cox, "Parish Registers" pp.30,34
3   County of Hertford Review Orders, HRO. ref. L.S.L.L.2013, Order 693 & 693a, Map numbers OFF.ACC.88 & 610
4   HRO. ref. X.C.7a
5   Report by Mr. H. D. Wood, copy kept by the Redbourn Parish Council and kindly copied for me.
6   Most of this information is taken from a letter written by Mr Heather to Miss Palmer in 1973; Copy held by the author
7   Films edited, with minimal loss of length, by the author and now held by the Village Museum
8   Matthew Paris, "Chronica Majora" Vol. 4 pp. 51-3
9   PRO. Calendar of Charter Rolls Vol.1, 15 Jun. 1249 and Vol. 2, 20 March 1300
10 Thomas Walsingham, "Gesta Abbatum", Vol. 3, page 328
11 Herts Advertiser, 22 June 1990 – "130 years ago"
12 Victoria County History, Hertfordshire, Vol. 1, p. 349 and Gwennah Robinson, "The Barracuda Guide to the County" History Series, Vol. III, p. 82
13 D. Hodson, "The Printed Maps of Hertfordshire 1577-1900", map 103
14 HRO, ref. Miscellaneous 73438
15 Hertfordshire Countryside, vol. 12, No. 47, frontispiece and ref. 13, p. 18
16 Eric Edwards, "Friars Wash Point-to –point Races", p. 13
17 As 9, Vol. 1, p. 365
18 W. Brigg, "The Herts Genealogist & Antiquary", Vol. III, p. 295
19 John Richardson, "The Local Historian's Encyclopedia" A.256
20 D. Baker-Jones "Old Hertfordshire Calendar" p. 7
21 "Common Round" parish magazine, July 1965
22 May Walker, "Redbourn", p. 46
23 As 19
24 As 18, August 1965
25 W. Branch Johnson, "Companion into Hertfordshire", p. 198
26 As 9, Vol. 1, p. 372
27 Parish Magazine August 1948, p. viii
28 Redbourn Parish Council Minutes, HRO. ref. CP.78.1/3 and 1/7
29 As 18, September 1966
30 As 12, Vol. 22, No. 104 page 33
31 Mid-Herts Football Association official programme, Redbourn Village Museum, ref. 00.292
32 Helen Keeley, "The Story of the Redbourn Playing Fields trust"
33 Redbourn Council minutes, HRO. ref. CP.78/1
34 Gorhambury Manorial Records, HRO. Ref. II.A.6, and Close Roll 5 Chas. I, pt
35 Gorhambury sale brochure, 1930
36 The account of this event is taken from the Herts Advertiser for 2nd April 1948 as recordedby the 'Redbourn History Group'

BIBLIOGRAPHY

The following books will provide further information on some of the subjects covered in this book. Most are available in local libraries, though some may be for reference only, and therefore not available for loan. For other books, magazines etc., I refer the reader to the reference lists for each chapter

Addison, Sir William - "The Old Roads of England",1980

Auckland, R. G - Sandridge Workhouse, 1986

Bagshawe, Richard W. – "Roman Roads", Shire Archaeology, 1979

Bates, Alan (Compiler) "Stage Coach Services - 1836", 1969

Bennett, H. S. - "Life on the English Manor", Alan Sutton, Gloucester, 1987

Brigg, W. (Ed) - "The Herts Genealogist and Antiquary" in 3 volumes, 1897

Brunskill, R. W. - "Timber Buildings in Britain" , Victor Gollancz Ltd., London, 1985

Burg, Judith – Religion in Hertfordshire 1847-51" (William Upton's survey), 1995

Campbell, James (Ed.) - "The Anglo-Saxons", 1982 - Many other books on this subject

Cannon, James & Hedley "The Nicky Line" 1977

Clutterbuck, R. - "The History and Antiquitaries of Hertford", 1815

Copeland, John - "Roads & their Traffic, 1750-1850" 1968

Corbett, James – "A History of St Albans", 1997

Cox, John G. C. – "St Alban & West Herts News of 1890"

Cussans, J. E. - History of Hertfordshire", 1879

Darby, H. C. - "Domesday England" (1977) and "The Doomsday Geography of SE. England" (1962)

Davis, Jean – "Straw Plait" 1978

du Maurier, Daphne – "The Golden Lads", 1975

Dugdale, Sir William – "Monasticon Angulatum", 1817-30

Eden, Sir F. M. – "State of the Poor", 1928

Edwards, Eric - "Friars Wash Point-to-Point Races, 1996

Featherstone, Alan – "The Mills of Redbourn", 1993

Finn, R Wellden (1986) "Domesday Book - A Guide" Phillimore & Co. Ltd.

Freeman, Charles – "Luton and the Hat Industry", 1976

Friar, Stephen - "A Companion to the English Parish Church" 1996

Gardener, H. W. – "The Agriculture of Hertfordshire"

Hartley, Dorothy - "The Land of England", Book Associates, London, 1979

Henwood, George - "Abbot Richard Wallingford, Pie powder press 1988

Hodson, D - "The Printed Maps of Hertfordshire 1577-1900"

Hoskins, W. G. - "The Making of the English Landscape" 1977

Hunn. J. R. – "Reconstruction & measurement of Landscape change" 1944

James, Justin – "Redbournbury Mill"

King, Nora – "The Grimston's of Gorhambury", 1983

Laing, Lloyd and Jennifer - "The Origins of Britain" 1980

Levett, A. E. - "Studies in Manorial History, 1924

McLaughlin Guides, -"The Poor are always with us", 1994; "Annals of the Poor", 1994

Morris, John (Ed) "Domesday Book, 12 Hertfordshire", 1976

Muir, Richard & Nina – "Fields"

Muir, Richard - "Shell Guide to Reading the Landscape", 1971

Newcome, Rev. Peter - "The History of the Ancient Foundation called The Abbey of St Albans", 1795

Pevsner, Nikolaus – "The Buildings of England – Hertfordshire", 1978

Powrie, Jean - "Eleanor of Castile", Brewin Books, 1990

Rackham, Oliver – "The History of the Countryside", 1997

Reville, Andre - "The Rising of the Workers of Hertfordshire in 1381", 1981

Richardson, John – "The Local Historian's Encyclopaedia, 1989

Roberts, Dr. Eileen - "The Hill of the Martyr", The Book Castle, Dunstable, 1993
    -"Images of ALBAN", Fraternity of The Friends of St Albans Abbey, 1999

Robinson, Bruce - "Norfolk Origins 1 - Hunters to Farmers", Acorn Editions, 1981

Rook, Tony - "A History of Hertfordshire", 1984

Sanctuary, Gerald - "The Monastery of St Albans",
    - "St Albans & the Wars of the Roses", 1985

Scarisbrick J.- "The Dissolution of the Monasteries, the case for St Albans"

Scott, Valerie G. & Tony Rook – "County Maps & Histories of Hertfordshire", 1989

Smith, J. T. – "Hertfordshire Houses, a selective inventory", 1993
    -"English Houses, 1200-1800, the Hertfordshire evidence", 1992

Sorrell, Alan - "Reconstructing the past" 1981

Staniforth, Arthur – "Straw Craftsmen" 1976

Swinson, Arthur - "The Quest for St Alban", Fraternity of the Friends of St Albans Abbey, 1971

Talbot, C. H. (Ed./Trans) – "The Life of Christina of Markyate", 1959

Tate, W. E. - "The Parish Chest", Phillimore 1983

Thompson, P. - "It happened in a Hertfordshire Village" 1976

Urwick, William – "Nonconformity in Hertfordshire", 1884

The Viatores – "Roman Roads in the South-East Midlands"

Walker, May – "Redbourn", 1960

Warrand, D. (Ed.) - "Victoria County History, Vol. 2, Hertfordshire, 1907

Watts, Martin – "Corn Milling", 1998

Williams, Geoffrey - "The Iron-Age Hillforts of England", Images 1993

Wood, Michael "A Search for the roots of England", 1987

Woodward, Sue & Geoff - "The Harpenden to Hemel Hempstead Railway, The Nickey Line" 1990

Wright, Geoffrey N. – "Turnpike Roads" Shire Album No. 283, 1992

    Books not listed under author's names

"Building Stone in St Albans" - St Albans City Museum, 1979

"Hertfordshire Puddingstone" -St Albans City Museum, Information sheet No.2

"Hertfordshire Village Book", Hertfordshire Federation of Women's Institutes –

"Markyate's Past" a series of booklets produced by the Markyate Local History Society -

"The Peasants' Revolt in Hertfordshire 1381" - A symposium, Hertfordshire publications

"The Place Names of Hertfordshire", 1938

Potters Bar Historical Series, a series of booklets published by the Potters Bar & District Historical Society

"The Story of Redbourn" Redbourn Tutorial Class

INDEX